Generative AI with LangChain

Build smart AI apps using LangChain and Python tools

Dr. Priyanka Singh

Hariom Singh

bpb

www.bpbonline.com

First Edition 2025

Copyright © BPB Publications, India

ISBN: 978-93-65896-497

LIMITS OF LIABILITY AND DISCLAIMER OF WARRANTY

To View Complete
BPB Publications Catalogue
Scan the QR Code:

www.bpbonline.com

Dedicated to

To the brilliant minds exploring LangChain and shaping the future of AI—your bold questions and boundary-pushing ideas inspire innovation.

To the curious students, passionate professionals, and relentless creators—your drive for knowledge lights the path forward.

To our families—your unwavering support fuels our journey. And to ourselves—for daring to start, for growing through each challenge, and for believing in the power of intelligent transformation.

About the Authors

- **Dr. Priyanka Singh** is a dynamic leader in artificial intelligence, cloud computing, and technical education, with over a decade of experience bridging the gap between industry and academia. A Ph.D. in cloud computing and an engineering manager (AI) at Universal AI, she has led innovative AI-driven projects across transportation, logistics, healthcare, and manufacturing. Her work emphasizes ethical AI development, governance, and impact-driven solutions. Dr. Singh is also a published author and technical reviewer in AI and NLP and a passionate mentor shaping the next generation of technologists. She was recognized as one of the Top 100 Women in Tech (AI) and is the creator of the #AIforLife movement, promoting the use of AI for societal good. Currently, she is transitioning into K-12 education in Arkansas, empowering students as an AP Computer Science educator.

- **Hariom Singh**, the co-author, brings over 15 years of strategic leadership experience in business transformation, technology integration, and AI adoption. With an MBA and a certified PMP/RMP, he excels in bridging business needs with technical execution across various domains. Known for his strategic mindset and data-driven leadership, Hariom champions the responsible use of AI to drive enterprise innovation. He is also a mentor, blogger, and advocate for clear communication and the ethical adoption of AI. His writing and thought leadership can be explored on Medium and LinkedIn.

Together, they bring a powerful blend of technical depth, business insight, and educational impact—committed to shaping a future where AI empowers, educates, and elevates society.

About the Reviewers

❖ **Sai Chaitanya** is a data scientist with 7 years of experience (8.5 years overall) in building machine learning models and solving real-world problems. He is currently pursuing a masters in data science at Scaler Academy, focusing on **data structures and algorithms (DSA)**, machine learning, deep learning and generative AI.

Sai is an aspiring technical author with plans to write a machine learning book that simplifies complex algorithms using a unique visual approach. His aim is to make learning intuitive and long-lasting for readers. This exciting project is set to begin in 2025, reflecting his passion for demystifying data science concepts.

In addition to his professional pursuits, Sai has recently embarked on a journey to enhance his overall well-being, balancing physical, mental, and spiritual health while expanding his knowledge in personal finance. He is also exploring the stock market and is dedicated to personal growth. Sai envisions a future where his journey inspires others to pursue excellence in the data science field and personal growth.

❖ **Nabil Tadili** is an accomplished lead developer at SPVIE Assurances, with extensive experience in software architecture and full-stack development. Over the years, he has contributed to a variety of impactful projects, including the integration of AI solutions to streamline business operations. Notably, he led initiatives to deploy machine learning models for defect detection and utilized **large language models (LLMs)** to automate document creation processes, enhancing operational efficiency.

Currently pursuing a master of science in computer science with a specialization in machine learning at Georgia Tech through the OMSCS program, Nabil is deeply invested in advancing his expertise in artificial intelligence. His work reflects a passion for harnessing cutting-edge technology to solve complex challenges and deliver innovative solutions.

Beyond his technical endeavors, Nabil remains committed to fostering collaboration and staying at the forefront of emerging trends in AI, software engineering, and digital transformation.

❖ **Vineet Jaiswal**, vice president of generative AI at India's largest bank, is a distinguished leader with over 17 years of experience in AI, machine learning, and software development. Recognized for his deep expertise across all major cloud platforms, he has made significant contributions to generative AI, deep learning, computer vision, MLOps, and backend technologies. His work spans collaborations with multiple Fortune 500 clients, driving innovation and scalable solutions. In addition to his professional achievements, he holds a masters degree and has completed various certifications, further solidifying his expertise in the field.

Acknowledgements

This book would not have been possible without the unwavering support of my family. I am deeply grateful to my husband and co-author, **Hariom Singh**, whose expertise in cloud architecture and AI brought invaluable depth to this work. His partnership and vision were instrumental throughout this journey.

As an author, I, **Dr. Priyanka Singh**, would like to thank my sons, **Gopi** and **Aaditya**, and my brother, **Sushil**, for their constant encouragement, patience, and love.

We extend our heartfelt thanks to the students, professionals, and innovators whose passion for learning and technology inspired the creation of this book. To our mentors, colleagues, and collaborators—your insights challenged and enriched our thinking.

To the publishers, editors, and everyone who helped bring this book to life, your dedication has turned our vision into reality.

This book is for the pioneers of today and the leaders of tomorrow. May it inspire, guide, and empower you as you shape the future of AI.

Preface

This book is a practical guide to building intelligent language applications using artificial intelligence and the LangChain framework. From foundational AI concepts and Python essentials to deploying real-world solutions on AWS, Azure, Snowflake, and Athena, each chapter is crafted to equip readers with both the knowledge and tools to create scalable, ethical, and impactful AI systems.

You will explore neural networks, LangChain workflows, DevOps/MLOps integration, and enterprise use cases, all through hands-on examples and strategic insights. Whether you are a beginner or a professional, this book is your roadmap to mastering AI-powered applications in today's fast-evolving tech landscape.

Chapter 1: Introduction to Artificial Intelligence and LangChain - This chapter introduces the core concepts of **artificial intelligence (AI)** and the LangChain framework. It explains AI fundamentals, its real-world applications, and its impact across industries. The chapter also presents LangChain as a powerful tool for building AI-driven language applications, emphasizing its flexibility, ease of use, and community support. Ethical considerations and responsible AI usage are also discussed to set the foundation for future learning.

Chapter 2: Getting Started with Python - This chapter lays the groundwork for using Python in AI development. It covers Python basics such as variables, data types, control structures, functions, and modules. The chapter also explains why Python is the preferred language in the AI community and walks through hands-on coding examples to help readers build confidence. It prepares learners to write clean, readable code for AI tasks and introduces Python's role in building intelligent systems.

Chapter 3: Understanding LangChain Basics - This chapter provides a comprehensive overview of the LangChain framework. It covers its key components—LangChain libraries, templates, LangServe, and LangSmith—and explains how developers can use these tools to create, debug, and deploy language applications. The chapter highlights LangChain's workflow, including building chains, integrating models, and serving applications via APIs. Hands-on examples and installation guidance make it easy for readers to get started.

Chapter 4: Neural Network with LangChain - This chapter explores the integration of neural networks with LangChain to build advanced language applications. It explains how neural networks work—covering layers, activation functions, and training processes—and demonstrates their role in NLP. The chapter introduces modular neural networks and showcases real-world implementations like sentiment analysis using LSTM. Readers also learn how LangChain supports scalable, customizable, and ethical AI development.

Chapter 5: LangChain and AWS Integration - This chapter explores how to deploy LangChain applications on **Amazon Web Services** (**AWS**). It covers the cloud setup process, explains integration with services like EC2, Lambda, and S3, and guides readers through infrastructure management, deployment strategies, and cost-effective scaling of AI applications using AWS.

Chapter 6: LangChain and Azure Integration - This chapter covers the step-by-step integration of LangChain applications into Microsoft Azure's cloud ecosystem. It explains how to deploy, scale, monitor, and secure AI services in Azure. Real-world examples show how to use LangChain alongside Azure services such as Azure Functions, Blob Storage, and Application Insights.

Chapter 7: Real-world Data Science with Snowflake and Athena - This chapter demonstrates how LangChain can be combined with modern data warehousing tools like Snowflake and Amazon Athena. It explains how to use LangChain to perform scalable data retrieval, intelligent querying, and downstream AI processing for enterprise-scale datasets.

Chapter 8: AI in DevOps and MLOps - This chapter explains the role of LangChain in the CI/CD and MLOps landscape. It covers topics like automated testing, continuous integration of AI models, versioning, model monitoring, deployment automation, and how to build resilient AI pipelines for production environments.

Chapter 9: Future Trends in AI and LangChain - This chapter explores the emerging trends and innovations in AI and LangChain—from advancements in machine learning and generative models to enterprise use cases in healthcare, agriculture, finance, and education. It emphasizes the importance of ethical and responsible AI, offering insights into what lies ahead in the evolving AI landscape.

Code Bundle and Coloured Images

Please follow the link to download the
Code Bundle and the *Coloured Images* of the book:

https://rebrand.ly/e5bad2

The code bundle for the book is also hosted on GitHub at
https://github.com/bpbpublications/Generative-AI-with-LangChain.
In case there's an update to the code, it will be updated on the existing GitHub repository.

We have code bundles from our rich catalogue of books and videos available at **https://github.com/bpbpublications**. Check them out!

Errata

We take immense pride in our work at BPB Publications and follow best practices to ensure the accuracy of our content to provide with an indulging reading experience to our subscribers. Our readers are our mirrors, and we use their inputs to reflect and improve upon human errors, if any, that may have occurred during the publishing processes involved. To let us maintain the quality and help us reach out to any readers who might be having difficulties due to any unforeseen errors, please write to us at :

errata@bpbonline.com

Your support, suggestions and feedbacks are highly appreciated by the BPB Publications' Family.

Did you know that BPB offers eBook versions of every book published, with PDF and ePub files available? You can upgrade to the eBook version at www.bpbonline. com and as a print book customer, you are entitled to a discount on the eBook copy. Get in touch with us at :

business@bpbonline.com for more details.

At **www.bpbonline.com**, you can also read a collection of free technical articles, sign up for a range of free newsletters, and receive exclusive discounts and offers on BPB books and eBooks.

Piracy

If you come across any illegal copies of our works in any form on the internet, we would be grateful if you would provide us with the location address or website name. Please contact us at **business@bpbonline.com** with a link to the material.

If you are interested in becoming an author

If there is a topic that you have expertise in, and you are interested in either writing or contributing to a book, please visit **www.bpbonline.com**. We have worked with thousands of developers and tech professionals, just like you, to help them share their insights with the global tech community. You can make a general application, apply for a specific hot topic that we are recruiting an author for, or submit your own idea.

Reviews

Please leave a review. Once you have read and used this book, why not leave a review on the site that you purchased it from? Potential readers can then see and use your unbiased opinion to make purchase decisions. We at BPB can understand what you think about our products, and our authors can see your feedback on their book. Thank you!

For more information about BPB, please visit **www.bpbonline.com**.

Join our book's Discord space

Join the book's Discord Workspace for Latest updates, Offers, Tech happenings around the world, New Release and Sessions with the Authors:

https://discord.bpbonline.com

Table of Contents

CHAPTER 1

Introduction to Artificial Intelligence and LangChain

Introduction

With this chapter, let us begin your journey into **artificial intelligence** (**AI**) and LangChain. We will simplify AI's complex concepts, making them easy to understand. Imagine AI as a fascinating puzzle; this chapter is your guide to solving it. It is designed to be clear and user-friendly, perfect for beginners. By the end, you will grasp what AI is and see how LangChain makes creating AI projects easier. Prepare to learn, enjoy, and discover AI's real-world applications!

Structure

In the upcoming chapter, we will explore the following subjects:

- Introduction to artificial intelligence
- Overview of LangChain
- Applications of AI in the modern world
- Ethical considerations in AI
- Establishing your environment

Objectives

This chapter will introduce you to AI, simply and excitingly. Whether you are a beginner or have some knowledge, we will provide the basics and guide you through learning more about AI. AI to ensure you understand its impact on society and the importance of using it responsibly. We invite you to join the AI community, a fantastic place for sharing, learning, and collaborating.

By the end of this chapter, you should clearly understand AI's basics, potential, and key ethical considerations. We aim to prepare you for further exploration and applying AI to your projects.

Introduction to artificial intelligence

AI is like teaching computers to think and solve problems like us. It is about making them smart enough to handle jobs from simple to complex tasks. They can learn from information, figure out patterns, make choices, and fix issues. AI is everywhere, changing the way we use technology and how we connect with each other. We will explore what AI is all about, see how it is used in real life, and think about the right and wrong ways to use it. Also, we will get to know how this tech works and introduce you to LangChain, a tool that makes creating AI easier.

Remember that AI machines do not get things the way we do. They do not feel anything and are not aware. They look at data and make decisions based on their programming and what they have learned from the data. Sometimes, if the data has biases, AI might not make the best decisions.

Historical context

The idea of AI has existed for centuries, evident in myths, tales, and conjectures about the creation of artificial entities with intelligence or consciousness by skilled artisans. The phrase AI originated in 1956, coined by *John McCarthy* and *Marvin Minsky*, among others, during a conference at *Dartmouth College*. They had an optimistic view of the future, thinking that creating a machine with intelligence comparable to a human was an imminent achievement.

- **Initial progress**: In the early years, AI research focused on symbolic methods and problem-solving. Researchers believed encoding knowledge and developing the ability to reason would lead to AI. This period saw the development of algorithms that are still used today.

- **AI winter and rebirth**: AI has gone through periods of extreme optimism followed by disappointment and reduced funding, known as **AI winters**, mainly due to the high expectations and subsequent failure to meet these expectations. However, interest in AI has always rebounded, thanks to breakthroughs and the relentless belief in its potential.

- **Modern AI**: Today, AI has significantly grown thanks to improvements in computational power and large amounts of data. **Machine learning** (**ML**), a subset of AI, has become very popular. This involves creating algorithms to learn from and make predictions or decisions based on data. Deep learning is an expert area within ML that has driven significant progress in computer vision and **natural language processing** (**NLP**). AI has become pervasive daily, from smartphone virtual assistants to personalized website recommendations.

- **Looking ahead**: The field of AI continues to grow and evolve. Scientists are investigating innovative methods in AI that could result in broader and more flexible types of intelligence, commonly referred to as **artificial general intelligence** (**AGI**). The objective is to design systems capable of understanding, learning, and utilizing knowledge in a manner that closely resembles human intelligence.

Overview of LangChain

LangChain is a toolkit designed for building applications involving language understanding and generation. It is a toolbox that helps developers create and manage how machines understand and use human language. It is used to make AI systems that can chat, write, summarize, or even translate languages.

Distinctive attributes of LangChain

LangChain stands out in the world of AI development for its unique features that simplify and enhance the process of creating language-based applications. Let us explore the distinctive attributes that make LangChain an invaluable tool for developers and innovators alike:

- **Ease of use**: LangChain is known for making the complex world of language AI more accessible. It provides tools and functionalities that simplify creating sophisticated language applications, so even those new to AI can jump in and start building.

- **Flexibility**: It is not a one-size-fits-all tool. LangChain is designed to be flexible and customizable. This means that whether you are building a simple chatbot or a complex system that understands medical reports, LangChain can be tailored to fit the needs of your project.

- **Community-driven**: LangChain is developed and used by a community of AI enthusiasts and professionals. This community contributes to its growth and evolution, ensuring it stays updated with the latest AI and language processing developments.

- **Integration friendly**: One of the biggest strengths of LangChain is its ability to integrate with various AI models and systems. This means you can plug in different language models or connect to other AI tools, making your projects even more powerful.

The allure of LangChain: A user's perspective

From the perspective of those who use it, LangChain offers a range of appealing features that make it a go-to choice for developing language-based AI applications. Here are why users are drawn to LangChain and how it benefits their projects:

- **Innovation**: LangChain enables innovation and the development of novel language-based applications. Whether creating a new language game or building a tool that helps analyze legal documents, LangChain provides the foundation for creative and innovative projects.

  An example of innovation with LangChain is as follows:

  o A team of developers used LangChain to create *Chatventures*, an interactive, AI-driven storytelling game. This game dynamically generates unique storylines based on player choices, combining elements of traditional role-playing games with advanced **natural language understanding** (**NLU**). By utilizing LangChain's capabilities, the team was able to innovate in the gaming industry, offering players an engaging experience where their words directly influence the game world.

- **Community and support**: The LangChain community is active and supportive. Users appreciate the sense of camaraderie and the shared goal of making language AI better and more accessible. Plus, having a community means there is always someone to turn to for help or inspiration.

  An example of community: LangChain enthusiasts:

  o LangChain enthusiasts is a vibrant and supportive community of developers, researchers, and AI enthusiasts dedicated to exploring and advancing the capabilities of the LangChain framework. This community, accessible through platforms like GitHub, specialized forums, and dedicated Slack or Discord channels, fosters a collaborative environment. The members regularly share insights, offer assistance with technical challenges, and discuss innovative uses of LangChain. From beginners seeking guidance to experts sharing cutting-edge applications, LangChain enthusiasts is a hub for anyone passionate about harnessing the power of language AI.

- **Keeping up with AI**: AI and language technology move fast. LangChain users value staying at the forefront of technology, using the latest methods and models for their projects. It is not just about keeping up but about leading and innovating.

Applications of AI in the modern world

AI has revolutionized numerous aspects of our daily lives and industries, offering innovative solutions and enhancing efficiencies across the board. From healthcare to finance and from manufacturing to customer service, AI's applications are vast and varied, demonstrating its transformative power. Here is a closer look at how AI is making significant impacts in the modern world.

Healthcare

AI's influence in healthcare is substantial and swiftly increasing, particularly in medical diagnostics. AI systems are specifically trained to analyze complex medical images, including x-rays, MRIs, and CT scans. These systems can detect patterns and irregularities that might elude human observation. For example, in cancer detection, AI algorithms can scrutinize mammograms or skin lesions with high precision, often detecting early signs of cancer more accurately and quickly than medical professionals. Early detection provided by these systems is critical, enabling prompt treatment and improving patient outcomes. Furthermore, AI plays a significant role in forecasting patient outcomes by processing extensive amounts of patient data. This analysis is instrumental in customizing treatment plans to individual needs. This customization leads to more effective treatments with fewer side effects, significantly improving patient care.

AI's role in healthcare is wider than diagnostics and treatment planning. It also extends to areas like drug discovery, where AI algorithms can predict how different drugs might interact with the body, speeding up the development of new medications. Moreover, AI-powered chatbots and virtual health assistants provide 24/7 support and guidance to patients, helping them manage their conditions and medications more effectively. These advancements illustrate AI's potential to transform healthcare, making it more efficient, accurate, and personalized.

Implementing a healthcare AI application with LangChain

In the upcoming chapter, we will understand the basics of LangChain. We will explore a practical example showcasing how the LangChain framework can be leveraged to develop a healthcare AI application. This application will focus on patient interaction and diagnostics. Using LangChain, we will build a system that can understand and process NLP from patients, extracting key medical information and symptoms. The system will then use this information to provide preliminary assessments or advice. We will explore how LangChain's tools and features can handle complex language understanding tasks, integrate with medical databases for accurate information retrieval, and ensure secure and ethical handling of sensitive patient data. This example will serve as a comprehensive guide to understanding the practical applications of AI in healthcare, demonstrating the capabilities of LangChain in creating advanced, user-friendly AI solutions in a critical sector like healthcare.

Finance

AI in finance transforms how we manage money, investments, and security. One key area is algorithmic trading, where AI systems analyze vast amounts of financial market data to make rapid and informed investment decisions. These systems can spot trends and market trends more rapidly than humans, enabling the development of more efficient and profitable trading strategies.

Another crucial application of AI in finance is fraud detection. Here, AI algorithms continuously monitor banking and credit card transactions to identify unusual patterns that might indicate fraudulent activity. For instance, if a card typically used in one city suddenly purchases in another country, the AI system flags this as suspicious and alerts the bank and customer. This real-time monitoring greatly reduces the risk of financial fraud, protecting financial institutions and their customers.

AI is also revolutionizing personalized banking services. Banks use AI to analyze customers' spending habits, income, and financial behaviors to offer customized advice and product recommendations. This might include suggesting a budgeting plan, recommending a new type of savings account, or advising on investment opportunities.

Implementing a finance-related AI application with LangChain

Furthermore, in *Chapter 4, Neural Network with LangChain,* we will practically implement a finance-related AI application using the LangChain framework. This application will focus on personal finance management. We will use LangChain to develop an AI tool that assists users in understanding their spending habits, provides financial advice, and helps in budget planning. This tool will utilize NLP to interact with users conversationally, making financial management more accessible and user-friendly. We will explore integrating financial data sources, implementing security measures for handling sensitive financial information, and creating an intuitive user interface using LangChain's capabilities.

This practical example will demonstrate AI's power in finance and provide a step-by-step guide to building a functional AI application in this domain. It will showcase the adaptability and effectiveness of the LangChain framework in real-world scenarios.

Retail

AI has emerged as a transformative force in improving customer experiences and optimizing operational efficiency in the retail sector. A prominent application is in providing personalized shopping recommendations. AI systems analyze a customer's purchases, browsing history, and interactions with various online products. Based on this analysis, the AI suggests products the customer will likely be interested in. This personalization improves the customer's shopping experience and boosts retailers' sales.

Inventory management is another significant area where AI is making a mark in retail. AI tools can predict product demand based on various factors like seasonality, market trends, and past sales data. This assists retailers in maintaining optimal inventory levels, cutting costs associated with excess stock, and ensuring that in-demand items are always available.

AI also significantly contributes to enhancing logistics management within the retail industry. It helps forecast the best delivery routes, estimate the right amount of stock to be sent to different stores, and even automate the warehousing processes. This optimization leads to faster delivery times, improved customer satisfaction, and reduced operational costs.

Implementing a retail-based AI application

Chapter 6, LangChain and Azure Integration, will demonstrate the implementation of a retail-based AI application using the LangChain framework. This application will focus on creating a smart shopping assistant that provides personalized product recommendations and answers customer queries. We will explore using LangChain to process and analyze customer data, integrate with retail databases, and build a conversational interface to engage with customers effectively. This practical example will illustrate the application of AI in enhancing retail experiences and offer insights into developing a user-centric AI tool in the retail industry.

Manufacturing

AI's introduction into the manufacturing sector is revolutionizing how goods are produced. One of its most impactful applications is in optimizing production processes. AI algorithms can analyze real-time production workflows, identify bottlenecks, and suggest improvements. This results in a more efficient production line, reducing waste and increasing output.

Predictive maintenance is another vital area where AI makes a difference in manufacturing. Traditional maintenance schedules are based on general estimates of when equipment might fail. In contrast, AI uses real-time data from machinery sensors to predict when a machine will need maintenance. This foresight significantly reduces downtime because maintenance can be performed before a breakdown occurs, ensuring continuous production and saving costs associated with unexpected repairs.

AI is also integral to the manufacturing sector's quality control process. By analyzing images of products as they come off the line, AI systems can identify defects or quality issues that might be invisible to the human eye. This allows for immediate correction and prevents defective products from reaching customers, ensuring a high-quality standard.

Implementing an AI application

In *Chapter 7, Real-world Data Science with Snowflake and Athena,* we will demonstrate the practical implementation of an AI application in the manufacturing sector using the LangChain framework. This application will focus on enhancing a manufacturing process through AI-driven predictive maintenance and quality control. We will explore how LangChain can process data from manufacturing equipment sensors, apply ML algorithms for predictive analysis, and integrate with existing manufacturing systems to provide real-time feedback and alerts. This hands-on example will guide understanding the real-world application of AI in manufacturing, showcasing how LangChain can be instrumental in transforming traditional manufacturing processes into smart, AI-enabled operations.

Transportation

The field of transportation is experiencing significant advancements because of AI. A major development is the emergence of autonomous vehicles. These self-driving cars use AI to interpret sensor data, allowing them to understand their surroundings and navigate roads safely without human intervention. This technology promises to increase safety by reducing human error, a leading cause of accidents.

AI is also essential in managing and optimizing traffic flow. AI systems can optimize traffic flows by analyzing traffic data in real-time, reducing congestion and improving travel times. To predict and manage traffic, these systems analyze patterns from various sources, including road cameras, vehicle GPS data, and historical traffic information. They can adjust traffic signal timings dynamically, suggest alternative routes to drivers, and even help plan urban infrastructure more effectively.

Moreover, in the transportation sector, AI is used to predict the maintenance of vehicles and public transport systems. By anticipating maintenance needs, AI helps reduce downtime and extend the lifespan of transport infrastructure.

Implementing a transportation-related AI application

In *Chapter 5, LangChain and AWS Integration,* we will explore the practical implementation of a transportation-focused AI application using the LangChain framework. This application will focus on traffic management and route optimization. We will utilize LangChain to process real-time traffic data, apply ML models to predict traffic patterns and develop a system that can provide optimal routing suggestions to ease congestion. This example will demonstrate the practical application of AI in transportation and provide a step-by-step guide on leveraging the LangChain framework to build a sophisticated, real-world AI solution in this sector.

Impact on jobs and industries

The advent of AI is significantly reshaping the job market and various industries, bringing both opportunities and challenges. Here is a closer look at AI's multifaceted impact.

Enhancement and efficiency

Integrating AI tools and systems across various sectors profoundly transforms the job landscape and industry operations. One of the key impacts of AI is the enhancement of efficiency. AI excels in handling repetitive and mundane tasks, which are often time-consuming for humans. In manufacturing, retail, and finance industries, AI algorithms can quickly process vast amounts of data, perform complex calculations, and manage routine tasks, such as sorting products or analyzing financial trends. This automation significantly reduces the time and cost associated with these activities.

Another major benefit of AI is the improvement in decision-making processes. AI systems are adept at synthesizing data from various sources, offering insights that may take time to become apparent to humans. For instance, AI can help doctors reach more accurate diagnoses by consolidating and examining data from medical records, academic research, and patients' historical health information. AI-driven analytics can reveal market trends and customer preferences in business, aiding in more strategic planning and targeted marketing.

Job creation

The advent of AI technology, while automating various tasks, simultaneously opens new avenues for job creation, particularly in fields that directly or indirectly interact with AI systems. The introduction of AI into the workforce is not just about technology taking over tasks; it is sparking a significant evolution in job landscapes across various industries. Here is a glimpse into how AI-related jobs are burgeoning and transforming roles in sectors as diverse as healthcare, finance, and beyond:

- **AI maintenance and development**: As more businesses and industries adopt AI systems, there is a growing need for professionals skilled in maintaining and improving these systems. This includes roles like AI engineers and developers who design, build, and fine-tune AI models. These professionals are crucial in ensuring that AI systems function smoothly and continue to meet the evolving needs of the business.

- **Data science and analysis**: Data is the backbone of any AI system. Consequently, there is a high demand for data scientists and analysts who can interpret complex datasets. These professionals are vital in transforming raw data into meaningful insights to train and improve AI models. Their role is critical in making AI systems more accurate and effective.

- **AI ethics and governance**: With the increasing use of AI, there is an increased emphasis on the ethical considerations surrounding AI technology. This concern has led to new roles focused on AI ethics, governance, and policy. Professionals in this field ensure that AI systems are designed and used responsibly, without bias, and in compliance with legal and ethical standards.

- **AI-enhanced roles**: Beyond the tech-specific jobs, AI is also transforming traditional roles. For example, AI tools assist doctors and nurses in diagnosis and treatment in healthcare, creating a demand for healthcare professionals who can effectively work alongside AI. In sectors like finance and law, AI's ability to process vast amounts of data leads to more data-driven decision-making, requiring professionals to possess skills in interpreting AI-generated insights.

- **Education and training**: As AI continues to evolve, so does the need for continuous learning and education in this field. Educators and trainers specializing in AI and related technologies are essential to preparing the current and future workforce for an AI-driven world.

Ethical considerations in AI

AI's rapid advancement and integration into various facets of our lives and industries brings myriad ethical considerations to the forefront. These concerns are critical to ensuring the responsible development and use of AI technologies.

Transparency

AI systems should be transparent enough that users and affected parties understand how and why decisions are made. There is an expanding demand for **explainable AI (XAI)**, which aims to make AI decisions more understandable to humans. This is crucial in healthcare or criminal justice sectors, where decisions significantly impact individuals' lives.

An example of transparency in AI ethics is as follows:

Consider a scenario in the healthcare sector involving an AI system used to diagnose diseases using medical imaging. A patient, *Emma*, undergoes an MRI scan, and the AI system analyzes the images to detect the presence of a tumor. Based on complex algorithms, the AI model indicates a high likelihood of a malignant tumor.

In a traditional, non-transparent AI setup, Emma and her doctor would receive this diagnosis without any insight into how the AI arrived at this conclusion. This lack of transparency can be distressing and confusing, especially if the diagnosis conflicts with other medical opinions or tests.

In this scenario, the AI system provides the diagnosis and clearly explains its decision-making process. For example, it might highlight the specific patterns or anomalies in the MRI scan that led to its conclusion, perhaps even comparing them to a database of similar cases. This transparency allows Emma and her doctor to understand why the AI made its diagnosis, fostering trust in the technology.

Furthermore, in a situation where the diagnosis requires critical medical decisions, the clarity provided by XAI becomes even more vital. It aids the medical professionals in making informed decisions about Emma's treatment plan and allows them to communicate these decisions effectively to her.

This example illustrates the importance of transparency in AI, especially in areas with significant consequences for human lives. By making AI decisions more understandable, we build trust in these systems and empower users to make informed choices about their health, legal matters, or any other critical areas where AI is employed.

Fairness and bias

AI must be free from biases that can lead to unfair treatment of individuals, particularly concerning race, gender, or age. Developers must ensure that AI systems are trained on diverse datasets and regularly checked for biases. As AI systems learn and evolve, continuous monitoring is necessary to ensure fairness.

An example addressing fairness and bias in AI is as follows:

Let us consider a real-world application in the recruitment industry, where an AI system screens job applications. The AI model is designed to evaluate resumes and shortlist candidates for interviews. However, if the AI is trained on historical hiring data that contains biases—for instance, a predominance of male employees in certain roles—it might inadvertently learn to favor male candidates over female ones.

When a qualified candidate, *Sarah*, applies for a technical position, the AI system, influenced by its biased training data, might undervalue her application simply because she is a woman. This results in unfair treatment of Sarah and a missed opportunity for the company to hire a skilled candidate.

To address this, developers must first ensure that the AI system is trained on a diverse and unbiased dataset. This means including various profiles in the training data representing different genders, ethnicities, ages, and backgrounds. After deployment, the AI system should be regularly audited for biases. In this case, the recruitment AI would undergo periodic reviews to assess if it is shortlisting candidates fairly, without any gender bias.

Additionally, implementing a feedback mechanism is crucial. For instance, if Sarah receives an unfavorable review from the AI, she should have the option to flag this for human review. This feedback helps identify and correct biases the AI might develop over time.

This example underscores the importance of actively ensuring fairness in AI systems. By continually monitoring for and correcting biases, developers can ensure that AI not only assists in making efficient decisions but also upholds the values of fairness and equality in critical processes like hiring.

Privacy and security

As AI often deals with large amounts of personal data, maintaining confidentiality and ensuring robust security against data breaches is crucial. This involves securing data handling practices and respecting individuals' consent and rights over their data.

An example of privacy and security in AI is as follows:

Consider a smart home assistant, an AI-powered device to manage household tasks and personal schedules. These assistants typically require access to various personal information, including calendars, shopping habits, and even voice recordings. Let us follow *John*, a user of one of these smart home assistants.

John enjoys the convenience of his AI assistant, which he uses to set reminders, shop online, and control smart appliances. However, the assistant collects and stores much of John's data. If this data is not handled securely, it could be vulnerable to breaches, risking John's privacy. Moreover, John might need to know how his data is used or shared with third parties.

To address these concerns, the company behind the smart home assistant needs to implement robust data security measures. This encompasses encrypting data both during transmission and while stored, conducting frequent security audits, and implementing stringent access control measures. Additionally, the company should be transparent with users about the use of their data. This could be achieved through clear, user-friendly privacy policies and consent forms, ensuring that John and other users are informed and in control of their data.

Furthermore, the AI assistant should be designed to function effectively with minimal data or by anonymizing the data it collects. For instance, instead of storing specific voice recordings, the assistant could process voice commands in real time and only store anonymized command logs.

This example highlights the dual responsibility of AI developers and companies: To ensure stringent security measures to protect user data from breaches and to respect user privacy by being transparent and seeking informed consent for data usage. This approach is vital in maintaining trust in AI technologies and protecting users' rights in an increasingly data-driven world.

Accountability

When AI systems make a mistake, clear accountability mechanisms are important. Determining whether the responsibility lies with the developers, users, or the AI itself is complex but essential. This is especially important in high-stakes areas like autonomous vehicles or medical treatment, where errors can have severe consequences.

An example of accountability in AI is as follows:

Take autonomous vehicles as an example. If a car controlled by AI crashes, we must ask who is responsible: The AI developers, the car manufacturers, the vehicle owners, or the AI itself.

In a scenario where the car's AI misunderstands a road sign due to a software glitch, causing an accident, the responsibility could lie with:

- The AI's programming (developer's fault)
- The vehicle's hardware (manufacturer's fault)
- The owner's maintenance or use of the car
- The inherent risks of using AI for driving

To manage these issues, we need:

- Specific laws for autonomous vehicles.
- Transparent AI systems to trace decisions.
- Ethical standards in AI development.
- Adapted insurance and legal frameworks.

The responsibility might fall on developers or manufacturers if it is a technical flaw or on the owner in negligence cases. This highlights the need for clear accountability in AI, especially in critical applications like self-driving cars.

Ethical considerations are crucial

The following ethical considerations lie at the heart of AI development and deployment, guiding us toward responsible use and ensuring technologies benefit humanity while minimizing harm:

- **Trust and adoption**: For AI to be successfully integrated into society, people must trust that it is safe, reliable, and fair. Ethical considerations are not just about avoiding harm but also about building trust and encouraging wider adoption of AI technologies.

- **Social impact**: AI has the potential to significantly impact society, from changing job markets to influencing political campaigns. Ethical considerations help ensure this impact is positive, promoting a more equitable and just society rather than exacerbating existing inequalities.

- **Innovation and longevity**: A focus on ethics in AI does not just prevent harm; it encourages more innovative and sustainable approaches to AI development. Developers can create beneficial and relevant AI over time by considering the long-term impacts and societal needs.

- **Regulation and compliance**: As AI becomes more prevalent, governments and international bodies seek to regulate its use to protect citizens. Ethical AI practices are becoming a requirement, not an option, and understanding and implementing these practices is crucial for legal compliance and maintaining a positive public image.

Establishing your environment

In this section, we will explore the role of AI in setting up an environment where you can learn, experiment, and develop AI models. Here are the steps and considerations for getting started:

1. **Educational foundation**: Begin by learning the basics of AI, ML, and data science through online courses, tutorials, or books. Understanding fundamental concepts and terminology is crucial.

2. **Hardware setup**: Consider your hardware. While many initial AI and ML projects do not require powerful hardware, as you progress, you might need a computer with a good CPU and, ideally, a **graphics processing unit (GPU)** for more intensive computing tasks.

3. **Install Python**: Python is a favorite language for AI due to its simplicity and the powerful libraries available. Make sure you have the latest version of Python installed.

Installing Python is usually a straightforward process, although the specific steps can differ slightly depending on the operating system. The steps can vary marginally depending on your operating system, whether it is Windows, macOS, or Linux. Here is a general guide to installing the latest version of Python:

1. For all users, visit the official Python website:

   a. Go to **https://www.python.org/**:

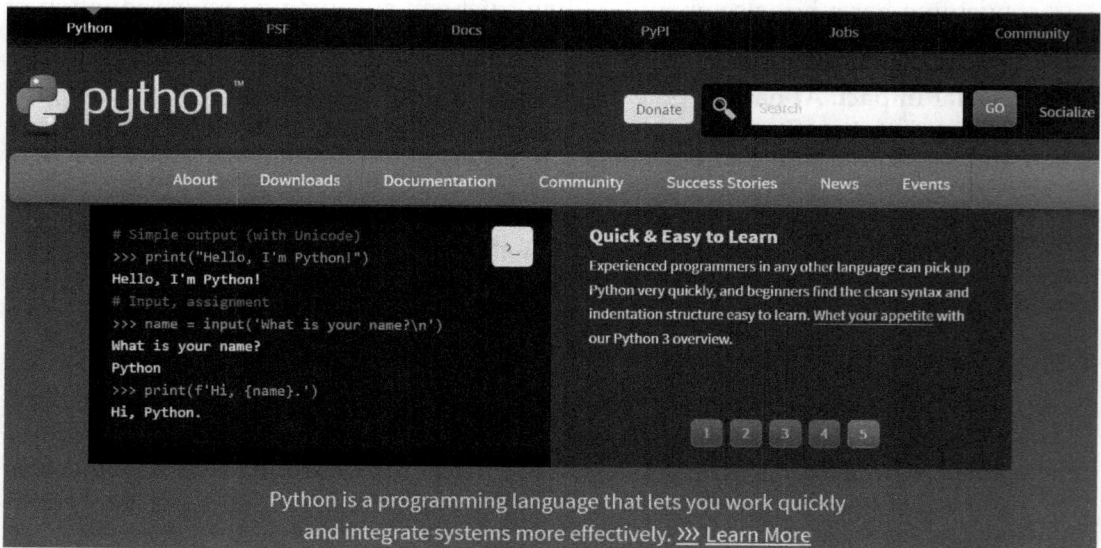

Figure 1.1: Install Python

b. **Download**:

i. Navigate to the **Downloads** section. The website should automatically offer you the latest version of your operating system. For instance, it might say, **Download Python 3. x.x** (where 3. *x.x* is the newest version).

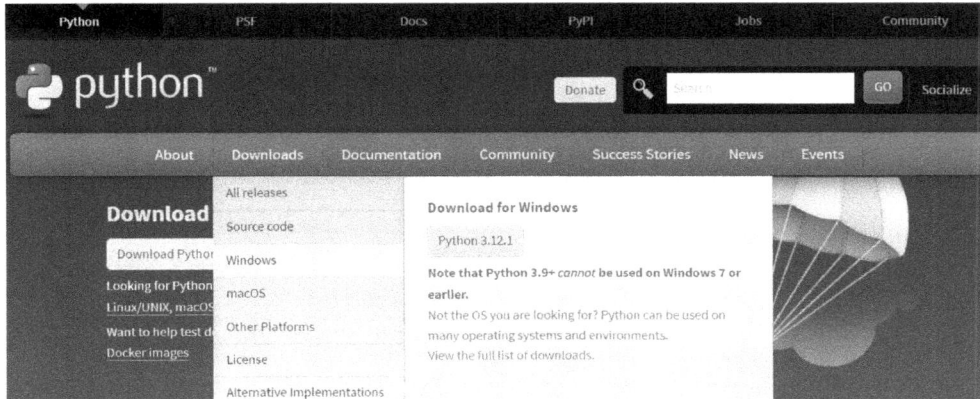

Figure 1.2: Download Python

2. **For Windows users**: Run installer:

a. Once downloaded, run the installer.

b. **Important**: Check the box that says **Add Python 3. x to PATH** before you click **Install Now**. This step is crucial as it allows you to run Python from the Command Prompt.

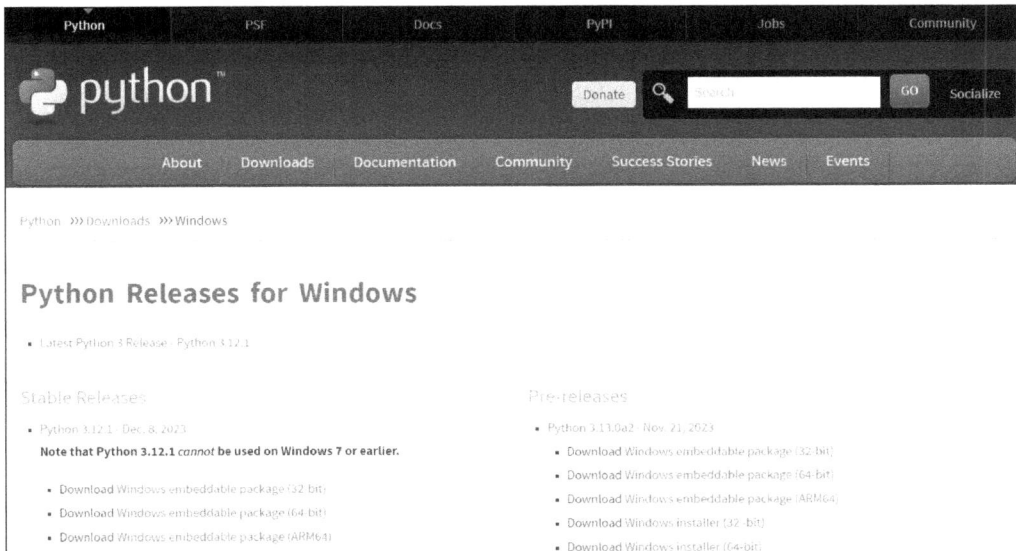

Figure 1.3: Install Python for Windows user

c. **Verify installation**:

  i. Launch the Command Prompt, enter the **Python --version**, and press the *Enter* key. If Python is correctly installed, this command will display its version number.

3. **For macOS users**:

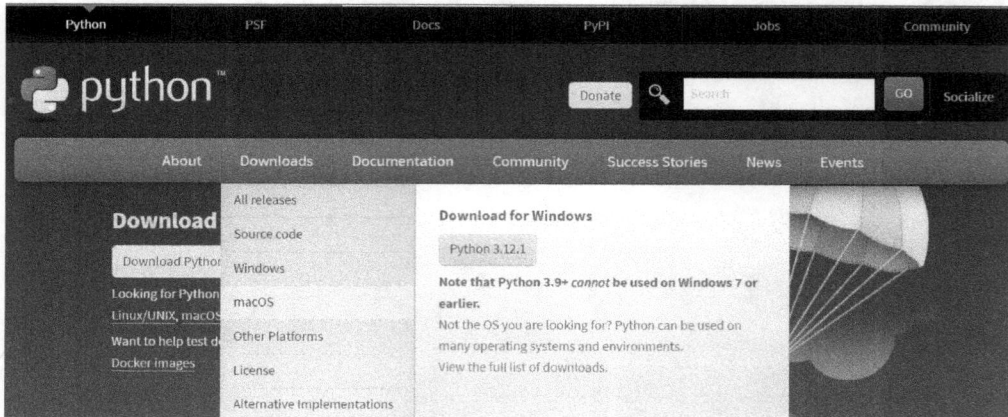

Figure 1.4: *Install Python for macOS user*

a. **Run the installer**:

  i. Open the downloaded file and follow the on-publicly instructions to install Python on your system.

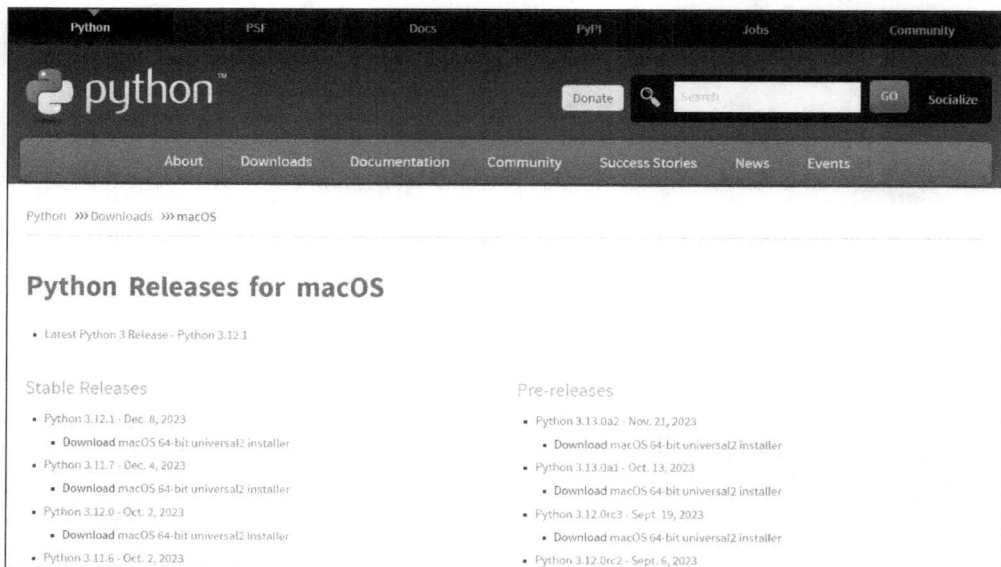

Figure 1.5: *Run the installer for macOS*

b. **Verify installation**:

    i. Open Terminal and type **python3 --version** and press *Enter*. The version number should appear to show whether the installation was successful.

4. **For Linux users**:

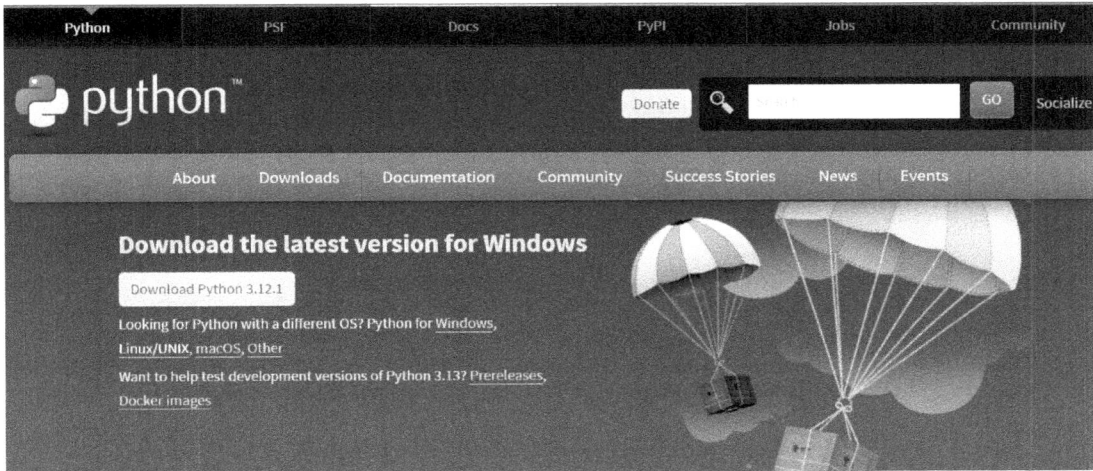

Figure 1.6: Download Linux

a. **Use package manager (for most Linux distributions)**:

    i. Python usually comes pre-installed on Linux. You can use the pack manager to install the latest version or verify.

    ii. For Ubuntu and other Debian-based distributions, you can use commands like **sudo apt-get update** followed by **sudo apt-get install python3**.

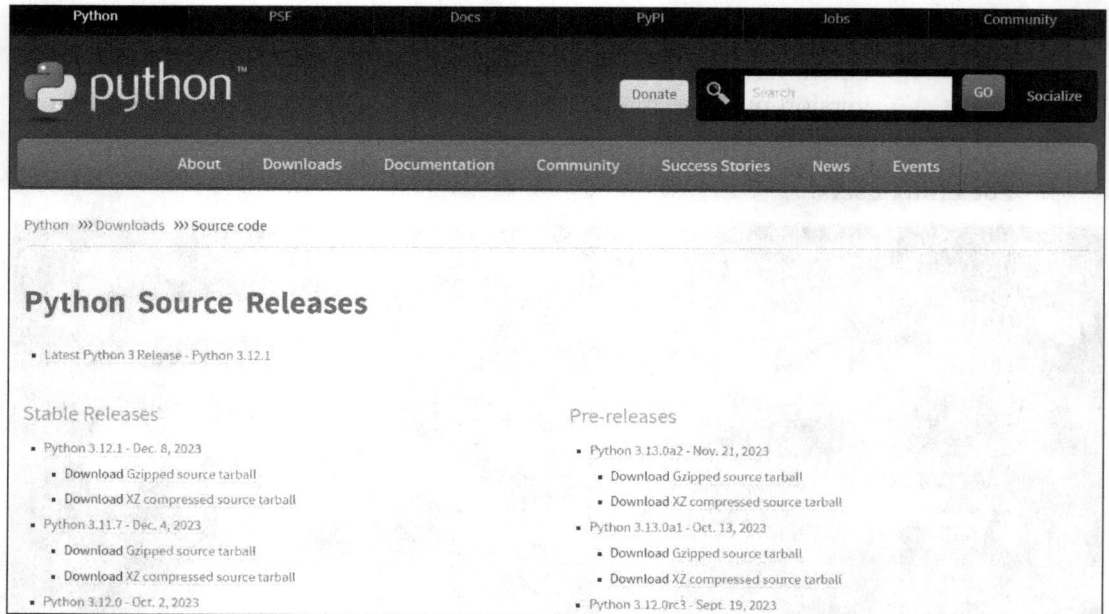

Figure 1.7: Run installer for Linux

   b. **Verify installation**:

      i. Open Terminal and type **python3 --version** and press *Enter*. You should see the version number.

5. **Additional steps**: Install **pip** (If not installed):

   a. **pip** is Python's package installer, usually included in recent Python versions.

      i. You can validate its installation by typing **pip --version** or **pip3 --version** in your command line or terminal.

   b. **Update Python and pip**:

      i. Regularly update Python and **pip** to the latest versions to ensure you have all the latest features and security updates.

Development environment

Setup a development environment that suits your style. This might be an **integrated development environment** (**IDE**) like PyCharm or **Visual Studio Code** (**VS Code**) or a more interactive setting like Jupyter Notebooks.

Setting up a development environment tailored to your preferences and the needs of your project is crucial for efficient programming and learning, especially in AI and Python development.

Integrated development environment

When setting up your workspace for AI projects, choosing the right IDE is key to a smooth and efficient workflow. Here is a breakdown of popular IDEs and how to get started with them:

1. **PyCharm**:

    a. **Download and install**:

        i. Visit the *JetBrains PyCharm* website (**https://www.jetbrains.com/pycharm/download/**) and download the version suitable for your OS (Community edition is free).

        ii. Run the installer and follow the instructions.

    b. **Setup**:

        i. Open PyCharm and configure it according to your preferences. You can select the theme, plugins, and other settings.

        ii. Build a new project and start a virtual environment within PyCharm for more efficient package management.

2. **VS Code**:

    a. **Download and install**:

        i. Visit the VS Code website (**https://code.visualstudio.com/**) and download the version for your OS.

        ii. Run the installer and follow the instructions.

    b. **Setup**:

        i. Once installed, open VS Code. You may customize it with themes and extensions from the marketplace. For Python specifically, make sure to install the Python extension.

        ii. Open or create a new folder for your project, then open the terminal within VS Code to setup a virtual environment and start coding.

Interactive environment:

1. **Jupyter Notebooks**:

    a. Install Jupyter via `pip` with `pip install jupyter` in your command line.

    b. To get a comprehensive set of tools, including Jupyter, installing Anaconda, which bundles Python, Jupyter, and other frequently used packages essential for scientific computing and data science, is advisable.

2. **Usage**:

   a. Once installed, launch Jupyter Notebook by running `jupyter notebook` in your command line. This will open a new tab in your default web browser with the Jupyter interface.

   b. Create a new notebook and start typing your Python code in cells. Jupyter is great for experiments and data analysis because you can see the output of each code cell right below the cell.

Figure 1.8: *Install Jupyter*

3. **Choosing the right environment**:

   Selecting the right development environment is important for a smooth coding experience. Your choice depends on the type of project, personal preference, and required features.

   • **Popular options**: PyCharm and VS Code are great for development and debugging, while Jupyter Notebooks is ideal for data science.

   • **Try different tools**: Experiment with various environments to see which one works best for you.

   • **Learn and install libraries**: Essential Python libraries for AI include NumPy, Pandas, Matplotlib, TensorFlow, and PyTorch.

   • **Practice with datasets**: Use datasets from platforms like *Kaggle* to gain practical AI experience.

4. **Join communities**:

   a. Participate in AI and ML online communities for learning and updates.

5. **Embrace Python for its unparalleled versatility and robust features**:

a. Popular in AI for its simplicity and extensive AI and data science libraries.

b. Python offers a loaded set of libraries and strong community support.

Getting started with Python

Here is a guide to get you started on the right path with Python, from installation to building your first AI model:

1. **Connect Python**: Download and install the latest version of Python from the official website. Ensure you have **pip** installed, which is Python's package installer.

2. **Understand Python basics**: Ensure you are comfortable with Python's basic concepts and syntax. Understanding how to work with variables, data types, functions, and control flow would be best.

3. **Explore Python libraries**: Begin exploring Python libraries that are essential for AI:

    a. NumPy for numerical operations.

    b. Pandas for data handling and manipulation.

    c. Matplotlib or Seaborn for data visualization.

    d. Scikit-learn for ML.

    e. TensorFlow or PyTorch for more advanced ML and deep learning.

4. **Build your first AI model**: Start with simple projects like building a linear regression model with scikit-learn. As you gain confidence, progressively tackle more complex problems.

5. **Continuous learning**: AI and Python both evolve rapidly. Keep learning new libraries, techniques, and best practices. Follow blogs, attend webinars, and practice regularly to hone your skills.

Conclusion

The field of AI has transcended mere trendiness to become an integral aspect of modern technology, driving practical innovations that reshape industries and everyday life. Recognizing AI's historical evolution, potential, and limits is crucial, along with considering its impact and ethical challenges. The future of AI promises exciting possibilities, prompting us to explore its full potential. Moreover, the developer-friendly features of AI, simplifying the integration of diverse components and adding complex skills like NLP, underscore its adaptability and accessibility.

As we transition to the next chapter, the focus shifts to LangChain, a powerful tool tailored to create AI applications centered around language. With its user-friendly design catering to experts and beginners in language AI, LangChain stands out as a versatile platform that encourages innovation in the dynamic field of AI. It serves as a reminder that industries and individuals alike must proactively prepare for an AI-centric future, embracing the transformative possibilities.

Points to remember

- **AI fundamentals**: AI enables machines to perform tasks requiring human intelligence, like pattern recognition and decision-making, but lacks consciousness or emotions.

- **Historical development**: The concept of AI dates back centuries, with significant milestones in the 1950s and periods of fluctuation known as **AI winters**.

- **Modern AI and ML**: Advances in computational power and data availability have propelled AI forward, particularly through ML and deep learning techniques.

- **LangChain overview**: LangChain is a toolkit designed for building language understanding and generation applications, emphasizing ease of use, flexibility, community support, and integration capabilities.

- **Ethical considerations**: It is crucial to address transparency, fairness, privacy, security, and accountability in AI development to ensure its responsible use.

Multiple choice questions

1. **What is AI not capable of?**

   a. Making decisions based on data

   b. Recognizing patterns

   c. Having consciousness

   d. Learning from previous data

2. **What was a significant period of disillusionment in AI's history called?**

   a. AI spring

   b. AI summer

   c. AI autumn

   d. AI winter

3. **Which is not a feature of LangChain?**

   a. Customizable for various projects

   b. Provides a physical toolkit for AI development

      c.   Community-driven development

      d.   Integration with various AI models

4.   **What is a key ethical consideration in AI?**

      a.   Increasing processing power

      b.   Transparency in decision-making

      c.   Data storage costs

      d.   Speed of computations

5.   **Which area has AI not impacted significantly?**

      a.   Healthcare diagnostics

      b.   Autonomous vehicle development

      c.   Enhancing human emotions

      d.   Fraud detection in finance

Answers

1	c
2	d
3	b
4	b
5	c

Key terms

- **Artificial intelligence**: The simulation of human intelligence in machines programmed to think and learn.

- **LangChain**: A toolkit designed for building applications with advanced language understanding and generation capabilities.

- **Machine learning**: A subset of AI that allows systems to learn and improve from experience without being explicitly programmed.

- **Natural language processing**: A branch of AI focused on the interaction between computers and humans through natural language.

- **Ethical AI**: Designing, developing, and deploying AI considering ethical principles like transparency, fairness, and accountability.

Join our book's Discord space

Join the book's Discord Workspace for Latest updates, Offers, Tech happenings around the world, New Release and Sessions with the Authors:

https://discord.bpbonline.com

## CHAPTER 2

Getting Started with Python

Introduction

Welcome to the comprehensive and in-depth exploration of Python, a language crucial in advancing **artificial intelligence (AI)**. This chapter is designed to guide beginners and seasoned programmers through the essential fundamentals of Python, providing you with a comprehensive understanding of its role in AI. It explains why Python is highly regarded within the AI community and demonstrates how its capabilities make it an integral tool in AI development.

Throughout this chapter, you will gain a thorough understanding of Python's syntax, key programming constructs, and how these elements are applied in AI contexts. By delving into Python's versatile features, you will learn how to effectively harness this language to build sophisticated AI models and applications. This initial knowledge sets the stage for a deeper commitment to Python's role in cutting-edge AI innovations.

Structure

The chapter covers the following topics:

- Introduction to Python
- Python basics
- Control structures in Python

- Functions and modules
- Python for AI

Objectives

This chapter provides an in-depth examination of Python and its pivotal role in AI. It aims to elucidate Python's significance as not just a tool but a foundation for more advanced applications and techniques in AI, which will be discussed in subsequent chapters. Understanding Python is key to unlocking the potential of AI, and this chapter is your first step towards that.

Prepare to embark on an informative and empowering journey. Python's robust features and its synergy with AI technologies form a powerful duo that facilitates significant advancements and discoveries in the field. This chapter imparts knowledge and engages you in practical AI applications, enhancing understanding and skills. The exploration into Python's capabilities in AI begins now.

Introduction to Python

Python is widely recognized as a cornerstone of AI. Its popularity among developers stems from several compelling attributes that distinguish it as a preferred programming language in the AI community. This section will explore the specific features and capabilities that make Python particularly effective and why it has become a top choice for AI professionals.

Discovering Python's appeal in AI

Imagine Python as your friendly sidekick in the AI journey. It is known for being super friendly and versatile. Unlike other coding languages, Python lets you express your ideas using fewer lines of code, like telling your computer what to do in a language it easily understands. This is a big deal in AI's fast-paced and tricky world, where writing clear and simple code can greatly vary how quickly you can build and maintain cool AI stuff.

Exploring simplicity and readability

Python is crafted for easy reading and writing, akin to conversing with your computer, without the cryptic nature of traditional programming languages. This inherent simplicity offers significant advantages, particularly in the field of AI. The focus in Python is not on the complexity of the code but on the effectiveness and efficiency of its execution. Python's readability paves a clear path forward, enabling developers to think about the imaginative aspects of AI development.

Python is an essential tool in AI development, akin to a superhero cape that simplifies and enhances the programming experience. It is easy syntax and great capabilities make it a choice ally for learners and seasoned AI professionals. This chapter delves deep into Python, demonstrating its pivotal role in effortlessly and effectively transforming AI concepts into practical applications.

Python basics

In *Chapter 1, Introduction to Artificial Intelligence and LangChain*, we set the stage by understanding Python basics. Now, it is time for hands-on practice. Prepare to write your first lines of code and explore the core elements that make Python a fantastic language.

Let us start with writing your first Python code by saying hello to the world, as shown in the following command:

```python
print("Hello, World!")
```

The output of the code is as follows:

```
Hello, World!
```

Essential concepts and basic operations

In Python programming, grasping critical concepts and basic operations is crucial for effectively manipulating data and implementing logic.

- **Variables**: Variables store information that can be retrieved or modified later. In Python, variables do not need to be declared with any specific type, and their type can change based on the data they are assigned.

- **Data types**: Understanding different data types, such as integer (**int**), floating-point numbers (**float**), strings (**str**), and lists (**list**), is essential for appropriate data manipulation and storage.

- **Operators**: Python uses operators to perform operations on variables and values. These include:

    o Arithmetic operators (**+, -, *, /, //, %, ****)

    o Comparison operators (**==, !=, >, <, >=, <=**)

    o Logical operators (**and, or, not**)

- **Control structures**: These guide execution flow based on conditions. Key control structures include:

    o If statements (**if, elif, else**)

    o Loops (**for, while**)

    o Loop control statements (**break, continue, pass**)

- **Functions**: Functions are blocks of code designed to perform a specific task, improving reusability and organization. Functions can accept arguments and return results.

Variables

Variables are containers for storing data values in Python, providing a flexible way to work with information.

Creating variables

Unlike some programming languages, Python does not require a specific command to declare a variable, shown as follows:

```python
x = 5
y = "John"
print(x) # Output: 5
print(y) # Output: John
```

Variables in Python do not need a predefined type and can change type after being set.

Variable names

A variable in Python can have a short name, like **x** and **y**, such as **age**, `carnage`, or `total_volume`. Here are the rules for naming variables in Python:

- A variable name should start with a letter or the underscore character.
- A variable name cannot start with a number.
- It can only contain alpha-numeric characters and underscores (A-Z, a-z, 0-9, and _).
- Variable names are case-sensitive (**Age**, **Age**, and **AGE** are three different variables).
- A variable name cannot be any of the Python keywords.
- **Legal variable names**: You must follow this pattern when declaring variable names:
  ```python
  myvar = "Priya"
  my_var = "Priya"
  _my_var = "Priya"
  myVar = "Priya"
  MYVAR = "Priya"
  myvar2 = "Priya"
  ```

- **Illegal variable names**: The format for declaring the variable name is wrong:

```python
2myvar = "Priya"
my-var = "Priya"
my var = "Priya"
```

Note: Remember that variable names are case-sensitive.

Multi-words variable names

Variable names with more than one word can be challenging to read. Here are three common techniques to make them more readable:

- **Camel case**: Each word, except the first, starts with a capital letter, shown as follows:

```python
myVariableName = "Priya"
```

- **Pascal case**: Each word starts with a capital letter, shown as follows:

```python
MyVariableName = "Priya"
```

- **Snake case**: An underscore character separates each word, shown as follows:

```python
my_variable_name = "Priya"
```

Choose the naming style that suits your preference or follows the convention of your project, as shown in the following command:

```python
a = 5       # a is of type int
a = "Sally" # a is now of type str
print(a)  # Output: Sally
```

Casting

Casting in Python is used when you explicitly need to convert a variable from one datatype to another. This can be necessary in cases where Python's implicit type conversion is not applicable or when precise control over data types is required for operations or function calls. Here is a deeper look at how casting works in Python:

Casting in Python

Casting is done using constructor functions:

- **int()**: Converts a compatible value into an integer. For example, **int(3.5)** converts the floating-point number **3.5** to the integer **3**. It can also convert strings representing integer values, like **int("10")**, into integer **10**.

- **float()**: Converts an integer or a numerical string into a floating-point number. For example, **float(5)** turns the integer **5** into the float **5.0**. Similarly, **float("2.5")** converts the string **"2.5"** into the floating-point number **2.5**.

- **str()**: Converts practically any data type into a string. For instance, **str(10)** would convert the integer **10** to the string **"10"**.

Casting is particularly useful when Python's automatic type determination does not work as intended. For instance, when receiving numerical input from a user, Python treats it as a string, necessitating a cast to **int** or **float** for mathematical operations. Here are examples to illustrate this:

```python
# Converting float to int might result in data loss
number = 3.764
print(int(number)) # Outputs: 3

# Converting int to float for more precise calculations
integer = 7
print(float(integer)) # Outputs: 7.0

# Ensuring output is in string format
number = 15
print("The number is " + str(number))  # Correctly concatenates string with number
```

Understanding how and when to use casting in Python can help manage type-related errors and ensure that operations on data are performed as expected. This makes your Python code more robust and error-resistant.

Getting the type

You can retrieve the data type of a variable using the **type()** function, shown as follows:

```python
x = 5
y = "John"
print(type(x)) # Output: <class 'int'>
print(type(y)) # Output: <class 'str'>
```

Single or double quotes

String variables in Python can be declared using either single or double quotes, shown as follows:

```python
x = "rohn"
# is the same as
x = 'Rohn'
```

Case-sensitive

It is important to note that variable names in Python are case-sensitive, shown as follows:

```python
a = 4
A = "Sally"
```

- **Assign multiple values**: Python provides a convenient way to assign values to various variables in a single line.

- **Many values to multiple variables**: You can assign values to multiple variables in one line. You need to make sure the number of variables matches the number of values.

  ```python
  x, y, z = "Orange", "Banana", "Cherry"
  print(x)
  print(y)
  print(z)
  ```

  Note: Ensure the number of variables matches the number of values, or you will encounter an error.

- **One value to multiple variables**: You can assign the same value to multiple variables in one line, shown as follows:

  ```python
  x = y = z = "Orange"
  print(x)
  print(y)
  print(z)
  ```

Unpack a collection

In Python, when you have a set of values stored in a list, tuple, or similar data structure, you can extract these values into separate variables. This process enhances your code's readability and usability.

```python
fruits = ["orange," "mango," "cherry"]
x, y, z = fruits
print(x)
print(y)
print(z)
```

This way, you can easily distribute the elements of a collection into individual variables for further use.

Exploring and mastering these concepts will pave the way for more effective use of variables in Python. You will gain a deeper understanding of data types and their manipulation.

Data types

Python is renowned for its diverse array of built-in data types, which enable developers to handle various data efficiently. Here is an overview of the main data types available in Python, which are foundational for simple tasks and complex system developments.

Built-in data types in Python

Python provides several built-in data types that help store and manage different kinds of information efficiently. These data types form the foundation of programming in Python:

- **String (`str`)**: Used for textual data. It is a sequence of Unicode characters enclosed in single, double, or triple quotes.

Numeric types:

- **Integer (`int`)**: Represents whole numbers without a fractional part.
- **Floating-point (`float`)**: Used for decimal or floating-point numbers.
- **Complex (`complex`)**: Handles complex numbers like those used in certain mathematical computations, represented by $a + bj$.

Sequence types:

- **List (`list`)**: A mutable sequence typically used to store collections of homogeneous items.
- **Tuple (`tuple`)**: An immutable sequence generally used for fixed collections of items.

- **Range (`range`):** Represents a sequence of numbers and is commonly used for looping a specific number of times in for loops.

Mapping type:

- **Dictionary (`dict`):** A collection of key-value pairs, each unique key.

Set types:

- **Set (`set`):** An unordered collection of unique elements.
- **Frozen set (`frozenset`):** Immutable and hashable, meaning it can be used as a key in a dictionary.

Boolean type:

- **Boolean (`bool`):** Represents the truth values false and true.

Binary types:

- **Bytes (`bytes`):** Immutable sequences of bytes commonly used for raw binary data.
- **Bytearray (`bytearray`):** A mutable counterpart of bytes.
- **Memory view (`memory view`):** Allows direct read and write access to an object's byte-oriented data without copying it first, which is efficient for large datasets.

None type:

- **None (`NoneType`):** Represents the absence of a value, often used to signify empty or no value here.

Getting the data type:

To determine the data type of any Python object, you can use the **type()** function. For example:

```python
x = 5
print(type(x)) # Output: <class 'int'>
```

Understanding these data types is crucial as they directly influence how data is manipulated and stored within a program, impacting both the functionality and performance of Python scripts.

Setting the data type:

In Python, the data type is determined when assigning a variable value, shown as follows:

```python
a = "Hello World"     # str
```

```
a = 20                   # int
a = 20.5                 # float
a = 1j                   # complex
a = ["apple", "banana", "cherry"]     # list
a = ("apple", "banana", "cherry")     # tuple
a = range(6)             # range
a = {"name" : "John", "age" : 36}     # dict
a = {"apple", "banana", "cherry"}     # set
a = frozenset({"apple", "banana", "cherry"})   # frozenset
a = True                 # bool
a = b"Hello"             # bytes
a = bytearray(5)         # bytearray
a = memoryview(bytes(5))  # memoryview
a = None                 # NoneType
```

Exploring and experimenting with these data types will enhance your ability to work with diverse information in Python.

Control structures in Python

Now that we have taken our first steps in Python, let us explore control structures. These tools bring decision-making capabilities to your code, allowing it to handle repetitive tasks efficiently.

Python if-else

In Python, conditions and **if** statements are fundamental for controlling the flow of your program. Here is a breakdown of the key concepts:

Logical conditions

The following are common logical conditions from mathematics that Python supports:

- **Equals:** a == b
- **Not equals:** a != b
- **Less than:** a < b
- **Less than or equal to:** a <= b
- **Greater than:** a > b
- **Greater than or equal to:** a >= b

If statement

An **if** statement is written using the **if** keyword. It allows you to execute a code block-based on a specified condition, shown as follows:

```python
a = 33
b = 200
if b > a:
  print("b is greater than a")
```

Indentation

Python uses indentation (whitespace at the beginning of a line) to define code scope, unlike other languages that use curly brackets, shown as follows:

```python
a = 33
b = 200
if b > a:
    print("b is greater than a")
```

Elif

The **elif** keyword is used when the previous conditions are false. It allows you to check additional conditions, shown as follows:

```python
a = 33
b = 33
if b > a:
  print("b is greater than a")
elif a == b:
  print("a and b are equal")
```

Else

The **else** keyword catches anything not caught by the preceding conditions, shown as follows:

```python
a = 200
```

```
b = 33
if b > a:
  print("b is greater than a")
elif a == b:
  print("a and b are equal")
else:
  print("a is greater than b")
```

Shorthand if

If you have only one statement to execute, you can place it on the same line as the **if** statement. For example:

- One line **if** statement is shown as follows:

```python
if a > b: print("A is greater than B")
```

Shorthand if ... else

If you have only one statement for both **if** and **else**, you can condense it into a single line using a ternary operator. For example:

- One line if-else statement is shown as follows:

```python
a = 2
b = 390
print("X") if a > b else print("Y")
```

These are recognized as **ternary operators** or **conditional expressions** in Python. Including multiple else statements within the same line for concise and efficient code is possible. For example:

- One line if-else statement with three conditions is shown as follows:

```python
x = 390
b = 390
print("A") if x> b else print("=") if a == b else print("BY")
```

Logical operators

Logical operators in Python allow for combining conditional statements, which is fundamental when you need to check multiple conditions simultaneously. Here are the three primary logical operators:

- **and**: This operator returns true if both operands are true. For example, `if age > 18 and age < 65:` checks if a person is officially considered an adult but not yet of retirement age.

- **or**: Returns true if at least one of the operands is true. It is useful when a condition can be satisfied by multiple scenarios. For example, `if day == "Saturday" or day == "Sunday":` checks if it is the weekend.

- **not**: This operator inverts the truth value of the operand. It is used to express a condition that is not true, such as `if not done:` would execute if done is false.

These logical operators are crucial for making decisions within your programs when evaluating multiple conditions simultaneously. They enhance the flexibility and power of conditionals in programming logic.

Examples:

- **and**: Combines conditional statements, shown as follows:

```python
if a > b and c > a:
print("Both conditions are True")
```

- **or**: Combines conditional statements, shown as follows:

```python
  if a > b or a > c:
    print("At least one of the conditions is True")
```

- **not**: Reverses the result of the conditional statement, shown as follows:

```python
  if not a > b:
    print("a is NOT greater than b")
```

- **Nested if**: You can have if statements inside other if statements, creating nested if statements, shown as follows:

```python
x = 41
if x > 10:
  print("Above ten,")
  if x > 20:
    print("and also above 20!")
  else:
    print("but not above 20.")
```

- **The pass statement**: If you need an if statement without content, use the pass statement to avoid errors, shown as follows:

```python
a = 33
b = 200

if b > a:
  pass
```

Exploring loops for repetitive tasks

Python offers two fundamental loop commands: While loops and for loops. Let us discuss both briefly.

While loop

The **while** loop allows the execution of a set of statements if a specified condition is true.

For example, print **i** as long as **i** is less than **6**:

```python
i = 1
while i < 6:
  print(i)
  i += 1
```

Note: It is crucial to increment i within the loop to avoid an infinite loop.

Break statement

The **break** statement allows us to exit the loop prematurely, even if the while condition is still true.

For example, exit the loop when **i** is **3**:

```python
i = 1
while i < 6:
  print(i)
  if i == 3:
    break
  i += 1
```

Continue statement

The **continue** statement stops the recent repetition and proceeds with the next one.

For example, **continue** to the next iteration if **i** is **3**:

```python
i = 0
while i < 6:
  i += 1
  if i == 3:
    continue
  print(i)
```

Else statement

The **else** statement in a **while** loop runs a code block once the condition is no longer true.

For example, write a code to print a message once the condition is false:

```python
j= 1
while j < 6:
  print(j)
  j+= 1
else:
  print("j is no longer less than ")
```

Understanding these loop constructs and their associated statements provides powerful tools for controlling the flow of your Python programs.

For loops

In Python, a for loop is used for repeating throughout a sequence, such as a list, tuple, dictionary, set, or string. Unlike traditional loops in some languages, Python's for loop operates more like an iterative method in object-oriented programming languages.

For example, **print** each fruit in a fruit list:

```python
fruits = ["apple", "banana", "cherry"]
for x in fruits:
  print(x)
```

The for loop eliminates the need for an indexing variable, making it simpler and more intuitive.

Looping through a string

Even strings are iterable objects, allowing you to loop through their characters.

For example, loop through the letters in the word **banana**:

```python
for x in "banana":
  print(x)
```

Break statement

The **break** statement can stop the loop before it completes all iterations. For example, exit the loop when **x** is **"banana"**:

```python
fruits = ["apple", "banana", "cherry"]
for x in fruits:
  print(x)
  if x == "banana":
    break
```

Exit the loop when **x** is **"banana"**, placing the **break** before the **print**:

```python
fruits = ["apple", "banana", "cherry"]
for x in fruits:
  if x == "banana":
    break
  print(x)
```

Continue statement

The **continue** statement allows you to skip the current iteration and proceed with the next.

For example, do not print **"banana"**:

```python
fruits = ["apple", "banana", "cherry"]
for x in fruits:
  if x == "banana":
    continue
  print(x)
```

range() function

The **range()** function is used to loop through a set of code a specified number of times.

For example, using the **range()** function:

```python
for x in range(6):
  print(x)
```

Note: range(6) represents values from 0 to 5.

Another example is using the start parameter:

```python
for x in range(2, 6):
  print(x)
```

Increment the sequence with **3**:

```python
for x in range(2, 30, 3):
  print(x)
```

Else in for loop

The **else** keyword in a for loop states a code block to be performed when the loop is finished.

For example, write a code in Python to display all numbers from 0 to 6, and print a message when the loop has ended:

```python
for x in range(6):
  print(x)
else:
  print("Finally finished!")
```

Example for break:

```python
for y in range(6):
  if y== 3: break
  print(y)
else:
  print("Break  end! ")
```

Nested loop

A nested loop is a loop within a loop.

For example, print each adjective for every fruit:

```python
adj = ["red", "big", "tasty"]
fruits = ["apple", "banana", "cherry"]

for x in adj:
  for y in fruits:
    print(x, y)
```

Pass statement

For loops cannot be blank, but if you have a for loop with no content, you can use the **pass** statement to avoid errors.

For example, **for** loop with **pass**:

```python
for x in [0, 1, 2]:
  pass
```

Understanding these **for** loop features provide you with versatile tools for efficient iteration and control flow in your Python programs.

These control structures empower your code to adapt and handle different scenarios. You can make decisions with **if** statements, and with loops, you efficiently repeat tasks. You can create more dynamic and responsive Python programs as you practice these concepts. If you face any difficulty, remember that **https://www.w3schools.com/** is a valuable resource for additional support.

Functions and modules in Python

We must explore functions and modules as we advance in our Python journey.

In Python, a function is like a mini-program within your program. It helps you organize your code and make it more manageable. Let us create a simple function to greet someone, shown as follows:

```python
def greet(name):
    print("Hello, " + name + "!")

# Now, we can use our function
greet("Alice")
```

Another example is as follows:

```python
def my_funct():
    print("Hello from a function in python")
```

If you want to call a function, you can call it by Using the function name followed by parentheses. This is also known as **calling a function**.

For example:

```python
def my_funct():
    print("Hello from a function")

my_funct()
```

Understanding function arguments in Python

In Python, arguments allow us to pass information into functions, making them more dynamic and reusable. They are specified inside the parentheses when defining a function.

- **Arguments:** Help transfer data into a function for processing.
- **Syntax:** Defined within parentheses after the function name.
- **Example: `def greet(name): print("Hello, " + name)`** where **name** is an argument.

  For example:

  ```python
  def my_function(fname):
      print(fname + " Refsnes")

  my_function("Emil")
  my_function("Tobias")
  my_function("Linus")
  ```

- **Parameters or arguments**: The terms parameter and argument can be wasted interchangeably. A parameter is a variable inside the parentheses in the function definition, while an argument is the value passed to the function when called.

- **Number of arguments**: A function requirement must be called with the correct number of arguments by default.

  For example:

  ```python
  ```

```
def my_function(fname, lname):
    print(fname + " " + lname)

my_function("Emil", "Refsnes")
```

- **Arbitrary arguments (args)**: If the number of arguments is unknown, you can use args to receive a tuple of arguments.

  For example:

  ```python
  def my_function(kids):
      print("The youngest child is " + kids[2])

  my_function("Emil", "Tobias", "Linus")
  ```

- **Keyword arguments**: You can send arguments with the **key=value** syntax, allowing you to specify the order of the arguments.

  For example:

  ```python
  def my_function(child3, child2, child1):
      print("The youngest child is " + child3)

  my_function(child1="Emil", child2="Tobias", child3="Linus")
  ```

- **Arbitrary keyword arguments (**kwargs)**: If the number of keyword arguments is unknown, you can use ****kwargs** to receive a dictionary of arguments.

  For example:

  ```python
  def my_function(**kwargs):
   for key, value in kwargs.items():
    print(f"{key}: {value}")
  my_function(name="a", age=30, occupation="Engineer")
  ```

- **Default parameter value**: You can set default values for parameters.

  For example:

  ```python
  def my_function(country="Norway"):
      print("I am from " + country)

  my_function("Sweden")
  ```

```
my_function("India")
my_function()
my_function("Brazil")
```

- **Passing a list as an argument**: You can send any data type as an argument to a function.

  For example:

  ```python
  def my_function(food):
      for x in food:
          print(x)

  fruits = ["apple", "banana", "cherry"]

  my_function(fruits)
  ```

- **Return values**: A function can return a value using the **return** statement.

  For example:

  ```python
  def my_function(x):
      return 5 * x

  print(my_function(3))
  print(my_function(5))
  print(my_function(9))
  ```

- **Pass statement**: If a function definition is empty, you can use the **pass** statement to avoid errors.

  For example:

  ```python
  def myfunction():
      pass
  ```

- **Positional—only and keyword-only arguments**: You can specify that a function can have only positional or keyword arguments.

  For example:

  ```python
  # Positional-Only Arguments
  ```

```
def my_function(x, /):
    print(x)
my_function(3)
```

```python
# Keyword-Only Arguments
def my_function(, x):
    print(x)

my_function(x=30)
```

- **Combine positional-only and keyword-only**: You can combine both argument types in the same function.

  For example:
  ```python
  def my_function(a, b, /, c, d):
      print(a + b + c + d)

  my_function(5, 6, c=7, d=8)
  ```

- **Recursion**: Python supports function recursion, where a function calls itself.

  For example:
  ```python
  def tri_rec(k):
      if k > 0:
          result = k + tri_rec(k - 1)
          print(result)
      else:
          result = 0
      return result

  print("\n\n Example Results")
  tri_rec(6)
  ```

Understanding these concepts empowers you to create modular and reusable code in Python.

Functions make your code cleaner and easier to understand. If you find defining functions challenging, **https://www.w3schools.com/** can provide additional clarity.

Uncovering the power of Python modules

Modules are like toolboxes filled with useful functions and variables you can use in your programs. Python has a vast standard library, and you can create your own modules, too.

Let us explore a basic example, shown as follows:

```python
# Create a module named my_math.py
# my_math.py
def add(x, y):
    return x + y

def subtract(x, y):
    return x - y
```

Now, you can use these functions in your main program, shown as follows:

```python
# Main program
import my_math

result_add = my_math.add(5, 3)
result_subtract = my_math.subtract(8, 2)

print("Sum:", result_add)
print("Difference:", result_subtract)
```

In this example, **my_math** is a module we created. Importing it allows us to use our main program's **add** and **subtract** functions.

These concepts, functions, and modules enhance the organization and functionality of your code. Functions let you break down tasks into manageable parts, and modules allow you to reuse and share these parts across different programs. As you explore these concepts, you will unlock powerful tools for building more sophisticated Python applications.

Python for AI

As our Python exploration deepens, it is crucial to grasp the pivotal role Python plays in AI.

Understanding Python's role in AI development

Python has emerged as a cornerstone in AI development due to its versatility and ease of use. Its syntax resembles natural language, making it accessible for beginners and efficient for seasoned developers. Python's vast ecosystem and robust libraries make it the language of choice for AI practitioners. Its integration with other technologies effortlessly makes it a go-to tool for crafting intelligent solutions.

Exploring Python libraries and frameworks in AI

Python boasts an array of specialized libraries and frameworks tailored for AI projects. Let us take a glance at a few key players.

NumPy

NumPy is a cornerstone Python library for numerical computing, widely recognized for its powerful array of objects. It is fundamental in AI and **machine learning (ML)** projects for handling large, multi-dimensional arrays and matrices. NumPy offers a wide array of mathematical functions, enabling efficient execution of operations on array structures. This capability is crucial for scientific computing, where handling large datasets and complex mathematical calculations is common.

Beyond its core array-processing capabilities, NumPy integrates closely with other libraries, serving as the foundational layer for more specialized tools in data science and AI, such as Pandas for data manipulation, matplotlib for data visualization, and libraries, like TensorFlow and PyTorch for ML. Its efficiency and versatility make NumPy a critical tool for developers and researchers working in AI, facilitating complex mathematical computations and data processing tasks necessary for developing intelligent systems.

Pandas

Pandas is an essential Python library for data manipulation and analysis. It offers powerful tools to handle structured data, such as tables and time series, which are common in many data analysis contexts. With Pandas, you can easily import, clean, and manipulate datasets, paving the way for more in-depth analysis and modeling.

The following are the key features of Pandas:

- **Data structures**: Pandas provides two primary data structures, DataFrame for 2D data and Series for 1D data. These structures are designed to work efficiently with large datasets, allowing for intuitive indexing, slicing, and data reshaping.

- **Data cleaning**: It offers numerous functions to identify and fill missing values, remove duplicates, and perform data type conversions, significantly simplifying the data cleaning.

- **File I/O**: Pandas supports various file formats for data import and export, including CSV, Excel, SQL databases, and JSON, making it versatile for different data sources.

- **Data analysis**: Beyond manipulation, Pandas provides built-in functions for summarizing and exploring data, such as calculating means, medians, and other statistical measures, as well as more complex operations like group-by, merge, and pivot tables.

- **Time series analysis**: It has robust features for working with time series data, including date range generation, frequency conversion, moving window statistics, and lagging and leading data.

The following are the examples of using Pandas:

- **Data importing**: Easily load a CSV file into a Pandas DataFrame, instantly organizing your data into a tabular format that is easy to work with.

- **Data cleaning**: Quickly identify missing values and fill them with appropriate fill values or interpolate based on surrounding data, ensuring your dataset is complete and ready for analysis.

- **Data exploration**: Use Pandas to sort, filter, and group your data, enabling you to uncover patterns or insights that can guide further analysis or inform decision-making.

- **Data transformation**: Pandas makes it easy to change your data, whether you are adding new columns from existing data, summarizing data with aggregation, or rearranging data with pivot tables for a fresh view.

Pandas is a cornerstone for anyone in data science, offering a blend of performance and ease of use that accelerates data analysis. Whether cleaning a dataset, performing exploratory analysis, or preparing data for ML models, Pandas provides the functionality to make your task more manageable and your code more readable.

TensorFlow and PyTorch

TensorFlow and PyTorch are leading deep learning frameworks that have revolutionized how neural networks are built and trained, making them indispensable tools in AI. Both frameworks offer extensive libraries and tools designed to facilitate the development of sophisticated AI models, particularly in applications involving large-scale neural networks.

TensorFlow, hailing from the stables of *Google Brain*, is celebrated for its flexibility, resilience, and all-encompassing ecosystem. This versatile platform caters to a spectrum of ML and deep learning tasks, enabling the creation of intricate neural networks and deploying AI models into real-world applications.

The following are the key features of TensorFlow:

- **Graph execution**: TensorFlow uses a graph framework, representing computations as graphs, allowing for efficient parallel processing and optimization.

- **Eager execution**: For easier debugging and a more intuitive interface, TensorFlow supports eager execution, making it more Pythonic and user-friendly.

- **Scalability**: TensorFlow is designed to scale from running on single CPUs or GPUs to distributed computing environments, making it suitable for both research and production.

- **Tooling and libraries**: It comes with a vast array of tools for visualization (TensorBoard), model optimization, and deployment.

PyTorch, crafted by *Facebook AI Research* lab, has garnered acclaim for its user-friendly nature, dynamic computation graph, and robust community backing. Its intuitive design and flexibility make it a preferred choice, especially in academic research and prototyping.

The key features of PyTorch are:

- **Dynamic computation graph**: PyTorch operates with dynamic computation graphs (autograd system), allowing more flexibility in building complex models.

- **Pythonic nature**: PyTorch is designed to be deeply integrated with Python, making it more natural to learn for Python developers and promoting a cleaner, more straightforward coding experience.

- **Strong GPU acceleration**: PyTorch provides robust support for **Compute Unified Device Architecture (CUDA)** to ensure efficient computing on GPUs, which is essential for training large neural networks.

- **Comprehensive libraries**: Similar to TensorFlow, PyTorch provides an array of libraries tailored for specific AI tasks. Examples include torchtext for **natural language processing (NLP)** and torchvision for computer vision.

Python is so vast that it serves as the gateway to the expansive world of AI. Its user-friendly nature and powerful AI-focused tools make it the language of choice for crafting intelligent systems. As you progress into AI development, these Python tools will become your allies, empowering you to bring AI concepts to life.

Conclusion

The chapter on Python provides a comprehensive introduction to its critical role in AI, emphasizing the language's user-friendliness and versatility. Key learnings include Python's ability to handle complex AI tasks with simplicity and readability, making it an ideal choice for beginners and seasoned programmers. The chapter extensively covers Python basics, variables, data types, control structures, functions, and modules, equipping readers with the fundamental skills necessary to write effective Python code. Through hands-on examples and practical coding exercises, readers gain a solid foundation in Python, paving the way for more advanced AI applications.

Looking ahead, the next chapter delves into understanding LangChain basics. This will explore how Python can be integrated with LangChain to create sophisticated AI solutions, expanding Python's capabilities in AI development. The upcoming content aims to bridge theoretical knowledge with practical applications, demonstrating how Python's robust features can be leveraged in conjunction with LangChain to tackle real-world problems effectively. Readers are encouraged to continue their Python journey, unlocking new possibilities in AI.

Points to remember

- **Python's popularity in AI**: Python is widely recognized for its simplicity and readability, which are particularly advantageous in the fast-paced and complex field of AI.

- **Hands-on approach**: This chapter encourages a practical approach to learning Python, starting with basic commands, and gradually exploring more complex programming concepts.

- **Variables and data types**: Variables in Python do not require explicit declaration to reserve memory space. The data type is set when you assign a value to a variable. Python supports various data types, such as integers, strings, and floats.

- **Control structures**: Python's control structures, including if, elif, and else statements, are essential for programming decision-making processes.

- **Loops and iterations**: Understanding loops (for and while) and how to control them using break and continue statements allows for efficient repetition and iteration through data structures.

- **Functions and modularity**: Functions help organize code into blocks that are both reusable and easier to read. Python's flexibility allows parameters to be passed in various ways, supporting default, keyword, and args.

- **Error handling and debugging**: Emphasis on writing clean code that is easy to debug, using tools like Python's interactive shell or built-in libraries for debugging and testing.

- **Advanced data handling**: Introduction to handling complex data structures like lists, dictionaries, and sets in Python, which are crucial for data manipulation in AI applications.

- **Python libraries for AI**: Overview of Python libraries such as NumPy, Pandas, TensorFlow, and PyTorch, which are integral to developing AI applications.

- **Future learning path**: The chapter sets the stage for advancing into more sophisticated AI programming topics, encouraging continuous learning and exploration of Python's capabilities in AI.

Multiple choice questions

1. **What is Python widely recognized for in the AI community?**

    a. Its slow performance

    b. Its complex syntax

    c. Its simplicity and readability

    d. Its limited libraries

2. **Which Python data type is used to store text?**

    a. int

    b. list

    c. str

    d. bool

3. **What keyword is used in Python to check if a condition is true or false?**

    a. check

    b. validate

    c. if

    d. condition

4. **Which loop type allows you to execute a set of statements as long as a condition is true?**

    a. For loop

    b. Do-while loop

    c. While loop

    d. Repeat loop

5. **How can you assign the same value to multiple variables in one line in Python?**

    a. x = y = z = "Orange"

    b. x, y, z = "Orange"

    c. x + y + z = "Orange"

    d. x - y - z = "Orange"

6. **Which Python statement is used to handle different possibilities within a block of code?**

    a. for

    b. handle

c. switch

d. if-elif-else

7. **What is the correct way to declare a function in Python?**

a. function myFunction():

b. def myFunction():

c. create myFunction():

d. new myFunction():

8. **What Python keyword is used to create a new list?**

a. create

b. new

c. list

d. None of the above

9. **Which module is primarily used in Python for numerical computations?**

a. PyTorch

b. NumPy

c. Pandas

d. TensorFlow

10. **What allows Python functions to return multiple values at the same time?**

a. Arrays

b. Dictionaries

c. Tuples

d. None of the above

Answers

1	c
2	c
3	c
4	c
5	a
6	d
7	b

8	d
9	b
10	c

Key terms

- **Variable**: A storage location paired with an associated symbolic name containing some known or unknown quantity of information referred to as a value.

- **Data types**: Categories of data that determine the kind of operations that can be performed on them. Common data types in Python include integers (int), floating-point numbers (float), strings (str), and Booleans (bool).

- **Function**: A block of organized, reusable code to perform a single, related action. Functions provide better modularity for applications and a high degree of code reuse.

- **Module**: A file containing Python definitions and statements. The file name is the module name with the suffix .py added.

- **Control structures**: Tools that manage the direction of the execution flow through a program, such as if, elif, and else statements.

- **Loop**: A programming construct that repeats a code block multiple times until a specified condition is met. Python includes two primary types of loops: For and while.

- **Library**: A collection of related functionalities of Python code that allows for managing and performing many tasks without writing your code. For example, NumPy, Pandas, and TensorFlow are popular libraries for Python.

- **List**: An ordered collection of items of different types. Lists are mutable, which means their content can be changed after creation.

- **Tuple**: An ordered collection of items similar to a list, but tuples are immutable, meaning they cannot be edited after creation.

- **Dictionary**: A collection of key-value pairs where each key is unique. Dictionaries are used to store data values like a map.

- **Exception handling**: The process of responding to exceptions, or exceptional events requiring special processing, often disrupting the normal flow of a program's instructions.

- **Recursion**: A method of solving problems where the solution to a problem depends on solutions to smaller instances of the same problem.

CHAPTER 3
Understanding LangChain Basics

Introduction

In this chapter, we will explore LangChain, a groundbreaking **artificial intelligence (AI)** framework that simplifies and transforms AI development. This chapter is your gateway to understanding how LangChain makes creating AI solutions more intuitive and approachable, catering to seasoned developers and beginners. You will discover LangChain's unique features, learn about its critical role in modern AI, and see how it stands out from other tools. We will highlight its essential components and workflow, providing real-world examples to demonstrate its practical applications across various sectors. By the end, you will gain a comprehensive insight into LangChain, preparing you to harness its full potential in your AI projects.

Structure

The chapter covers the following topics:

- Introduction to LangChain
- Key components of LangChain
- LangChain workflow
- LangChain in action

- Installation
- Hands-on examples

Objectives

This chapter aims to introduce readers to LangChain, a cutting-edge tool transforming how we develop AI. It explains the critical role LangChain plays in AI and breaks down its main features and how they work. The chapter will walk readers through how LangChain is used through easy-to-understand examples to clarify the concepts. It also highlights how LangChain is applied in real-life situations and solves various AI challenges. By the end of this chapter, readers should have a good grasp of LangChain and feel confident about using it in their own AI projects, enhancing their skills and knowledge in this exciting area.

Introduction to LangChain

LangChain is a relatively new addition to AI. It is a comprehensive collection of tools and methods tailored to AI development. Think of LangChain as a toolkit, much like a set of essential tools in a mechanic's toolbox. It equips AI developers with the necessary resources to build more intelligent and sophisticated AI programs.

Here is a peek into what LangChain brings to the table:

- **Brainy apps in tune with context**: Picture creating a computer program that buddies with language models and scans through instructions, examples, and information. This magical connection allows the program to dish out savvy and spot-on responses based on what it learns.

- **Apps with a thought process**: LangChain excels in birthing applications that can ponder over problems using language models. It is similar to teaching your program to unravel the mysteries of answering questions or deciding on actions based on its knowledge.

Key components of LangChain

The components of LangChain are as follows:

- **LangChain libraries**: These are like the multilingual tools available in Python and JavaScript. They help weave together various components to make your program dance.

- **LangChain templates**: These are the ready-made blueprints for constructing different types of programs. It is like having plans for creating apps specializing in specific tasks.

- **LangServe**: This nifty tool lets you share your LangChain creations effortlessly, making them available to the world wide web. It is akin to transforming your program into a helpful service that others can tap into.

- **LangSmith**: Imagine this as a special hangout for developers. It aids them in tackling issues, experimenting with ideas, keeping tabs on how well their programs are doing, and overseeing their digital offspring. Plus, it plays nice with any big language model framework, making life easier for developers to whip up some cool stuff.

Components of LangChain are shown in the following figure:

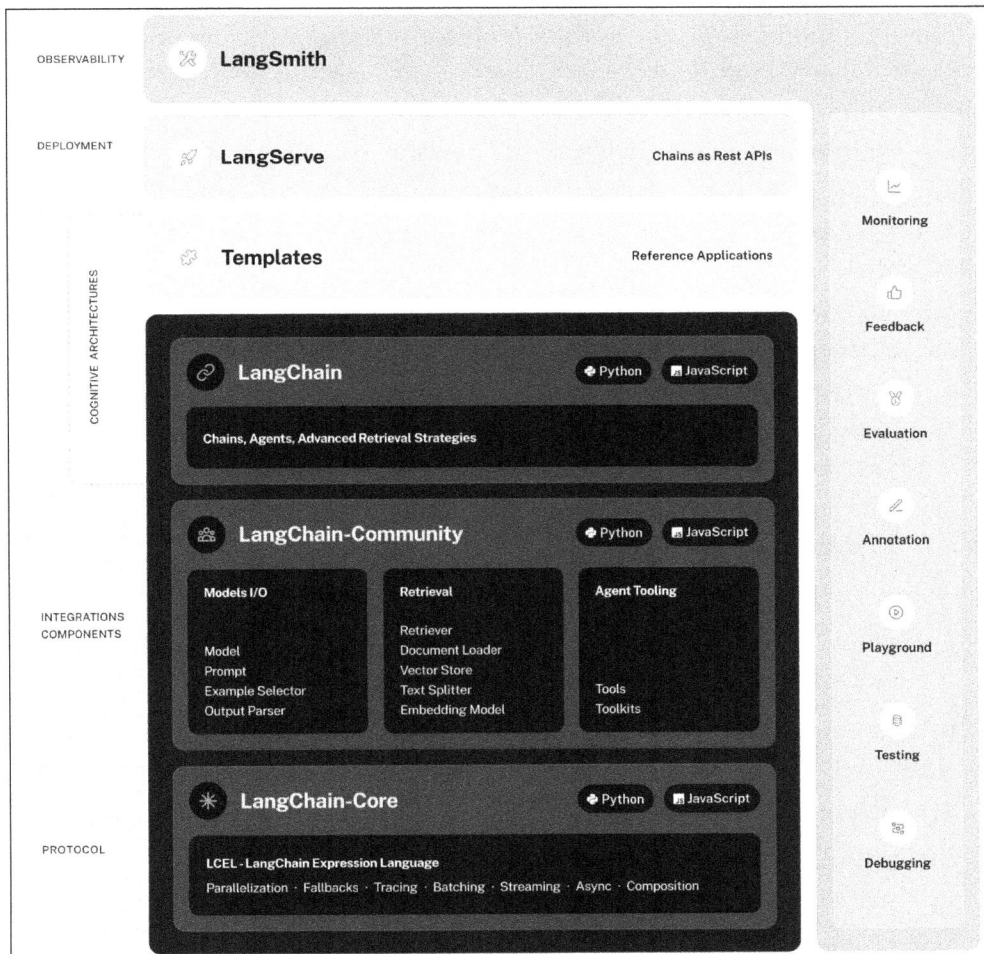

Figure 3.1: Components of LangChain

When it comes to your applications, these products team up to make the whole journey a breeze:

1. **Develop**: Kickstart your application creation by writing it in LangChain or LangChain.js. Explore with handy Templates as your guide for reference.

2. **Production**: Let LangSmith take the lead. Inspect, test, and monitor your chains to ensure you can always fine-tune and deploy confidently.

3. **Deploy**: Use LangServe to turn any chain into a user-friendly API, making it accessible and easy for everyone.

LangChain libraries

The LangChain packages offer tools and integrations you can mix and match like building blocks. These components are like magical tools for working with language models. They are super flexible and easy to use, whether diving into the full LangChain framework or picking and choosing what you need.

Now, let us explore the LangChain libraries. They are made up of different packages:

- **langchain-core**: This is like the foundation, providing the basic building blocks and the **LangChain Expression Language** (**LCEL**). It is where the essential ideas take shape.

- **langchain-community**: Consider this the ideal neighbor who brings something extra to the party. It is all about third-party integrations, adding more possibilities.

- **LangChain**: This is the powerhouse, housing everything you need for your application's brainpower. Chains, agents, and retrieval strategies—all working together to create the cognitive architecture of your application.

Advantages

The advantages of LangChain libraries are as follows:

- LangChain's key role is bridging the gap between complex AI theories and their practical applications.

- It simplifies transforming theoretical AI concepts into usable real-world applications.

- **Simplifying AI development**:
  o By offering an integrated set of tools, LangChain streamlines the development process.

  o It makes the intricacies of AI more approachable, especially for those who might find the technical aspects daunting.

- **Enhancing accessibility and understanding**:
  o LangChain contributes significantly to making AI technologies more accessible to a broader audience.

- o It plays a crucial role in demystifying AI, making it easier for more people to understand and work with AI technologies.

- **Advancing AI technologies**:

  - o LangChain is at the forefront of advancing AI technology through its facilitative role.

  - o It is instrumental in the ongoing evolution of AI, pushing the boundaries of what can be achieved with AI.

- **Widening the reach of AI**:

  - o By making AI development more user-friendly and less esoteric, LangChain expands the reach of AI technologies.

  - o It allows a broader spectrum of people and businesses to leverage AI's capabilities, resulting in various creative and innovative uses.

Limitations

Like any technology, LangChain comes with its set of limitations. These limitations can stem from its design, the current state of **natural language processing** (**NLP**) technology, and practical deployment considerations.

- **Dependency on underlying models**: LangChain's capabilities are directly tied to the performance and limitations of the underlying language models it utilizes. Any biases, inaccuracies, or constraints in understanding complex queries in the base models will also affect LangChain applications.

- **Computational resources**: Running advanced NLP models, especially large-scale language models, requires significant computational resources. This can lead to high operational costs and limit the ability to scale LangChain applications for startups or individuals with limited resources.

- **Data privacy and security**: LangChain applications often process sensitive or personal data. Indeed, maintaining data privacy and security poses significant challenges. Especially when using third-party models or deploying applications in environments requiring strict compliance with data protection regulations.

- **Complexity in customization and integration**: While LangChain aims to simplify the integration of language models into applications, there still needs to be a barrier to complexity when customizing these models or integrating them with existing systems, especially for users with a deep technical background in NLP or **machine learning** (**ML**).

- **Limited contextual understanding**: Language models, and by extension, LangChain applications, may need to help maintain context over long conversations or documents. This can affect the quality of responses in chatbot applications or any application requiring deep contextual awareness.

- **Model update and management**: Language models continually evolve, with new versions improving understanding and generating language. Keeping LangChain applications up to date with the latest models requires ongoing maintenance and can introduce compatibility issues.

- **Bias and ethical concerns**: Language models can inherit and amplify biases in their training data. LangChain applications must be carefully monitored and managed to prevent the propagation of harmful biases, which can be a significant challenge given the opaque nature of some AI models.

- **User expectations and experience**: The user experience with LangChain-based applications can vary significantly depending on the application's design and the underlying model's capabilities. Managing user expectations, especially when the model fails to understand or appropriately respond to queries.

- **Scalability and performance**: Scaling LangChain applications to handle high requests efficiently can be challenging, especially when using models requiring substantial computational power. Performance optimization is key but can only be achieved with compromising cost and accuracy.

- **Development and operational costs**: The cost of developing, deploying, and maintaining LangChain applications can be significant, especially for complex applications or those requiring high levels of customization. Operational costs, including computing resources and accessing proprietary models, can also be prohibitive for some users.

Despite these limitations, LangChain presents a powerful tool for leveraging the capabilities of language models in a wide range of applications. Awareness of these limitations allows developers to design more robust, effective, and ethical solutions. As the field of NLP continues to advance, it is expected that many of these limitations will be addressed through improvements in technology, model design, and application development practices.

LangChain workflow

This section includes a quick guide to explore how to begin working with LangChain, LangSmith, and LangServe. You will learn to utilize key LangChain features, such as prompt templates, models, and output parsers, and discover how to employ the LCEL for effective component integration. Moreover, we will guide you through creating a straightforward application, tracking it using LangSmith, and deploying it with LangServe.

Getting started

Setup with Jupyter Notebook: Our tutorials, including this one, are designed for Jupyter Notebooks, which provide an interactive learning experience. Although not mandatory, using Jupyter Notebooks is highly recommended for a hands-on approach to understanding

LangChain's workings. The installation instructions for Jupyter are available at: **https://jupyter.org/install**.

1. To install LangChain, run the following command:

```bash
!pip install langchain
```

2. **Introduction to LangSmith**: LangSmith is invaluable for dissecting complex multi-step LLM applications, allowing you to inspect the internals of your chain or agent. While not essential, it is a powerful tool for understanding and debugging your applications. After signing up, configure your environment variables for logging:

```bash
export LANGCHAIN_TRACING_V2="true"
export LANGCHAIN_API_KEY="..."
```

3. **Building applications with LangChain**: LangChain facilitates the creation of applications that connect external data and computation sources to LLMs. Starting with a basic LLM chain, we will progress to more complex applications, including retrieval chains and conversational agents, providing links to detailed documentation for deeper exploration. Follow the given steps:

   a. **LLM chain and OpenAI integration**: We integrate LangChain with *OpenAI*, using the `langchain-openai` package for model interaction. Setting up involves obtaining an API key and initializing the model with it. This foundation allows us to query the model and employ prompt templates for refined input processing.

   b. **Advanced chains retrieval and conversational agents**: Moving beyond basic models, we will explore creating retrieval chains for data fetching and conversational chains for dynamic interactions. This involves integrating vector stores for data retrieval and designing prompts that consider conversation history for more nuanced responses.

   c. **Building an agent**: We will also cover how to construct an agent that decides its action steps dynamically, utilizing tools such as a retriever and a search tool for comprehensive answer generation.

   d. **Serving with LangServe**: Finally, we transition from development to deployment. LangServe enables you to deploy your LangChain applications as REST APIs easily. We will guide you through creating a server with FastAPI, defining your application's logic, and serving it, complete with a built-in UI for testing.

LangChain in action

LangChain is revolutionizing the way developers and data scientists approach AI development by providing a robust, flexible framework for building and deploying language models. Following are some practical examples of LangChain in action, demonstrating its capabilities and advantages.

Installation

Follow the given steps:

1. To install LangChain run:

   `!pip install langchain`

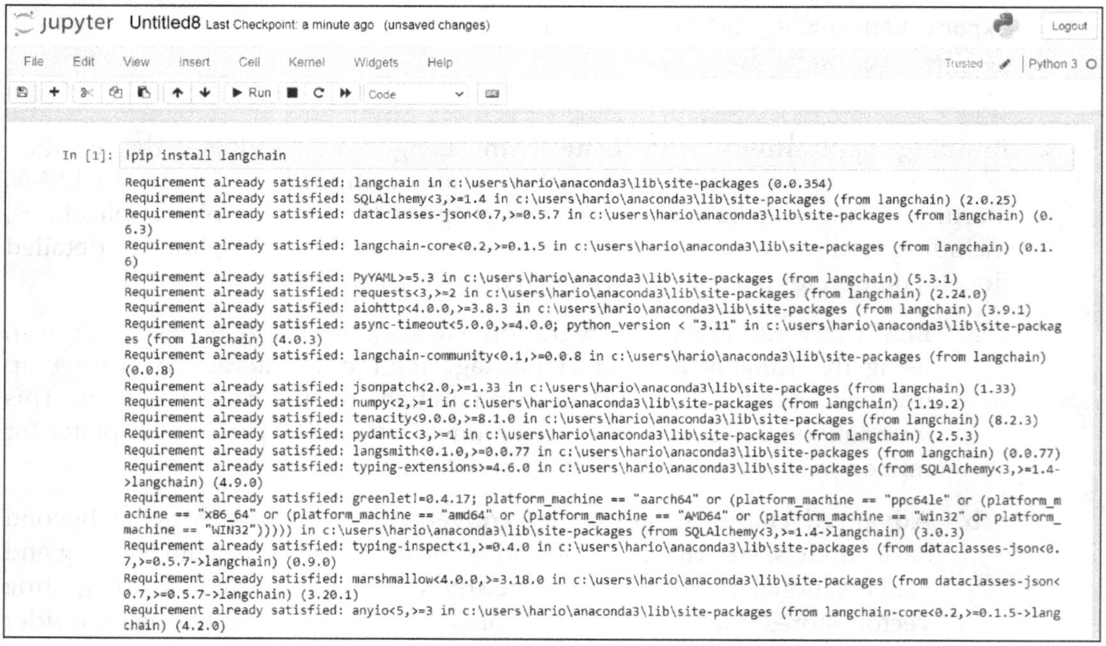

Figure 3.2: Install LangChain

Installing LangChain gives you the essentials—the basic building blocks—like setting up the foundation of a house. But here is the cool part: LangChain's real magic happens when you link it up with different model providers, data stores, and more. So, when you install LangChain, you get the core, but the extra goodies—like specific integrations for different tasks—are not automatically thrown in.

2. **Clone the repository**: Make a copy of the **LangChain** repository. Think of it as grabbing your toolkit directly from the workshop.

```bash
git clone https://github.com/LangChain/LangChain.git
```

This command fetches all the juicy bits from the LangChain workshop to your local space.

3. **Navigate to the LangChain directory**: Once you have cloned the repository, go into the LangChain directory.

```bash
cd PATH/TO/REPO/langchain/libs/langchain
```

Replace **PATH/TO/REPO** with the path where you cloned the **LangChain** repository.

4. **Run the installation**: Now, setup LangChain directly from the source:

```bash
python setup.py install
```

This command does the trick, ensuring all the necessary parts are in place.

5. **langchain-community**: The `langchain-community` package offers additional third-party integrations for LangChain users. You can add it separately or include it when you install LangChain. Use the following command to install:

```bash
pip install langchain-community
```

6. **LangChain core essentials**: The `langchain-core` package provides foundational elements and the LCEL essential for the LangChain framework. This package is a prerequisite installed with LangChain but is also available for individual installation:

```bash
pip install langchain-core
```

7. **LangChain experimental features**: The `langchain-experimental` package is a repository for cutting-edge features under development within the LangChain project aimed at research and testing. Install it using:

```bash
pip install langchain-experimental
```

8. **Deploying with LangServe**: LangServe facilitates the deployment of LangChain applications and frameworks via a REST API, simplifying the process for

developers. It is included with the LangChain CLI installation or can be installed separately for both client and server needs using:

```bash
pip install "langserve[all]"
```

Or for specific client or server requirements:

    a. **Client code**: `pip install "langserve[client]"`

    b. **Server code**: `pip install "langserve[server]"`

9. **LangChain command line interface (CLI)**: The LangChain CLI streamlines working with LangChain projects and templates. Install this tool with:

```bash
pip install langchain-cli
```

10. **LangSmith software development kit (SDK)**: LangSmith SDK comes pre-installed with LangChain to extend its capabilities. If you are working outside the LangChain environment, you can install it separately:

```bash
pip install langsmith
```

Hands-on examples

Building a chatbot:

1. Initialize LangChain and integrate a NLP model.
2. Input and manage conversational data.
3. Develop the chatbot interface, customizing responses and interactions.
4. Test the chatbot, debug any issues, and then deploy it for user interaction.
5. Monitor its performance and iteratively improve based on user feedback.

Demo

Building a chatbot involves several steps, from initializing a language model to deploying and monitoring the chatbot. To create a basic chatbot, we will outline a simplified process using LangChain and a hypothetical NLP model. This example will assume you are working in a Python environment and have basic familiarity with programming concepts.

Follow the given steps:

1. **Initialize LangChain and integrate an NLP model**: First, ensure you have LangChain and any necessary packages installed. We will use a generic NLP

model for demonstration purposes. Still, in a real scenario, this could be a specific model like GPT-3 from OpenAI or any other suitable model for conversational AI:

```python
# Install LangChain if you haven't already
# pip install langchain

from langchain.llms import YourModelWrapper # Hypothetical wrapper for your NLP model

# Initialize your NLP model
nlp_model = YourModelWrapper(api_key="your_api_key_here")
```

2. **Input and manage conversational data**: Managing conversational data involves keeping track of the conversation's context so the chatbot can provide relevant responses. For simplicity, we will use a basic approach to store conversation history:

```python
conversation_history = []

def add_to_conversation(speaker, text):
    conversation_history.append((speaker, text))
```

3. **Develop the chatbot chatbot backend**: The chatbot interface will receive user input, process it with the NLP model, and generate responses. This example uses a simple CLI, but you might develop a web or mobile app interface in a real app:

```python
def generate_response(user_input):
    add_to_conversation("user", user_input)

    # Combine conversation history into a single string
    context = "\n".join([f"{speaker}: {text}" for speaker, text in conversation_history])

    # Use the NLP model to generate a response based on the
    conversation context
    response = nlp_model.generate_response(context + "\nbot:", max_length=50)  # Hypothetical method

    add_to_conversation("bot," response)
    return response

def chatbot_interface():
    print("Chatbot initialized. Type 'quit' to exit.")
```

```
While True:
    user_input = input("You: ")
    if user_input.lower() == 'quit':
        break
    response = generate_response(user_input)
    print(f"Bot: {response}")
```

4. **Test and debug the chatbot**: Testing involves interacting with the chatbot through the interface developed in *Step 3* and identifying any issues or areas for improvement. Debugging might require adjusting the conversation management logic or the parameters used for generating responses:

```python
# Run this to start the chatbot interface and interact with it
chatbot_interface()
```

5. **Deploy and monitor performance**: Deployment could mean integrating the chatbot into a web service, a social media platform, or any other interface where users can interact. Monitoring its performance involves analyzing the conversations, user feedback, and other metrics to identify opportunities for improvement:

```python
# Deployment and monitoring will depend on your specific platform and
infrastructure.
# This may involve deploying the chatbot to a cloud service (e.g.,
AWS, GCP), setting up webhooks, or configuring other platform-specific
tasks.

# Example of deployment (simplified)
def deploy_chatbot(model, platform):
    """

    Deploy the trained chatbot model to the specified platform.
    Platform could be cloud services or on-premise infrastructure.
    """

    if platform == 'cloud':
        # Example: Deploying the model to a cloud service
        print("Deploying chatbot to cloud service...")
    elif platform == 'local':
        # Example: Deploying the model to a local server
        print("Deploying chatbot to local server...")
    else:
        print("Unknown platform")
```

```
# Example of a function to setup monitoring (simplified)
def monitor_chatbot():
    """
    Setup monitoring to track chatbot performance and user
interactions.
    This may include collecting data on response time, user
satisfaction, and conversation history.
    """
    print("Monitoring chatbot performance...")

# Call deploy and monitor functions (simplified)
deploy_chatbot(model="chatbot_model", platform="cloud")
monitor_chatbot()
```

Iterative improvement

You can iteratively improve the chatbot based on user feedback and performance monitoring. This might involve fine-tuning the NLP model, enhancing the conversation management logic, or adding new features to the chatbot interface:

```python
You can collect user feedback and monitor performance metrics to improve
the chatbot over time. Based on these insights, you can make improvements
to the NLP model or the chatbot's behavior```
# Example of feedback and performance monitoring
def improve_chatbot(feedback, metrics):
    """
    Continuously improve the chatbot based on user feedback and performance
metrics.
    This could include fine-tuning the NLP model, adjusting conversation
logic, or updating the user interface.
    """
    if feedback['positive'] > 80:
        print("Chatbot is performing well, consider adding new features.")
    else:
        print("Chatbot needs improvements, consider adjusting NLP model or
logic.")

    if metrics['response_time'] > 2:
        print("Improve response time by optimizing the model or
infrastructure.")
```

```
# Example feedback and metrics (simplified)
feedback = {'positive': 75, 'negative': 25}
metrics = {'response_time': 3.5}

# Call the improve function
improve_chatbot(feedback, metrics)
```

This demo provides a basic framework for building a chatbot with LangChain and an NLP model. The actual implementation details will vary depending on the specific NLP model you use, the deployment platform, and the complexity of the chatbot you wish to create.

Developing a recommendation system:

1. Setup LangChain and select an AI model suited for pattern recognition.
2. Input product and user data, organizing it for efficient processing.
3. Develop the recommendation algorithm, tailoring it to user preferences.
4. Test the system to ensure accurate recommendations, then deploy.
5. Continuously monitor and refine the system based on user interactions and feedback.

Demo

Developing a recommendation system with LangChain, it involves leveraging AI models for pattern recognition to suggest products or content tailored to user preferences. This process includes setting up the environment, inputting and organizing data, creating the recommendation logic, testing, deploying, and iterating-based on feedback. Consider the following steps to get an overview of implementation in Python:

1. **Setup LangChain and select an AI model**: First, ensure LangChain is installed, and then select an AI model that is good at identifying patterns within data. Models capable of understanding user behavior or item similarities are ideal for recommendations:

    ```python
    # Ensure LangChain is installed
    # pip install langchain

    From langchain. llms import YourPatternRecognitionModel  #
    Hypothetical model wrapper.

    # Initialize the AI model for pattern recognition
    ai_model = YourPatternRecognitionModel(api_key="your_api_key_here")
    ```

2. **Input product and user data**: Organize your product and user data in a format your system can easily process. This might involve setting up databases or in-memory data structures to hold user profiles, product information, and interaction histories:

```python
products = {
    "product_id_1": {"name": "Product 1", "category": "Category A",
"features": ["feature1", "feature2"]},
    "product_id_2": {"name": "Product 2", "category": "Category B",
"features": ["feature3", "feature4"]},
    # Add more products as needed
}

users = {
    "user_id_1": {"name": "User 1", "preferences": {"Category A": 5,
"Category B": 1}, "history": []},
    "user_id_2": {"name": "User 2", "preferences": {"Category A": 2,
"Category B": 4}, "history": []},
    # Add more users as needed
}
```

3. **Develop the recommendation algorithm**: This step involves creating the logic that uses the AI model to generate personalized user recommendations. The algorithm should consider user preferences, product features, and the user's interaction history:

```python
def generate_recommendations(user_id):
    user_preferences = users[user_id]['preferences']
    recommended_products = []

    # Example logic for recommending products based on user
preferences
    for product_id product_details in products.items():
        category_score = user_preferences.get(product_
details['category'], 0)
        if category_score > 3:  # Assuming a score higher than 3
indicates interest
            recommended_products.append(product_id)

    # Optionally, use ai_model to refine further recommendations
based on complex patterns
    # refined_recommendations = ai_model.refine_recommendations(user_
```

```
   id, recommended_products)

       return recommended_products
   ```
```

4. **Test and deploy the recommendation system**: Before deploying, test the system thoroughly to ensure it accurately reflects user preferences in its recommendations. Then, the system can be deployed to a production environment to interact with real users:

```python
# Test the recommendation system with a few users
test_user_id = "user_id_1"
print(f"Recommendations for {users[test_user_id]['name']}:
{generate_recommendations(test_user_id)}")

# Deployment will depend on your specific environment and needs
```

5. **Monitor and refine**: Monitor the system's performance and gather user feedback after deployment. Use this information to refine the recommendation logic, increase the accuracy of the AI model, and better meet user needs:

```python
# Monitor user interactions, gather feedback, and analyze system
performance
# Update the recommendation algorithm and AI model as needed based
on insights gained
```

This demo outlines the foundational steps for creating a recommendation system with LangChain and a pattern recognition AI model. The specific implementation details, including the AI model selection and the recommendation logic, will vary based on the application's unique requirements and the available data.

Real-world examples

LangChain is a theoretical concept and a practical tool utilized across various sectors. Its capabilities in analyzing complex datasets and enhancing decision-making processes have been harnessed in different industries, inspiring developers and AI enthusiasts with its real-world impact.

Healthcare: Patient data analysis

LangChain analyzes patient data in a hospital for better diagnosis and treatment planning. It processes vast amounts of medical records, identifying patterns and correlations that might need to be noticed by human analysis. This application helps in the early detection of diseases and personalized treatment strategies.
```

Demo with a dummy dataset

To build a LangChain-based solution for analyzing patient data in a hospital setting for better diagnosis and treatment planning, we must focus on LangChain's ability to manage data processing workflows, connect various data sources, and provide intelligent insights through content generation. LangChain excels in applications that require dynamic content processing and interaction, such as analyzing medical records and generating insights or recommendations.

This is a complete example of using LangChain with a dummy dataset to analyze patient data for better diagnosis and treatment planning. This example demonstrates how LangChain can be used for early disease detection, pattern recognition, and treatment recommendations:

```python
# Install required libraries
# pip install langchain openai

from langchain.chains import LLMChain
from langchain.prompts import PromptTemplate
from langchain.llms import OpenAI

# Dummy patient data for demonstration
patient_data = [
    {"patient_id": 1, "name": "John Doe", "age": 45, "history":
"Hypertension, Diabetes", "symptoms": "Chest pain, Shortness of breath,
Fatigue"},
    {"patient_id": 2, "name": "Jane Smith", "age": 60, "history": "Asthma,
Family history of heart disease", "symptoms": "Severe chest pain,
Dizziness, Sweating"},
    {"patient_id": 3, "name": "Emily Johnson", "age": 30, "history":
"None", "symptoms": "Fatigue, Shortness of breath, Lightheadedness"}
]

# Initialize OpenAI LLM (you can replace with your preferred LLM)
llm = OpenAI(temperature=0.5)

# 1. Early Disease Detection
# Define a prompt to detect diseases based on symptoms
disease_detection_prompt = PromptTemplate(
    input_variables=["patient_data"],
    template="Detect any potential diseases based on the following symptoms
and medical history: {patient_data}"
)
```

```
disease_detection_chain = LLMChain(prompt_template=disease_detection_
prompt, llm=llm)

# Analyzing patient data to detect diseases
for patient in patient_data:
    patient_info = f"Patient: {patient['name']}, Age: {patient['age']},
History: {patient['history']}. Symptoms: {patient['symptoms']}"
    disease_alert = disease_detection_chain.run(patient_info)
    print(f"Patient: {patient['name']} - Disease Detection: {disease_
alert}\n")

# 2. Pattern Recognition in Symptoms Across Multiple Patients
# Example: Recognizing patterns or common diseases from multiple patient
records
def analyze_patient_trends(patients_data):
    symptoms_list = [patient['symptoms'] for patient in patients_data]
    treatment_plan = "Based on patient trends, we recommend reviewing for
cardiovascular diseases and diabetes."
    return treatment_plan

patient_trends_analysis = analyze_patient_trends(patient_data)
print("Patient Trend Analysis: ", patient_trends_analysis)

# 3. Personalized Treatment Recommendations
# Define a prompt to recommend treatment based on patient data
treatment_recommendation_prompt = PromptTemplate(
    input_variables=["patient_data"],
    template="Based on the patient's data, recommend a treatment plan:
{patient_data}"
)

treatment_chain = LLMChain(prompt_template=treatment_recommendation_prompt,
llm=llm)

# Generate treatment plans for each patient
for patient in patient_data:
    patient_info = f"Patient: {patient['name']}, Age: {patient['age']},
History: {patient['history']}. Symptoms: {patient['symptoms']}"
    treatment_plan = treatment_chain.run(patient_info)
    print(f"Patient: {patient['name']} - Treatment Recommendation:
{treatment_plan}\n")
```

```
# 4. Iterating Based on Feedback
# Example of refining treatment plan based on feedback (e.g., feedback from
doctors)
def refine_treatment_plan(feedback):
    updated_treatment = f"Updated treatment plan based on feedback:
{feedback}"
    return updated_treatment

# Example feedback from doctor
feedback = "Increase dosage for John Doe's hypertension and add medication
for his chest pain."
updated_plan = refine_treatment_plan(feedback)
print("Refined Treatment Plan: ", updated_plan)
```

Explanation:

1. **Early disease detection**: LangChain is used to analyze symptoms and medical history to generate disease detection alerts. This allows for early diagnosis of potential diseases.

2. **Pattern recognition**: The function **analyze_patient_trends** examines the symptoms of multiple patients, identifying trends like common cardiovascular diseases and diabetes.

3. **Personalized treatment recommendations**: For each patient, LangChain generates personalized treatment plans based on their medical history and symptoms.

4. **Iterating-based on feedback**: After the treatment plan is generated, feedback (e.g., from doctors) is used to refine the treatment recommendations.

5. **Retail**: Customer behavior prediction:

   a. A retail chain implements LangChain to predict customer buying behaviors. By analyzing past purchase data and browsing habits, LangChain helps tailor marketing strategies and stock management, improve customer satisfaction, and increase sales.

6. **Finance**: Fraud detection:

   a. LangChain is applied to detect fraud in the financial sector. By integrating with transaction systems, it monitors and analyzes transaction patterns to identify potentially fraudulent activities. This proactive approach protects financial institutions and their customers from financial losses.

Conclusion

This chapter concludes with a comprehensive overview of LangChain's capabilities, advantages, limitations, and practical applications. We explored AI development, making it accessible to a wider audience and highlighting the importance of understanding LangChain's limitations for effective application development. The chapter emphasizes LangChain's role in simplifying AI integration into applications despite challenges such as dependency on underlying models, computational resources, and data privacy concerns.

The next chapter will focus on integrating LangChain with AWS and explore how cloud computing resources can enhance LangChain applications. It will cover setting up LangChain environments in AWS and leveraging AWS services for improved scalability, security, and efficiency in AI projects. This integration addresses some of LangChain's limitations by utilizing AWS's robust cloud infrastructure, particularly around computational resources and deployment.

Points to remember

- **Introduction to LangChain**: LangChain is described as a comprehensive toolkit for AI development that helps simplify the creation of AI applications. It is likened to a set of essential tools in a mechanic's toolbox.

- **Components of LangChain**: The chapter details various components of LangChain, including LangChain libraries, LangChain templates, LangServe, and LangSmith, which support the development, production, and deployment of AI applications.

- **LangChain workflow**: The workflow involves using Jupyter Notebooks for an interactive learning experience, integrating with LangSmith for debugging, and deploying applications with LangServe.

- **Practical examples**: The document provides hands-on examples, such as building a chatbot and developing a recommendation system, to demonstrate the practical application of LangChain in real-world scenarios.

- **Advantages and limitations**: LangChain bridges the gap between AI theory and practice, simplifies AI development, and makes AI more accessible. However, it also has limitations, such as dependency on underlying models, the need for significant computational resources, and challenges in customization and integration.

- **Real-world applications**: Examples are provided from the healthcare, retail, and finance sectors, where LangChain is used for tasks like analyzing patient data, predicting customer behavior, and detecting fraud.

Multiple choice questions

1. **What is LangChain primarily designed for?**

   a. Web development

   b. AI development

   c. Mobile app development

   d. Game development

2. **LangChain libraries are comparable to:**

   a. Physical tools in a mechanic's toolbox

   b. Ingredients in a recipe

   c. Multilingual tools available in programming languages like Python and JavaScript

   d. A collection of books in a library

3. **What does LangServe primarily facilitate?**

   a. Debugging of LangChain applications

   b. Deployment of LangChain applications as a REST API

   c. Installation of LangChain libraries

   d. Creation of LangChain templates

4. **LangSmith is designed for:**

   a. Managing databases

   b. Assisting developers in debugging and monitoring their applications

   c. Enhancing the graphical user interface of applications

   d. Speeding up the processing power of applications

5. **Which package contains the foundational elements and LCEL?**

   a. langchain-community

   b. langchain-core

   c. langchain-experimental

   d. langserve

6. **One of the key advantages of LangChain is:**

   a. Reducing the need for data privacy measures

   b. Simplifying the AI development process

    c.   Eliminating all AI development costs

    d.   Completely automating the AI development workflow

7. **A limitation of LangChain is:**

    a.   Its inability to work with language models

    b.   Dependency on the performance and limitations of underlying language models

    c.   Lack of support for any programming languages

    d.   Its exclusive focus on web development

8. **The LangChain workflow involves:**

    a.   Avoiding the use of Jupyter Notebooks

    b.   Direct deployment without testing

    c.   Using Jupyter Notebooks for an interactive learning experience

    d.   Solely focusing on theoretical AI concepts

9. **In the context of building a chatbot with LangChain, what is the first step?**

    a.   Deploying the chatbot

    b.   Monitoring its performance

    c.   Initializing LangChain and integrating an NLP model

    d.   Designing a user interface

10. **What is crucial for generating personalized recommendations when developing a recommendation system with LangChain?**

    a.   Ignoring user preferences

    b.   Focusing solely on product features

    c.   Considering user preferences and product features

    d.   Using a single algorithm for all users

Answers

1	b
2	c
3	b
4	b
5	b
6	b

7	b
8	c
9	c
10	c

Key terms

- **LangChain**: A comprehensive toolkit designed to simplify the creation and deployment of AI applications. It provides developers with essential tools, templates, and libraries to enhance the integration of AI technologies into various applications.

- **LangChain libraries**: These are collections of tools and methods in LangChain comparable to multilingual tools available in programming languages like Python and JavaScript. They facilitate the integration of various components, making application development more modular and efficient.

- **LangChain templates**: Ready-made blueprints within LangChain that guide developers in creating specific types of AI-driven applications. These templates simplify development by providing a structured approach to building applications.

- **LangServe**: A tool within LangChain that enables the deployment of applications as REST APIs. It simplifies making LangChain applications accessible and user-friendly by turning them into web-accessible services.

- **LangSmith**: A platform for developers to monitor, debug, and manage their LangChain applications. It assists in understanding the internal workings of applications and provides tools for efficient debugging and performance optimization.

- **Jupyter Notebook**: Recommended for an interactive learning experience with LangChain, Jupyter Notebooks facilitate hands-on practice and exploration of LangChain's functionalities.

- **LCEL**: Foundational elements within the LangChain core package that provide the basic building blocks for creating and manipulating application logic in LangChain.

Join our book's Discord space

Join the book's Discord Workspace for Latest updates, Offers, Tech happenings around the world, New Release and Sessions with the Authors:

https://discord.bpbonline.com

Neural Network with LangChain

Introduction

Welcome to our journey exploring neural networks and LangChain, where we will see how these two powerful technologies transform language applications. Think of neural networks as the brain of computers, learning and making decisions, while LangChain helps build language apps easily and effectively. Together, they create smart tools for understanding and generating human language, like translating on the fly or powering lifelike chatbots.

This chapter will break down how these technologies work and show real-world examples of their use, from improving customer service to generating insightful reports. We will also tackle the ethical considerations and challenges of AI and language tech, guiding you to use these tools responsibly. By the end, you will understand the potential of neural networks and LangChain and be inspired to join this technological evolution.

Structure

The chapter covers the following topics:

- Introduction to neural networks and LangChain
- Integrating neural networks with LangChain
- Mechanics of neural networks in language processing

- Learning and adaptation in LangChain
- Applications and use cases
- Challenges and ethical considerations
- Future directions and innovations

Objectives

This chapter offers a thorough look at how combining neural networks with LangChain unlocks new opportunities for building advanced language applications. Whether you are making apps, researching, or just keen on technology, the insights here will give you a clearer view of where language technology is headed, thanks to the power of neural networks.

Introduction to neural networks and LangChain

Understanding the integration of neural networks with LangChain is crucial for grasping how modern language applications achieve their remarkable capabilities. Given the expansive nature of both subjects, focusing on their essential aspects provides a solid foundation without overwhelming detail. Here is a concise overview to capture the essence of how neural networks and LangChain are transforming language technology applications.

Neural networks

Neural networks are a technology inspired by how the human brain works. Imagine your brain as a network of neurons connected to others, communicating through electrical signals. Whenever you learn something new or remember information, these neurons fire signals to each other, creating a pattern. Neural networks in computers do something similar but with data.

They comprise layers of nodes (think of these as artificial neurons), each having a job. The first layer receives the input data, like text or images. The middle layers (hidden layers) process this data, making sense of it by recognizing patterns and features. The final layer gives us the output, such as identifying an object in a picture or translating a sentence from one language to another.

The cool part is that neural networks learn from examples. You feed them lots of data, and they adjust their internal settings (called **weights**) to improve their predictions or decisions. It is like teaching a child to recognize different fruits by showing them many pictures; over time, they learn to tell which is which.

Introduction to LangChain

LangChain is a framework specifically designed for building applications that work with language, leveraging the power of neural networks and other AI technologies. It acts as a bridge, making it easier for developers to create sophisticated language-based tools, from chatbots and practical supporters to language translation services and content creation tools.

The beauty of LangChain lies in how it simplifies working with language technologies. It provides a set of building blocks, so developers do not have to start from scratch every time. They can plug in different neural network models, work with various data sources, and use tools for processing and understanding language, all within the LangChain framework. Accelerating the development of applications capable of comprehending and producing human language naturally and intuitively enhances speed and efficiency in the process.

Combining neural networks with LangChain opens up possibilities for creating advanced language applications. Neural networks provide the brain-like ability to learn and make sense of language. At the same time, LangChain offers the structure and tools to bring these capabilities to life in practical, useful applications. Together, they are transforming how we interact with technology, making it more human-like in its understanding and use of language.

Bridging AI and language technology

LangChain is a cutting-edge framework designed to harness the power of AI to build language-based applications. Its core purpose is to serve as a foundational platform that simplifies and accelerates the development of sophisticated tools capable of understanding, processing, and generating human language. By standing at the crossroads of AI and language technology, LangChain pushes the boundaries of how we interact with machines, making these interactions more natural and intuitive.

The purpose of LangChain with neural networks

LangChain's primary goal is to democratize the development of language technologies, making it accessible for developers of all skill levels to create advanced language applications. It achieves this by providing an integrated environment combining the latest AI advancements, particularly neural networks, with the flexibility and tools needed to build diverse language applications. Whether automating customer support with chatbots, generating dynamic content, or creating sophisticated language understanding systems, LangChain is designed to make these tasks more manageable and efficient.

Capabilities of LangChain with neural networks

LangChain offers a wide range of capabilities like the following, making it a versatile tool for developers:

- **Integration with neural networks**: It seamlessly integrates with various neural network models, especially those designed for **natural language processing** (**NLP**) tasks, allowing developers to leverage state-of-the-art AI models for language understanding and generation.

- **Modular architecture**: The modular framework enables developers to plug in different components as needed. This could include different AI models, data processing tools, or even third-party APIs, providing the flexibility to tailor applications to specific needs.

- **Rapid prototyping**: With LangChain, developers can quickly prototype and iterate on language applications, reducing development time and making it easier to experiment with new ideas.

- **Scalability**: Designed to handle applications of varying sizes, from small projects to enterprise-level solutions, LangChain supports scalability, ensuring that applications can grow in complexity and user base without compromising performance.

Integrating neural networks with LangChain

Integrating neural networks into LangChain marks a significant step in developing advanced language applications. This combination harnesses neural networks' computational power and learning capabilities to enhance LangChain's framework, enabling it to tackle complex language processing tasks with greater sophistication.

Integrating neural networks into LangChain represents a powerful synergy that enhances the framework's capabilities in processing and generating natural language. This collaboration brings the sophistication of neural network models to the developers' fingertips, enabling them to create language applications that are more intelligent, engaging, and adaptable to the user's needs.

Here is a closer look at how this integration works and the benefits it brings to NLP and generation.

Neural networks are incorporated into LangChain

LangChain is not just another AI tool, it is a comprehensive framework designed to bridge the gap between large language models and real-world applications. It works by chaining together various components called **links** to provide a flow. Each link in the chain represents a step in the process, from input to output. This modular approach allows for flexibility and customization, making LangChain adaptable to a wide range of applications:

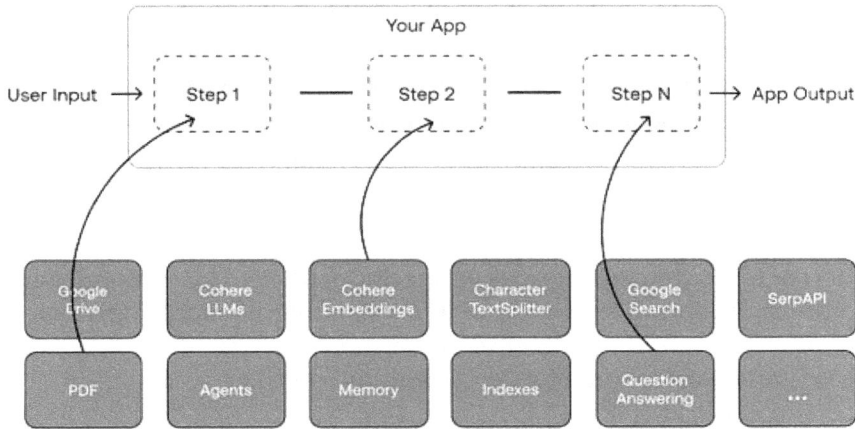

Figure 4.1: LangChain's modules

LangChain is designed with a modular architecture, allowing neural networks to be seamlessly integrated as one of the core components. Developers can choose from various pre-trained neural network models specialized in language tasks (such as **Bidirectional Encoder Representations from Transformers (BERT)**, **generative pre-trained transformer (GPT)**, or **Text-To-Text Transfer Transformer (T5)**) and plug them directly into their LangChain applications. This flexibility means that LangChain can easily adapt to include the latest neural network research and development advancements:

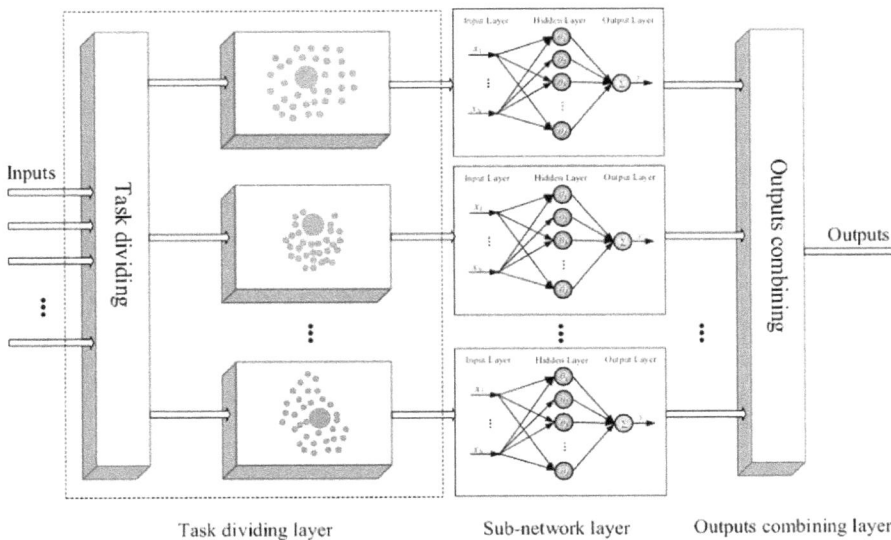

Figure 4.2: Modular neural networks

Modular neural networks (MNNs) are a new approach to building neural networks. Instead of using one big model for everything, MNNs break a problem into smaller tasks, each handled by a separate module. Each module is a small neural network trained to focus on a specific part of the problem. The results from these modules are then combined to create a complete solution.

In MNNs, each module is trained independently, allowing it to specialize. This is different from traditional neural networks, where one model handles everything.

- **Customizable neural network models**: In addition to using pre-trained models, LangChain also provides developers with the tools to train their neural network models or fine-tune existing ones on specific datasets. This customization is crucial for applications requiring a deep understanding of niche topics or specialized language use, ensuring that the neural network can accurately interpret and generate language tailored to the application's needs.

- **Unified API for language tasks**: LangChain simplifies the intricacies of engaging with neural networks by providing a unified API. This simplification facilitates developers in harnessing the capabilities of powerful models for diverse language-related tasks, eliminating the requirement for extensive expertise in neural network programming. This API covers tasks such as text classification, sentiment analysis, language translation, and more, enabling developers to focus on building their application's logic and user experience.

Benefits of integrating neural networks with LangChain

The following are the benefits of integrating neural networks with LangChain:

- **Improved language, understanding, and generation**: Neural networks demonstrate exceptional proficiency in grasping the subtleties of human language, encompassing context, tone, and semantics. By integrating such models, LangChain applications can attain unprecedented language understanding and generation. This advancement contributes to more natural and engaging interactions with AI.

- **Scalability and flexibility**: The integration allows LangChain to scale its language processing capabilities according to the application's demands. Whether processing simple queries or generating complex narratives, the neural network models can be scaled up or down, providing flexibility across various use cases and ensuring consistent performance.

- **Continuous learning and improvement**: Neural networks can learn and improve from data. As LangChain applications are exposed to more language data over time, the underlying neural network models can be retrained or fine-tuned, allowing the applications to improve their language processing capabilities continually. This continuous learning cycle means that LangChain applications can adapt to language use or user behavior changes, maintaining their relevance and effectiveness.

- **Accelerated development time**: By providing a streamlined way to integrate state-of-the-art neural network models, LangChain significantly reduces the development time for language applications. Developers can leverage the power of neural networks without extensive AI expertise, enabling them to bring innovative language applications to market faster.

Mechanics of neural networks in language processing

Let us simplify how neural networks work with LangChain to handle language tasks, using sentiment analysis as a practical example. Sentiment analysis helps determine whether words in reviews or posts have happy, sad, or neutral feelings. We will go through the steps to do this with LangChain and a neural network, touching on how we get data ready, train a model, and use special functions and algorithms to teach the model.

Example: Checking feelings with LangChain and neural networks.

Getting data ready

First up, we need data. For checking feelings in text, we gather many sentences and label each with the feeling it expresses (happy, sad, neutral). LangChain helps us prepare this data by:

- Breaking sentences into words or symbols (tokenizing).

- Turning words into numbers (vectorizing) because that is what neural networks understand.

- Splitting the data into two groups, i.e., teaching the model (training set) and testing how well it learned (testing set).

Teaching the model

Next, we pick a neural network model that works with text, like **long short-term memory (LSTM)** (good for remembering things from sentences) or BERT (a more advanced option for understanding context). Here is a simple way to setup an **LSTM** model for sentiment analysis:

```python
from tensorflow.keras.models import Sequential
from tensorflow.keras.layers import Embedding, LSTM, Dense
from tensorflow.keras.preprocessing.sequence import pad_sequences

# Pretend `X_train` is our data and `y_train` are our labels.
# `vocab_size` is how many different words we have.
```

```
# `max_length` is the longest sentence we need to look at.

model = Sequential()
model.add(Embedding(vocab_size, 100, input_length=max_length))  # Helps the
model understand word meanings
model.add(LSTM(100))  # This part remembers and uses sentence context
model.add(Dense(1, activation='sigmoid'))  # Decides if the sentence is
happy or sad

model.compile(loss='binary_crossentropy', optimizer='adam',
metrics=['accuracy'])

# Now we teach the model with our data
model.fit(X_train, y_train, epochs=10, batch_size=64)
# Dummy test data (X_test) for prediction or call url
 X_test = ['    '] #pass value
# Convert the test data to sequences of integers
X_test = tokenizer.texts_to_sequences(X_test)
 # Pad the test data to match the same length as the training data
 X_test = pad_sequences(X_test, maxlen=max_length)
 # Make predictions on the test data
predictions = model.predict(X_test)
 # Convert predictions to binary values (0 or 1)
predictions = (predictions > 0.5).astype(int)
 # Display predictions
print(f"Predictions: {predictions}")
```

This setup teaches the neural network to figure out feelings in sentences by understanding words, remembering sentence flow, and making a happy/sad decision.

Making it smart: Functions and learning tricks:

- **Special functions (activation functions)**: We used a **sigmoid** function to make the happy/sad decision. For more choices (like happy, sad, neutral), we would use a **softmax** function. These help the model decide what the text means.

- **Learning tricks (algorithms)**: We chose the Adam optimizer because it adjusts how fast the model learns, ensuring it gets smarter without getting confused.

Note: To help with this hands-on exercise, here is an example of a simple dummy dataset (X_train and y_train). We will also include the necessary parameters like vocab_size and max_length:

```
import numpy as np
from tensorflow.keras.preprocessing.text import Tokenizer
from tensorflow.keras.preprocessing.sequence import pad_sequences
```

```
# Dummy data: a list of short sentences (X_train)
X_train = ['I love programming', 'I hate bugs', 'Coding is fun', 'I enjoy
learning', 'Debugging is hard']
y_train = [1, 0, 1, 1, 0] # 1 = positive sentiment, 0 = negative sentiment

# Tokenizer to convert words into numbers
tokenizer = Tokenizer()
tokenizer.fit_on_texts(X_train)

# Convert texts to sequences of integers
X_train = tokenizer.texts_to_sequences(X_train)

# Pad sequences to make them the same length
max_length = max(len(s) for s in X_train)  # Find the max length of
sentences
X_train = pad_sequences(X_train, maxlen=max_length)

# Get the size of our vocabulary
vocab_size = len(tokenizer.word_index) + 1  # +1 to account for 0 padding
token

# Model definition (same as before)
from tensorflow.keras.models import Sequential
from tensorflow.keras.layers import Embedding, LSTM, Dense

model = Sequential()
model.add(Embedding(vocab_size, 100, input_length=max_length))  # Helps the
model understand word meanings
model.add(LSTM(100))  # This part remembers and uses sentence context
model.add(Dense(1, activation='sigmoid'))  # Decides if the sentence is
happy or sad

model.compile(loss='binary_crossentropy', optimizer='adam',
metrics=['accuracy'])

# Now we teach the model with our dummy data
model.fit(X_train, y_train, epochs=10, batch_size=2)
```

Explanation:

- **Dummy data (X_train)**: W created a small set of sentences with some positive and negative sentiment labels in **y_train**.

- **Tokenizer**: Converts words into integers for the model to understand.

- **Padding**: Ensures all input sequences are the same length (**max_length**), which is required for **LSTM** models.

- **Vocabulary size**: The number of unique words in the dataset plus one for the padding token.

> **Note: This walkthrough shows how LangChain and neural networks team up for a task like sentiment analysis, simplifying the complex parts of preparing data, choosing a model, and training it to understand language. This example highlights how LangChain helps make using neural networks for language tasks easier and more powerful.**

Learning and adaptation in LangChain

LangChain, with its neural network brain, is always learning and adapting. It refines its models through continuous interaction with language data to better understand and generate language. This continuous improvement process means that LangChain's applications become more efficient, accurate, and user-friendly, providing a dynamic solution that evolves with the users' needs.

LangChain, combined with the power of neural networks, is like a smart assistant that gets better the more you use it. This section will explain how LangChain learns from data and interactions over time and keeps improving its ability to handle language tasks.

LangChain learns

When you first start using LangChain with its neural networks, it is like giving a brain the basics of language. It knows some things, but not everything. As LangChain is exposed to more text, conversations, or language data, it starts to learn as a person does. Here is how it happens:

- **From data**: Every time LangChain processes text—articles, reviews, or chat messages, it pays attention to the patterns and details in the words. This could be how sentences are structured, or words are used in different contexts.

- **From interactions**: When people use applications built on LangChain, every question and response is a learning opportunity. LangChain notices which answers are helpful and which are not, adjusting its approach accordingly.

Continuous improvement

Imagine teaching a child to speak. Over time, with corrections and new vocabulary, they speak more clearly and correctly. LangChain does something similar with language, using continuous learning. Here is what that involves:

- **Feedback loop**: Just like a student learns from feedback, LangChain uses the reactions and corrections from users to understand what it needs to improve. If a user corrects a translation or provides a different answer, LangChain takes note.

- **Model refinement**: Behind the scenes, LangChain's neural networks are updated based on new data and interactions. This could mean adjusting how it understands sentence structures or the meanings of words in various contexts.

Model refinement in action

Let us say you are using a LangChain-powered chatbot for customer service. Initially, it might misunderstand some questions or provide less-than-perfect answers. However, as customers interact with it, LangChain starts to understand common questions and how best to answer them. Over time, it learns from the patterns in these conversations, becoming more accurate and helpful.

Logic behind continuous learning

Here is how continuous learning works:

- **Data analysis**: LangChain analyzes the data it gathers to identify areas for improvement. For example, if many users ask the same question but the chatbot's responses are frequently corrected, LangChain will flag this for learning.

- **Updating the model**: Specialists or automated systems review the flagged data and use it to update LangChain's neural network models. This might involve retraining the model with new data to understand certain phrases or concepts better.

Applications and use cases of LangChain and neural networks

LangChain, when combined with neural networks, opens up many possibilities across different industries. By understanding and generating natural language, this technology revolutionizes how businesses interact with data and customers. Here are some real-world applications and their impacts:

- **Customer service chatbots**:
    - **Application**: One of the most common uses of LangChain and neural networks is creating chatbots for customer service. These chatbots can understand customer queries in natural language and provide instant, accurate responses. They can handle many questions, from simple FAQs to more complex inquiries, reducing wait times and improving customer satisfaction.
    - **Impact**: Enterprises have witnessed substantial enhancements in customer service efficiency. Chatbots can manage numerous inquiries concurrently, operating 24/7 without succumbing to fatigue or making errors due to

exhaustion. Consequently, this results in quicker response times, enabling human customer service representatives to concentrate on addressing more intricate issues that demand a personalized approach.

- **Content creation and summarization**:
  - o **Application**: LangChain automates content creation and summarization tasks. For instance, it generates news summaries from long articles or creates product descriptions based on bullet points of features. This application saves time for content creators and ensures consistent quality and tone across all content.
  - o **Impact**: Companies in the media and e-commerce sectors have benefited from streamlined content production processes. Automated summarization helps readers quickly get the gist of long articles, improving user engagement. Meanwhile, automated product description generation helps e-commerce sites keep product listings up to date with minimal manual effort.

- **Language translation services**:
  - o **Application**: LangChain and neural networks power advanced language translation services that go beyond word-for-word translation to understand context and cultural nuances. This is crucial for businesses operating in multiple countries or regions, enabling them to communicate effectively with a global audience.
  - o **Impact**: Using neural network-powered translation services has significantly reduced language barriers, allowing companies to expand their reach and communicate with customers in their native language. This enhances customer experience and opens up new markets for businesses.

- **Sentiment analysis for market research**:
  - o **Application**: Sentiment analysis is used to gauge public opinion on products, services, or brands by analyzing social media posts, reviews, and comments. LangChain can process vast amounts of text data to identify general sentiment, providing valuable insights for marketing strategies.
  - o **Impact**: Companies have gained a deeper understanding of customer satisfaction and market trends, enabling them to make informed decisions. This real-time feedback loop allows businesses to quickly adjust their strategies, improve product offerings, and address customer concerns proactively.

- **Personalized education platforms**:
  - o **Application**: LangChain and neural networks create personalized learning experiences in education. The platform can tailor the curriculum, exercises, and feedback to individual needs by understanding students' strengths, weaknesses, and learning preferences.

     o **Impact**: Personalized education platforms have shown promising results in improving student engagement and learning outcomes. Students receive support tailored to their own pace and learning style, making education more accessible and effective for diverse learner populations.

These applications showcase the versatility and transformative potential of integrating LangChain with neural networks across various industries. The capabilities of AI to comprehend and generate human language empower businesses to boost efficiency, elevate customer experiences, and unlock fresh opportunities for growth and innovation. The continuous development of LangChain and neural network technologies promises even more exciting applications in the future, further illustrating the practical benefits of this advanced technology.

Challenges and ethical considerations

Deploying neural network-powered language applications comes with technical and ethical challenges. Developers and businesses must comprehend these challenges to utilize technologies like LangChain responsibly. Here is an overview of these challenges and strategies to address them:

- **Technical challenges**:

     o **Data bias and quality**: Neural networks learn from data, so AI will inherit these flaws if the data is biased or of poor quality. This can lead to biased or inaccurate outputs in language applications, affecting user trust and application reliability.

     o **Interpretability and transparency**: Neural networks, particularly deep learning models, are frequently perceived as black boxes due to the challenge of comprehending their decision-making processes. This opacity can pose issues, particularly in critical applications where understanding the reasoning behind AI decisions is crucial.

     o **Language complexity**: Natural language is complex and nuanced. Sarcasm, idioms, and cultural references can be challenging for AI to understand correctly, leading to misunderstandings or inappropriate responses.

- **Ethical considerations**:

     o **Privacy**: Language applications often process sensitive personal information. Ensuring the privacy and security of this data is crucial to protecting users' rights and maintaining trust.

     o **Consent and transparency**: Users should be informed about how their data is used, including whether their interactions are with AI or humans. Obtaining consent for data use and providing transparency about AI's role are key ethical considerations.

- o **Bias and fairness**: AI systems can perpetuate or exacerbate societal biases if not carefully monitored and corrected. Ensuring fairness and reducing bias in AI-generated language content are significant ethical challenges.

- **Strategies for overcoming challenges**: Addressing technical challenges:

  - o **Data quality and diversity**: Ensure the training data is as diverse and unbiased as possible. Regularly audit and update the data to include various languages, dialects, and cultural contexts to minimize bias.

  - o **Explainability tools**: Use and develop tools and methods that increase the interpretability of neural networks. This could involve techniques that visualize how models make decisions or simplified models that approximate the behavior of more complex systems.

  - o **Continuous testing and improvement**: Regularly test language applications in real-world scenarios to identify and correct misunderstandings or inappropriate responses. Incorporate user feedback for continuous improvement.

- **Tackling ethical considerations**:

  - o **Privacy and data protection**: Implement robust data protection measures, anonymize personal data where possible, and adhere to privacy regulations like GDPR. Ensure data is stored securely and used ethically.

  - o **Consent and transparency**: Communicate to users how their data will be used and obtain their consent. Give users choices to opt out of data collection or use AI in their communications.

  - o **Bias mitigation**: Regularly audit AI models for bias and take helpful actions to address any issues. This can include retraining models with more balanced data or developing algorithms specifically designed to reduce bias.

While neural network-powered language applications offer immense potential, navigating the technical and ethical challenges they present is crucial for their responsible deployment. By prioritizing fairness, transparency, and user privacy, developers can harness the power of AI in language technology to create inclusive, ethical, and effective solutions. These strategies address current challenges and lay the groundwork for a future where AI enhances human communication without compromising ethical standards.

Future directions and innovations

The integration of neural network technologies within LangChain is poised for exciting advancements and innovations. As we look toward the future, several trends and developments are expected to shape the language technology landscape. Here is a glimpse into the future of neural network-powered language applications.

Advancements in neural network technologies

The following are the advancements in neural network technologies:

- **Improved natural language understanding (NLU)**: Future neural networks will likely achieve a deeper understanding of human language. This includes a better grasp of context, nuances, and the subtleties of human communication, enabling more accurate and human-like interactions.

- **Enhanced multimodal capabilities**: The next wave of neural networks will be adept at processing and integrating multiple types of data (text, voice, images, and video) simultaneously. This multimodal approach will enable more sophisticated language applications to understand and generate content across different media formats.

- **Advancements in automated machine learning (AutoML) and neural architecture search (NAS)**: AutoML and NAS techniques will make designing and optimizing neural networks easier. This means creating more efficient models tailored to specific language tasks with less manual effort.

Emerging trends and new applications

The following are the emerging trends and new applications:

- **Real-time language translation and interpretation**: Future neural networks will power devices and applications capable of real-time translation and interpretation, breaking down language barriers in instant communication. This could revolutionize international relations, education, and global business.

- **Emotional AI and sentiment analysis**: Advancements in understanding emotional cues in text and speech will enable the development of AI that can respond to human emotions appropriately, opening new avenues in mental health support, customer service, and interactive entertainment.

- **Ethical AI advisors**: As ethical considerations become increasingly important. We might see the emergence of AI advisors trained to guide ethical dilemmas, leveraging neural networks to understand complex ethical frameworks and cultural norms.

- **Personalized content creation**: Neural networks will enable the creation of highly personalized content, from news articles tailored to individual interests to personalized learning materials that adapt to the student's knowledge level and learning style.

- **Enhanced accessibility tools**: Neural networks will drive innovations in accessibility, such as real-time sign language interpretation, advanced speech-to-text services, and context-aware assistive devices, making technology more accessible to people with disabilities.

The future of neural network technologies within LangChain promises to transform how we interact with language and technology. By pushing the boundaries of natural language understanding and generation, these advancements will enable more intuitive, intelligent, and accessible language applications. As we continue to explore and innovate, the potential applications and capabilities of neural networks in language technology will expand, leading to a future where AI-enhanced communication is seamlessly integrated into our daily lives.

Conclusion

In conclusion, integrating neural networks with LangChain paves the way for revolutionary advancements in language technology. This chapter covered the basics of neural networks and LangChain explained their integration and highlighted real-world applications, from customer service improvements to content creation and translation. We also addressed ethical considerations and the potential for breaking down language barriers.

This integration boosts the efficiency and personalization of language applications, promising a future where technology is more accessible and intuitive. The journey revealed vast opportunities for innovation, leading to more intelligent and empathetic language applications.

In the next chapter, readers will explore advanced techniques and case studies showcasing the most cutting-edge uses of LangChain and neural networks in various industries.

Points to remember

When discussing the integration of neural networks with LangChain for advanced language applications, here are some crucial points to remember:

- **Synergy between neural networks and LangChain**: The combination of neural network technology with the LangChain framework amplifies the capabilities of language applications, making them more intelligent, adaptable, and efficient.

- **Continuous learning and adaptation**: LangChain applications, powered by neural networks, learn from every interaction and piece of data, continuously improving their performance and accuracy over time.

- **Diverse applications across industries**: This integration finds applications across diverse domains, including customer service, content creation, language translation, and sentiment analysis. Such versatility demonstrates its broad-ranging impact across different fields.

- **Technical and ethical challenges**: Deploying neural network-powered language applications involves navigating technical hurdles like data bias and addressing ethical considerations like privacy and fairness.

- **Future innovations**: The field is ripe for future advancements, including improved natural language understanding, multimodal capabilities, and the development of ethical AI advisors, among others.

- **Data handling and preprocessing**: Effective data preparation, including tokenizing and vectorizing text, is essential for training neural networks in language applications, highlighting the importance of quality and diverse datasets.

- **Importance of activation functions and learning algorithms**: The choice of activation functions and optimizers, like the sigmoid function and Adam optimizer, is crucial for performing neural network models in language tasks.

- **Bias mitigation and model transparency**: Efforts to reduce bias and increase the interpretability of AI models are vital for building trust and ensuring the responsible use of technology.

- **User engagement and feedback**: Incorporating user feedback into the learning cycle is critical for refining and enhancing the performance of language applications over time.

- **Commitment to ethical AI development**: Ensuring the ethical use of AI, particularly in handling personal data and making AI's decision-making processes transparent, is essential for the sustainable development of language technologies.

These points encapsulate the essence of integrating neural networks with LangChain, highlighting this technology's transformative potential, challenges, and future direction in advancing language applications.

Multiple choice questions

Here are 10 multiple choice questions based on the chapter, along with their answers:

1. **What are neural networks inspired by?**

   a. Computer algorithms

   b. Human brain structure

   c. Animal instincts

   d. Plant communication

2. **What does LangChain primarily focus on?**

   a. Data analysis

   b. Language technology applications

   c. Financial forecasting

   d. Image recognition

3. **Which of the following is a common application of LangChain and neural networks?**

   a. Cryptocurrency trading

   b. Customer service chatbots

   c. Weather prediction

   d. Game development

4. **What is sentiment analysis used for?**

   a. Predicting stock market trends

   b. Diagnosing diseases

   c. Understanding emotions in text

   d. Enhancing internet speed

5. **Which technique converts sentences into a list of words or symbols?**

   a. Normalization

   b. Tokenizing

   c. Embedding

   d. Encrypting

6. **What type of neural network is particularly good for processing sequences like sentences?**

   a. CNN

   b. RNN

   c. LSTM

   d. Feedforward neural network

7. **Which activation function is commonly used for binary classification tasks?**

   a. ReLU

   b. Tanh

   c. Sigmoid

   d. Softmax

8. **What challenges does data bias pose in language applications?**

   a. Increases computational cost

   b. Reduces the model size

   c. Leads to biased or inaccurate outputs

   d. Improves model accuracy

9. **Which of the following is an ethical consideration in deploying neural network-powered language applications?**

   a. Increasing energy consumption

   b. Ensuring model portability

   c. Protecting user privacy

   d. Enhancing color schemes

10. **What future direction is anticipated for neural network technologies within LangChain?**

    a. Decreased reliance on data

    b. Improved natural language understanding

    c. Shift away from AI

    d. Reduced application areas

As discussed in the chapter, these questions cover the fundamentals, applications, challenges, and prospects of integrating neural networks with LangChain.

Answers

1	b
2	b
3	b
4	c
5	b
6	c
7	c
8	c
9	c
10	b

Key terms

Here are some key terms discussed in the chapter, each explained in simple words:

- **Neural networks**: Imagine a computer program that tries to think and learn like a human brain. Neural networks comprise many tiny parts working together to understand information, make decisions, or recognize patterns.

- **LangChain**: This toolbox is for making apps that can understand or use language in smart ways. It uses neural networks to help these apps improve at tasks like chatting, translating languages, or creating new sentences.

- **NLP**: This is all about teaching computers to understand human language. NLP enables computers to perform tasks such as reading text, processing speech, interpreting content, gauging sentiment, and identifying significant elements within the given information.

- **Sentiment analysis**: This is like teaching a computer to tell if a piece of writing is happy, sad, angry, etc. It is used to understand people's feelings about certain topics based on their online writing.

- **Tokenizing**: This is the first step in helping a computer understand text. It breaks down sentences into smaller pieces, like words or phrases, so the computer can look at them individually.

- **Vectorization**: This is a way to turn words into numbers. Computers are great with numbers, so this step changes words into a format that computers can work with to understand and analyze language.

- **LSTM**: This is a smarter part of a neural network that remembers information for a long time. It is especially good for understanding sentences or longer pieces of text.

- **BERT**: A very advanced type of neural network designed to understand the context of words in sentences. It looks at the words before and after each to better understand what each sentence means.

- **Activation functions**: These are like switches that help neural networks decide what information is important and what is not. They play a big role in helping the network learn from the data it sees.

- **Adam optimizer**: This smart tool helps neural networks learn faster and better. It adjusts how the network learns, ensuring it gets everything important.

- **Data bias**: This happens when the information used to teach a computer is not fair or balanced. It can make the computer's decisions biased or unfair because it is learning from slanted examples.

- **Black box**: This term describes when we do not understand how a computer makes its decisions. Even though it can give us an answer, how it got there is still being determined.

Understanding these terms gives you a good foundation for grasping the complexities and innovations of combining neural networks with LangChain to create advanced language technology applications.

CHAPTER 5

LangChain and AWS Integration

Introduction

LangChain helps with tasks like automating work and analyzing data using **artificial intelligence** (**AI**). It gets even better combined with the services and large infrastructure of **Amazon Web Services** (**AWS**). AWS provides the technology, storage, and networking necessary for large-scale AI applications. Using LangChain with AWS makes building, running, and expanding AI applications easier, improving development, performance, reliability, and security. LangChain is an AI application builder with AWS, a leading cloud platform. This combination offers great opportunities for application creators, businesses, and researchers.

This chapter will help you understand the process of integrating LangChain with AWS, focusing on setup, deployment, and management. It is aimed at developers, businesses interested in AI, and tech enthusiasts. You will learn about the initial steps, deploying LangChain on AWS, the helpful AWS services, dealing with challenges, and the advantages of this integration, with practical examples. By the end, you will be equipped to seamlessly integrate LangChain with AWS, leveraging AI and cloud technology to innovate and achieve your goals.

Structure

This chapter covers the following topics:

- Getting started with LangChain and AWS
- Setting up your AWS environment
- Deploying LangChain applications on AWS
- Managing and scaling the LangChain application
- Advanced integration techniques
- Case studies and real-world examples
- Challenges and solutions
- Future directions

Objectives

Merging LangChain's AI application capabilities with AWS's cloud services effectively will aim for seamless integration that enables scalable, cost-efficient, and secure AI solutions. This will support rapid development and global deployment of innovative applications, leveraging the strengths for enhanced performance and user experience for both of these applications.

Getting started with LangChain and AWS

Introduction to LangChain: LangChain serves as a framework specifically crafted to streamline the development of AI applications, focusing on those harnessing **natural language processing** (**NLP**) and language models. It offers tools and libraries that facilitate the integration of complex language models into applications, enabling developers to create sophisticated AI-driven solutions efficiently. LangChain can automate workflows, enhance data analysis, generate content, and facilitate conversational interfaces.

Overview of AWS: AWS is a massive cloud computing platform that provides diverse services. These services encompass computing power, storage options, and networking capabilities, offering a comprehensive solution for various cloud computing needs. For AI application development, AWS provides key services such as *Amazon Elastic Compute Cloud* (*EC2*) for scalable computing, *Amazon Simple Storage Service* (*S3*) for storage, *Amazon Relational Database Service* (*RDS*) for databases, and *Amazon Lambda* for running code in response to events. AWS also offers specialized AI and **machine learning** (**ML**) services like *Amazon SageMaker*, simplifying model building, training, and deployment.

Prerequisites for integration

The following section discusses the prerequisites for AWS and LangChain integration:

- **AWS account setup**: To begin using AWS, it is essential to have an AWS account. You can sign up on the AWS website if you do not already have one. For individuals new to AWS, a free trial is available. This requires an outstanding chance to experiment with various AWS services without incurring substantial costs.

Beginner steps for AWS account setup

The following are the steps for AWS account setup:

1. **Visit the AWS website**: Go to the official AWS website.

2. **Click on Create an AWS Account**:
   a. Look for the **Create an AWS Account** button on the homepage and click on it.
   b. If the button is not visible, you can directly access it through this link.

3. **Provide your email address and create a password**:
   a. Enter a valid email address to which you have access.
   b. Create a secure password (use a mix of uppercase, lowercase, numbers, and special characters).
   c. Enter an account name (this can be anything you want, e.g., `MyFirstAWSAccount`).

4. **Select the account type**:
   a. Choose personal account if you are an individual.
   b. Select business account if it is for an organization.

5. **Add contact information**:
   a. Enter your name, phone number, and address.
   b. Double-check for accuracy, as AWS may verify this information.

6. **Provide payment information**:
   a. Add a valid credit/debit card.
   b. Even though AWS Free Tier services are available, a payment method is required for account verification and billing purposes.
   c. AWS will charge you a small, refundable fee to verify your card.

7. **Verify your identity**:

   a. You may be asked to verify your phone number.

   b. AWS will send an OTP via SMS or voice call, which you must enter on the verification page.

8. **Choose a support plan**:

   a. AWS offers different support plans (Basic, Developer, Business, Enterprise).

   b. Select the Basic Support Plan for free services for beginners.

9. **Complete the setup**:

   a. After filling out all the details and verifying your information, AWS will confirm the creation of your account.

   b. This process may take a few minutes.

10. **Log in to the AWS Management Console**:

    a. Once your account is setup, log in to the AWS Management Console.

    b. Use your registered email and password to access your account.

11. **Explore AWS Free Tier**:

    a. AWS offers a Free Tier to help you explore services like EC2, S3, and RDS without incurring significant costs.

    b. Ensure you monitor usage within the Free Tier limits to avoid unexpected charges.

12. **Secure your account**:

    a. Activate **multifactor authentication (MFA)** for added security.

    b. This can be setup via my security credentials section in the AWS Management Console.

13. **Familiarize yourself with billing and cost management**:

    a. Check the Billing dashboard to track your usage and expenses.

    b. Use AWS Cost Explorer to understand which services you use most.

14. **LangChain installation**: Ensure LangChain is installed and properly configured in your development environment. The documentation for LongChain provides detailed instructions on how to get started, including any software dependencies.

15. **AWS, CLI, and SDKs**: Install the **AWS Command Line Interface (AWS CLI)** and relevant AWS **software development kits (SDKs)** for your programming language. These tools are essential for interacting with AWS services programmatically.

AWS CLI and SDKs

The following is the installation and setup for beginners:

1. **Install AWS CLI**: The AWS CLI allows you to manage AWS services from the command line.

    a. **Step**: Download and install the CLI:

        i. **For Windows**: AWS CLI Installer.

        ii. **For Mac/Linux**: Use curl or package managers like Homebrew (Mac).

        iii. **Command (Mac example)**:
```bash
brew install awscli
```

        iv. **Verify installation**:
```bash
aws -version
```

2. **Configure AWS CLI**:

    a. **Run the following command**:
```bash
aws configure
```

    b. **Provide**:

        i. Access key ID

        ii. Secret access key

        iii. Default region (e.g., **us-east-1**)

        iv. Output format (e.g., **JSON**)

3. **Install AWS SDK for your programming language**: SDKs help integrate AWS services with your application.

    a. Example for Python (Boto3):
```bash
code
pip install boto3
```

    b. Example for JavaScript (AWS SDK):
```bash
npm install aws-sdk
```

4. **Test the installation**:

    a. **CLI example**: List S3 buckets:

```bash
bash
aws s3 ls
```

b. **SDK Example (Python)**:

```python
#python

import boto3
s3 = boto3.client('s3')
print(s3.list_buckets())
```

Single-file Python script for expert

Single-file Python script to setup and interact with AWS using the AWS CLI and SDK (Boto3). This script assumes Python is installed on your system and guides you through installation, configuration, and testing:

```python
import os
import subprocess
import boto3
from botocore.exceptions import NoCredentialsError

def install_aws_cli():
    """Install AWS CLI using pip or system package managers."""
    print("Installing AWS CLI...")
    try:
        subprocess.run(["pip", "install", "awscli"], check=True)
        print("AWS CLI installed successfully.")
    except subprocess.CalledProcessError:
        print("Failed to install AWS CLI. Please try manually.")
        exit(1)

def verify_aws_cli():
    """ Verify AWS CLI installation."""
    try:
        subprocess.run(["aws", "--version"], check=True)
        print("AWS CLI verified successfully.")
    except FileNotFoundError:
        print("AWS CLI is not installed. Re-run this script.")
        exit(1)

def configure_aws_cli():
    """Configure AWS CLI."""
    print("Configuring AWS CLI...")
    subprocess.run(["aws", "configure"])
```

```python
def install_boto3():
    """Install Boto3 SDK for Python."""
    print("Installing Boto3 (AWS SDK for Python)...")
    try:
        subprocess.run(["pip", "install", "boto3"], check=True)
        print("Boto3 installed successfully.")
    except subprocess.CalledProcessError:
        print("Failed to install Boto3. Please try manually.")
        exit(1)

def list_s3_buckets():
    """List all S3 buckets using Boto3."""
    print("Listing S3 buckets...")
    try:
        s3 = boto3.client("s3")
        response = s3.list_buckets()
        print("S3 Buckets:")
        for bucket in response.get("Buckets", []):
            print(f"- {bucket['Name']}")
    except NoCredentialsError:
        print("No AWS credentials found. Run 'aws configure' to set them
up.")

if __name__ == "__main__":
    # Step 1: Install AWS CLI
    install_aws_cli()

    # Step 2: Verify AWS CLI installation
    verify_aws_cli()

    # Step 3: Configure AWS CLI
    configure_aws_cli()

    # Step 4: Install Boto3 (AWS SDK for Python)
    install_boto3()

    # Step 5: List S3 buckets as a test
    list_s3_buckets()
```

How to use:

1. Save this script as **aws_setup.py**.

2. Run it using Python:

```bash
python aws_setup.py
```

3. Follow the on-screen prompts to configure AWS CLI and interact with AWS.

   This script automates the setup and validation process for AWS CLI and Boto3, streamlining your AWS workflow.

4. **Security credentials**: Setup AWS **Identity and Access Management** (**IAM**) roles and policies to manage access to AWS services securely. This involves creating IAM users, groups, and roles with the necessary permissions for your LangChain applications.

5. **Familiarity with key services**: Familiarize yourself with the AWS services you plan to use, such as EC2, S3, Lambda, and SageMaker. Understanding these services and how they can support your LangChain applications is crucial for successful integration.

Advantages of cloud computing for AI

The following are the advantages of cloud computing for AI:

- **Scalability**: Cloud computing allows AI applications to scale seamlessly, accommodating varying workloads and data sizes.

- **Cost efficiency**: By using pay-as-you-go models, cloud services reduce the need for substantial up.

- Front investments in hardware.

- **Accessibility**: Cloud platforms enable easy access to AI tools and datasets from anywhere with an internet connection.

- **High performance**: Leveraging powerful cloud-based GPUs and TPUs enhances the processing speed and efficiency of AI tasks.

- **Storage**: Cloud services provide vast and flexible storage options, essential for managing large volumes of AI data.

- **Collaboration**: Cloud environments facilitate collaboration among teams by allowing shared access to AI resources and projects.

- **Integration**: Cloud platforms offer seamless integration with various AI frameworks and tools, simplifying development processes.

- **Security**: Advanced security measures and compliance standards protect sensitive AI data in the cloud.

- **Maintenance**: Cloud providers handle infrastructure maintenance, freeing AI developers to focus on innovation.

- **Rapid deployment**: Cloud computing enables the quick deployment of AI models and applications, accelerating time to market.

Setting up your AWS environment

Setting up your AWS environment properly is crucial for successfully integrating LangChain applications. Here is a guide to configuring AWS services and ensuring a secure and efficient setup:

1. **Configure AWS IAM for security**:

    a. **Create IAM roles**: Create IAM roles specific to your LangChain application. Assign policies that grant permissions to AWS services that the application will interact with.

    b. **Best practices for IAM**: Follow the principle of least privilege, only granting necessary permissions to each role. Regularly review and update IAM policies to maintain security.

2. **Setup Amazon EC2 instance**:

    a. **Launch EC2 instances**: Use Amazon EC2 to launch virtual servers for running your LangChain applications. Select an instance type that matches your computational needs.

    b. **Configure security groups**: Setup security groups for your EC2 instances, specifying which ports can be accessed and from which location. For LangChain applications, ensure ports for web services and any specific application ports are open.

3. **Utilize Amazon S3 for storage**:

    a. **Create S3 buckets**: Store application data, models, or any static files in Amazon S3 buckets. Organize your data with a clear name for ease of access.

    b. **Secure your buckets**: Implement S3 bucket policies to control access to your data. Use encryption for data at rest and enable logging to monitor access and usage.

4. **Deploy functions with AWS Lambda**:

    a. **Create Lambda functions**: For event-driven or on-demand processing, use AWS Lambda. You can run code in response to triggers from AWS services without provisioning or managing servers.

    b. **Lambda and LangChain**: Integrate LangChain functionalities into Lambda functions for scalable, serverless processing, like language model inference or data processing tasks.

5. **Networking and connectivity**:

   a. **Setup VPC**: Configure *Amazon Virtual Private Cloud (VPC)* to isolate your LangChain environment in a private network, enhancing security.

   b. **Connectivity**: Ensure proper connectivity between your EC2 instances, S3 buckets, and Lambda functions within the VPC. Use VPC endpoints for private connections to AWS services.

6. **Security considerations and best practices**:

   a. **Encrypt data**: Use AWS **Key Management Service (KMS)** to manage encryption keys and encrypt your data in transit and at rest.

   b. **Regular audits**: Use AWS CloudTrail and AWS Config to monitor and audit your AWS resources. Keep an eye on configurations and ensure compliance with your security policies.

   c. **Access management**: Regularly review access rights and IAM roles. Use MFA for an additional layer of security.

7. **Monitoring and management**:

   a. **Use CloudWatch**: Leverage *Amazon CloudWatch* for monitoring your AWS resources and applications. Setup alarms to get alerts on specific metrics or events.

   b. **AWS cost management**: Keep track of your AWS usage and costs. Use AWS Budgets to set cost alarms and AWS Cost Explorer to analyze your spending pattern.

Following these steps and considerations, you can create a robust AWS environment tailored for LangChain applications. This setup ensures security and efficiency and provides a scalable foundation for deploying and managing your AI-driven applications.

Deploying LangChain applications on AWS

Deploying LangChain applications on AWS involves leveraging various AWS services to efficiently host, manage, and scale your applications. This section provides a step-by-step guide and best practices for a successful deployment:

1. **Package your LangChain application**:

   To deploy your LangChain application effectively, you need to ensure all its dependencies are included. Packaging makes your application portable and easy to setup on any environment.

   a. **Setting up a virtual environment (Optional but recommended)**:

      i. **Create a virtual environment**: Use a virtual environment to manage dependencies specific to your project.

```bash
```

```bash
python -m venv langchain_env
source langchain_env/bin/activate # On Windows, use
`langchain_env\Scripts\activate`
```

ii. **Install dependencies**: Install LangChain and any other dependencies your application requires. For example:

```bash
```

```bash
pip install langchain openai requests
```

iii. **Freeze dependencies**: Save your dependencies in a **requirements. txt** file. This ensures that your application uses the same versions when deployed.

```bash
```

```bash
pip freeze > requirements.txt
```

b. **Dockerize your application (Optional but useful)**:

If you plan to deploy your application in containers (e.g., with AWS ECS), Docker is a great option:

i. **Create a Dockerfile**: Here is an example Dockerfile for a LangChain application:

```
#Dockerfile
# Use a lightweight Python image
FROM python:3.9-slim

# Set the working directory
WORKDIR /app

# Copy application files
COPY . /app

# Install dependencies
RUN pip install --no-cache-dir -r requirements.txt

# Expose a port if your applicationis a web service
EXPOSE 8080

# Command to run your application
CMD ["python", "app.py"]
```

ii. **Build the Docker image**: Run the following command in the directory containing your Dockerfile:

```bash
```
```bash
docker build -t langchain-application
```

   iii. **Test the Docker image locally**: Verify the image works as expected:
```bash
docker run -p 8080:8080 langchain-app
```

2. **Version control your LangChain application**:

Version control helps you track changes, collaborate with others, and manage updates or rollbacks.

  a. **Initialize a Git repository:**

    i. **Open your project directory and initialize Git**:
```bash
git init
```

    ii. **Add your application files to Git**:
```bash
git add
git commit -m "Initial commit of LangChain app"
```

  b. **Use AWS CodeCommit (or GitHub):**

AWS CodeCommit is a managed version control service. Alternatively, you can use GitHub or GitLab.

    i. **Create a repository**: In AWS Management Console, go to CodeCommit and create a new repository.

  c. **Push your code:**

    i. **Clone the repository locally**:
```bash
git remote add origin https://<your-repo-url>
git branch -M main
git push -u origin main
```

Example of a simple Git workflow:

- **After making changes to your app, commit and push them**:
```bash
git add
git commit -m "Updated Dockerfile and applicationdependencies"
git push origin main
```

- **Deploy on Amazon EC2**:
  - **Launch an EC2 instance**: Choose an appropriate EC2 instance type based on the resource your application needs. For compute-intensive LangChain models, consider using GPU instances.

o **Deploy your application**: Upload your application code or Docker container to the EC2 instance. Configure the instance to start your application automatically upon boot.

o **Load balancer**: To ensure high availability in your infrastructure, consider utilizing *Amazon Elastic Load Balancing (ELB)*. This service is designed to distribute traffic efficiently across numerous Amazon EC2 instances, enhancing the reliability and availability of your application or system. Use *AWS Elastic Beanstalk* for easy deployment:

o **Automated deployment**: Elastic Beanstalk automates the deployment process and covers various activities, from capacity provisioning and load balancing to auto scaling. Deploy your LangChain application by uploading your code, and Elastic Beanstalk handles the rest.

o **Environment configuration**: Customize the Elastic Beanstalk environment to suit the needs of your application, selecting the appropriate instance type, database, and storage options.

- **Serverless deployment with AWS Lambda**: For serverless components of your LangChain application, package your functions and any necessary dependencies. Upload your package to AWS Lambda and setup the appropriate triggers, such as HTTP requests via *Amazon API Gateway* or event triggers from other AWS services. Use Amazon API Gateway to create RESTful APIs for your Lambda functions, enabling your LangChain application to interact with other services or users.

Step-by-step guide for serverless deployment

The following are the steps for serverless deployment with AWS Lambda:

Serverless deployment with AWS Lambda is a powerful way to run your LangChain application without managing servers.

1. **Package your functions**:

   To deploy your code to AWS Lambda, you first need to package your application and its dependencies.

   a. **Write your Lambda function:**

      Create a Python script for your Lambda function. Let us assume the function generates responses using LangChain:

      Example: `lambda_function.py`

      ```python
      import json
      from langchain.llms import OpenAI
      ```

```python
def lambda_handler(event, context):
    # Initialize the LangChain LLM
    llm = OpenAI(temperature=0.7)

    # Get user input from the API Gateway event
    user_input = event['queryStringParameters']['input']

    # Generate a response
    response = llm(user_input)

    return {
        'statusCode': 200,
        'body': json.dumps({'response': response})
    }
```

2. **Package dependencies:**

   AWS Lambda requires dependencies to be packaged with your function.

   a. **Create a virtual environment:**

   bash

   python -m venv lambda_env

   source lambda_env/bin/activate # On Windows, use `lambda_env\ Scripts\activate`

   b. **Install dependencies:**

   bash

   pip install langchain openai

   c. **Package everything**: Zip your **lambda_function.py** and the dependencies:

   bash

   mkdir package

   pip install --target ./package langchain openai

   cp lambda_function.py package/

   cd package

   zip -r ../lambda_function.zip

   d. **Deploy to AWS Lambda**:

   Once your function is packaged, you can deploy it to AWS Lambda.

   i. Create a Lambda function

   ii. Go to the AWS Lambda console.

   iii. Click **Create function** and select **Author from scratch**.

   iv. **Provide:**

- Function name: e.g., `LangChainFunction`.
- Runtime: Choose Python 3.x.

e. Upload your code:

   i. Under the Code section, click Upload from `.zip` file.

   ii. Upload the `lambda_function.zip` file you created earlier.

   iii. Save the changes.

f. Set environment variables (Optional):

If your application uses API keys (e.g., for *OpenAI*), store them securely in Lambda:

   i. Go to the Configuration tab | Environment variables.

   ii. Add variables like `OPENAI_API_KEY`.

3. Setup API Gateway:

AWS API Gateway allows you to expose your Lambda function as an HTTP endpoint.

a. Create an API:

   i. Go to the API Gateway Console.

   ii. Click Create API | HTTP API (for simplicity).

b. Integrate with Lambda:

   i. Add a route to your API:

- Method: GET (or POST, depending on your application).
- Resource path: `/generate-response`.

   ii. Integrate it with your Lambda function:

Select your Lambda function (e.g., `LangChainFunction`).

c. Deploy the API

   i. Deploy your API by clicking Deployments | Create.

   ii. Note the API endpoint URL, e.g., `https://abcd1234.execute-api.us-east-1.amazonaws.com`.

4. Test your serverless application:

a. Open your browser or use a tool like Postman to send a request:

Example URL:

```bash
https://abcd1234.execute-api.us-east-1.amazonaws.com/generate-
response?input=Hello
```

The Lambda function should respond with a generated response from LangChain.

Use serverless:

- **Cost-efficient**: Pay only for the time your function runs.

- **Scalable**: Lambda scales automatically with demand.

- **No server management**: Focus on your application logic, not infrastructure.

Data storage and management

Amazon S3: Use S3 for storing static files, datasets, or model artifacts. Secure your data with bucket policies and encryption.

Step-by-step guide: Data storage and management with Amazon S3

1. **Setup an S3 bucket:**

   a. **Create an S3 bucket:**

      i. Go to the Amazon S3 console.

      ii. Click **Create bucket** button.

      iii. Fill in the required fields:

         - **Bucket name**: Choose a unique name (e.g., `my-langchain-data`).

         - **Region**: Select the AWS Region closest to you.

      iv. Enable bucket versioning (optional, but useful for tracking changes).

      v. Click **Create bucket** button.

   b. **Organize your data:**

      Once your bucket is created, organize your data into folders for easier management:

      Example folder structure:

```arduino
my-langchain-data/
```

```
├── static-files/
├── datasets/
└── model-artifacts/
```

2. **Upload data to S3:**

   a. **Upload files via the console:**

      i.   Open your bucket in the S3 console.

      ii. Click **Upload** | **Add files**.

      iii. Drag and drop files or browse to select them.

      iv. Under **Permissions** tab, choose whether the files should be publicly accessible or private.

   b. **Upload files using the AWS CLI:**

      The AWS CLI is a powerful tool for managing S3.

      i.   Install and configure the AWS CLI if you have not already:
           bash
           aws configure

           • Upload a file:
             bash
             aws s3 cp my_file.csv s3://my-langchain-data/datasets/

           • Upload a folder:
             bash
             **aws s3 cp my_folder/ s3://my-langchain-data/
             --recursive**

3. **Secure your data:**

   a. **Bucket policies define access permissions:**

      i. In the S3 console, select your bucket and go to the **Permissions** tab.

      ii. Under bucket policy, add a JSON policy. For example:

          • Grant read-only access:
            ```json
            {
              "Version": "2012-10-17",
              "Statement": [
                {
                  "Effect": "Allow",
                  "Principal": "*",
                  "Action": "s3:GetObject",
            ```

```
          "Resource": "arn:aws:s3:::my-langchain-data/*"
      }
    ]
  }
```

b. **Encryption ensures your data is safe from unauthorized access:**

    i.   In the **Properties** tab of your bucket, enable default encryption.

    ii.   Choose **server-side encryption with Amazon S3 managed keys (SSE-S3)** or **server-side encryption with AWS KMS (SSE-KMS).**

4. **Access data in your LangChain application:**

a. **Using Boto3 to access S3:**

Here is a Python example of how to interact with S3 using Boto3:

```python
#python
import boto3

# Initialize S3 client
s3 = boto3.client('s3')

# Download a file
bucket_name = "my-langchain-data"
file_key = "datasets/my_file.csv"
local_file_path = "my_file.csv"

s3.download_file(bucket_name, file_key, local_file_path)
print(f"Downloaded {file_key} to {local_file_path}")

# Upload a file
s3.upload_file(local_file_path, bucket_name, "static-files/
uploaded_file.csv")
print(f"Uploaded {local_file_path} to S3.")
```

b. **Public access (Optional):**

If your bucket or files are publicly accessible, you can share their URLs:

```bash
bash
https://<bucket-name>.s3.<region>.amazonaws.com/<file-key>
```

5. **Use case examples:**

- **Store model artifacts**: Save trained ML models to the `model-artifacts` folder for easy retrieval.

- **Store datasets**: Upload datasets (e.g., `.csv` or `.json`) used for training models.

- **Host static files**: Use S3 to store files like `.html`, `.css`, or `.js` for web-based applications.

Use S3:

- **Scalability**: Handles small files or petabytes of data effortlessly.

- **Security**: Offers encryption, bucket policies, and access control mechanisms.

- **Cost-effectiveness**: Pay only for what you use.

- **Database services**: To manage application data, choose an appropriate AWS database service, such as *Amazon RDS* for relational databases or *Amazon DynamoDB* for NoSQL.

Step-by-step guide

The following are the steps for managing application data with AWS database services.

Choosing the right database for your LangChain or other applications is key to ensuring smooth data management. Detailed and beginner-friendly guide to help you get started with Amazon RDS (for relational databases) and Amazon DynamoDB (for NoSQL databases).

1. **Choosing the right database service**:

   - **Amazon RDS**: Best for applications needing structured data stored in relational tables (e.g., MySQL, PostgreSQL). Use it for applications requiring SQL-based queries, data consistency, and relationships between tables.

   - **Amazon DynamoDB**: Ideal for applications needing fast and scalable NoSQL storage, such as key-value or document-based data storage. Great for applications with high throughput and low-latency requirements.

2. **Setting up Amazon RDS**:

   Amazon RDS provides managed relational databases like MySQL, PostgreSQL, or MariaDB.

   a. **Create an RDS database instance**:

      i. **Open the RDS console**: Amazon RDS console.

      ii. Click **Create database** button.

      iii. **Choose a database engine**:

   b. **Select the engine (e.g., MySQL or PostgreSQL)**:

      Set configuration:

      - **DB instance identifier**: A name for your database, e.g., `langchain-db`.

- **Username/password**: Set admin credentials to access your database.

c. **Choose instance class**:

    i. Select the size of your instance. For beginners, the Free Tier (**db. t2.micro**) is a great starting point.

    Storage: Specify storage capacity (start small, e.g., 20 GB).

    ii. **Networking**:

- Place the database in a VPC.

- Allow public access if your application runs outside the VPC (not recommended for production).

d. **Click Create database**.

e. **Connect to your database**:

    i. Find the endpoint in the RDS console (it is the URL to access the database).

    ii. Use a database client like MySQL Workbench or a Python library to connect:

Python example (MySQL with SQLAlchemy):

```python
from sqlalchemy import create_engine

# Replace with your RDS endpoint, username, and password
db_endpoint = "langchain-db.xxxx.us-east-1.rds.amazonaws.com"
db_user = "admin"
db_password = "yourpassword"
db_name = "mydatabase"

# Create the database connection
engine = create_engine(f"mysql+pymysql://{db_user}:{db_password}@{db_endpoint}/{db_name}")

# Test the connection
with engine.connect() as connection:
    result = connection.execute("SELECT 1;")
    print(result.fetchone())
```

3. **Setting up Amazon DynamoDB (NoSQL)**:

Amazon DynamoDB is a serverless NoSQL database perfect for fast and flexible key-value or document-based storage.

a. **Create a DynamoDB table**:

    i. **Open the DynamoDB console**: Amazon DynamoDB console.

    ii. Click **Create table** button.

    iii. **Define table structure**:

Table name: e.g., `LangChainData`.

- **Primary key**: Choose a key to uniquely identify records:

    i. **Partition key**: e.g., `RecordID` (for a unique identifier).

- **Sort key (optional)**: Use it for organizing related data.

    i. Enable default settings for throughput (DynamoDB scales automatically).

    ii. Click **Create table**.

b. **Insert data into DynamoDB:**

    i. Use the DynamoDB console to add items manually:

Go to your table | **Items** | **Create item**.

Add key-value pairs for your data.

    ii. Insert data programmatically using Boto3:

Python example (inserting data):

```python
import boto3

# Initialize DynamoDB client
dynamodb = boto3.resource('dynamodb')
table = dynamodb.Table('LangChainData')

# Add an item to the table
response = table.put_item(
    Item={
        'RecordID': '001',
        'UserInput': 'Hello, how are you?',
        'GeneratedResponse': 'I am doing well. How can I
assist you today?'
    }
)
print("Data inserted:", response)
```

a. **Python example (fetching data)**:

python

```
# Get an item by RecordID
response = table.get_item(Key={'RecordID': '001'})
print("Fetched item:", response['Item'])
```

4. **Security best practices**:

   a. **RDS**:

   - Use IAM roles and database security groups to control access.

   - Enable automatic backups to recover data in case of failures.

   b. **DynamoDB**:

   - Use IAM policies to restrict access to specific tables.

   - Turn on DynamoDB Streams to track changes to your data.

5. **Use cases**:

   - **Amazon RDS**:

     o Storing structured data for your LangChain application, like user data, logs, or conversation history.

     o Running SQL queries to retrieve data.

   - **Amazon DynamoDB**:

     o Storing high-volume, fast-changing data, such as session details or chatbot context.

     o Using key-value pairs to quickly access user-specific records.

Using AWS databases

The following are the steps and best practices:

1. **Amazon RDS**: Fully managed relational database, automatically handles backups, scaling, and patching.

2. **Amazon DynamoDB**: Highly scalable, low-latency NoSQL database for applications needing fast performance.

3. **Monitoring and scaling**:

   a. **Amazon CloudWatch**: Utilize CloudWatch to monitor application performance and set alarms for metrics like CPU usage, response times, or error rates.

b. **Auto scaling**: Implement auto scaling policies for your EC2 instances or use the automatic scaling on AWS Lambda to adjust capacity based on-demand, ensuring efficient resource use and cost management.

4. **Best practices for deployment and scalability**:

a. **Continuous integration/continuous deployment**: Use AWS CodePipeline or similar tools for **continuous integration/continuous deployment (CI/ CD)** to automate testing and deployment of your LangChain application.

b. **Infrastructure as code**: Leverage AWS CloudFormation or AWS CDK to define your **infrastructure as code (IaC)**, using IaC, making it easy to deploy and replicate environments.

c. **Security**: Ensure all application components follow AWS security best practices, including using security groups, network ACLs, and encryption.

d. **Cost optimization**: Regularly review your AWS usage and costs. Optimize resource usage with AWS Cost Explorer and consider purchasing reserved instances for long-term savings.

Following these steps and best practices, you can effectively deploy and manage your LangChain applications on AWS, taking full advantage of the scalability, reliability, and breadth of services on cloud.

Managing and scaling the LangChain application

Effectively managing and scaling LangChain applications on AWS ensures optimal performance, reliability, and cost efficiency. The following section includes key techniques, strategies for scaling applications, and cost optimization strategies for managing and scaling your applications to handle varying loads:

- **Techniques for managing LangChain applications**:

   o **Monitoring**:

      ▪ Utilize Amazon CloudWatch to monitor application performance metrics such as CPU usage, memory consumption, and request latency. Setup dashboards to visualize these metrics in real-time.

      ▪ Implement logging with Amazon CloudWatch Logs for detailed insight into application behavior and to facilitate troubleshooting.

- **Troubleshooting**:
  - Use AWS X-Ray or similar tools to trace requests through your LangChain applications, helping identify bottlenecks or sources of errors.
  - Leverage AWS CloudTrail to audit and track user activity and API usage, aiding in identifying changes that may affect application performance.
- **Automation**:
  - Automate deployment and updates using AWS CodePipeline and AWS CodeDeploy, reducing the potential for human error and ensuring consistent configurations.
  - Setup automated backups and snapshot management for databases and storage to prevent data loss and facilitate quick recovery.

- **Strategies for scaling applications**:
  - **Vertical scaling**: Increase or decrease the size of your Amazon EC2 instances based on performance requirements. This can be done manually or through automated tools based on specific triggers.
  - **Horizontal scaling**:
    - Use Auto Scaling groups to automatically adjust the number of EC2 instances in response to demand. Combine with ELB to distribute traffic evenly across instances.
    - AWS Lambda automatically scales for serverless components based on the number of requests, adjusting resources to maintain performance.
  - **Database scaling**:
    - Employ Amazon RDS read replicas to scale read operations and reduce the load on the primary database.
    - Consider Amazon DynamoDB for NoSQL databases, which offers built-in scaling capabilities to handle through demands.
- **Cost management and optimization tips**:
  - **Monitor and analyze costs**:
    - Use AWS Cost Explorer to track how your resources are utilized and identify areas where costs can be reduced.
    - Implement budgets and alerts with AWS Budgets to manage costs and avoid unexpected expenses proactively.

o **Optimize resource usage**:

- Implement reserved instances or savings plans for EC2 and RDS to save on long-term costs.

- Utilize Amazon EC2 spot instances for stateless, flexible, or fault-tolerant workloads to take advantage of lower prices.

o **Clean up unused resources**: Review and terminate unused or underutilized resources, including EC2 instances, EBS volumes, and Elastic IPs.

o **Leverage serverless and managed services**:

- Choose serverless services like AWS Lambda, which scales automatically and charges only for the computer time you use, reducing costs for intermittent workloads.

- Use managed services such as Amazon RDS and Amazon S3, which can reduce operational overhead and allow you to benefit from economies of scale of AWS.

By implementing these management, scaling, and cost optimization strategies, you can ensure that your LangChain applications on AWS perform optimally and are cost-effective and scalable to meet user demand.

Advanced integration techniques

Integrating LangChain with AWS offers many opportunities to leverage advanced features and techniques. These integrations enhance the functionality of LangChain applications and tap into the vast capabilities of AWS services, particularly in areas such as automation, scalability, and ML.

- **Customizing LangChain applications with AWS services**:

  o **Serverless functions with AWS Lambda**:

  - **Dynamic scaling**: Use AWS Lambda to handle event-driven tasks, such as processing data inputs or dynamically generating responses. Lambda functions scale automatically with the request volume, offering a cost-effective way to enhance LangChain applications.

  - **Microservices architecture**: Decompose your LangChain application into microservices using Lambda, allowing for easier management, deployment, and scaling of individual components.

  o **API integration with Amazon API Gateway**:

  - **RESTful API interfaces**: Create RESTful APIs for your LangChain applications using Amazon API Gateway. This facilitates secure and scalable access to your applications, enabling them to interact with other systems and services.

- **API Gateway and Lambda**: Combine API Gateway with Lambda to run LangChain functionalities in a serverless architecture, reducing the need to manage infrastructure.

- **Utilizing AWS ML services**:
  - **Enhancing LangChain with Amazon SageMaker**:
    - **Model training and deployment**: Use Amazon SageMaker to train and deploy ML forms into creation. SageMaker simplifies the entire process, from data preparation to model training and tuning.
    - **Direct integration**: Integrate SageMaker-trained models directly into your LangChain applications to add capabilities like sentiment analysis, text classification, or custom language models.

Example illustrating how to enhance LangChain with Amazon SageMaker for tasks like sentiment analysis or text classification:

1. **Prerequisites**:
   - **AWS account**: Ensure you have an AWS account with SageMaker enabled.
   - **IAM role**: Create an IAM role with appropriate permissions to access SageMaker, S3, and other services.
   - **Python libraries**: Install the required libraries:
     bash
     ```
     pip install boto3 langchain
     ```

2. **Train and deploy a SageMaker model**:

   Let us use a pre-trained BERT model for text classification as an example:

   Python script for training (`train_model.py`):
   ```python
   python
   import boto3
   import sagemaker
   from sagemaker.huggingface import HuggingFace

   # Specify SageMaker session and role
   sagemaker_session = sagemaker.Session()
   role = "<Your-IAM-Role-ARN>"

   # Define Hugging Face model parameters
   hyperparameters = {
   ```

```
        'epochs': 3,
        'train_batch_size': 32,
        'model_name': 'bert-base-uncased'
}

# Define training job
huggingface_estimator = HuggingFace(
        entry_point='train.py',  # Your training script
        source_dir='./source',  # Directory containing training code
        instance_type='ml.p3.2xlarge',
        instance_count=1,
        role=role,
        transformers_version='4.6',
        pytorch_version='1.7',
        py_version='py3',
        hyperparameters=hyperparameters
)

# Train the model
huggingface_estimator.fit({'train': 's3://<your-bucket>/train-
data/'})
```

After training, deploy the model as an endpoint:

```python
predictor = huggingface_estimator.deploy(
        initial_instance_count=1,
        instance_type='ml.m5.large'
)
endpoint_name = predictor.endpoint_name
print(f"Deployed SageMaker endpoint: {endpoint_name}")
```

3. **Integrate SageMaker with LangChain**:

Use the deployed model in your LangChain application.

LangChain integration

Here is how LangChain interacts with the SageMaker endpoint for predictions:

```python
import boto3
from langchain.llms import OpenAI
from langchain.chains import LLMChain
from langchain.prompts import PromptTemplate
```

```python
# Define SageMaker endpoint name
sagemaker_endpoint = "<Your-SageMaker-Endpoint-Name>"

# Initialize SageMaker runtime client
sagemaker_runtime = boto3.client('sagemaker-runtime')

def call_sagemaker_endpoint(input_text):
    """
    Call SageMaker endpoint for predictions.
    """
    response = sagemaker_runtime.invoke_endpoint(
        EndpointName=sagemaker_endpoint,
        ContentType="application/json",
        Body=json.dumps({"inputs": input_text})
    )
    result = json.loads(response["Body"].read())
    return result

# LangChain setup
prompt_template = PromptTemplate(
    input_variables=["text"],
    template="Classify the sentiment of the following text: {text}"
)

def custom_model_chain(input_text):
    """
    Use SageMaker for classification and LangChain for chaining.
    """
    # SageMaker prediction
    model_prediction = call_sagemaker_endpoint(input_text)

    # Generate LangChain response
    chain = LLMChain(llm=OpenAI(), prompt=prompt_template)
    final_response = chain.run(text=model_prediction)

    return final_response

# Example Usage
text_input = "I absolutely loved the service at the hospital!"
result = custom_model_chain(text_input)
print("Final response:", result)
```

Expected workflow

The following is the workflow:

1. **Input**: Text input (e.g., `I loved the service`).

2. **SageMaker**: The text is sent to the SageMaker endpoint, which performs sentiment analysis.

3. **LangChain**: Uses the SageMaker output to generate a final response or chain it with additional AI reasoning.

4. **Output example**: `The sentiment is positive, indicating a great user experience`.

Key benefits

The following are the key benefits:

- **Simplified training**: SageMaker automates the training and tuning process.

- **Direct integration**: LangChain can seamlessly utilize the SageMaker model output for further processing or chaining.

- **Scalable deployment**: SageMaker endpoints scale automatically based on-demand.

- **Incorporating Amazon Comprehend for NLP**: Leverage Amazon Comprehend within your LangChain applications for advanced NLP tasks such as entity recognition, sentiment analysis, and language detection.

- **Seamless integration**: Easily integrate the capabilities of Comprehend into LangChain workflows to process and analyze large volumes of text data without deep learning expertise.

- **Example**: Amazon Comprehend with LangChain for NLP tasks like entity recognition, sentiment analysis, and language detection.

The following are the prerequisites and steps:

1. **Prerequisites**:

    - **AWS account**: Ensure you have an active AWS account with permissions to use Amazon Comprehend.

    - **Python libraries**: Install the required libraries:
      ```bash
      pip install boto3 langchain
      ```

2. **Setting up Amazon Comprehend**:

   Amazon Comprehend is a managed NLP service. No training or model hosting is required; you can use its API directly.

3. **LangChain integration with Amazon Comprehend**:

   Python implementation:

```python
python
import boto3
from langchain.prompts import PromptTemplate
from langchain.chains import LLMChain

# Initialize Amazon Comprehend client
comprehend_client = boto3.client('comprehend')

# Function to call Amazon Comprehend
def analyze_text_with_comprehend(text, analysis_type):
    """
    Use Amazon Comprehend for NLP tasks like sentiment analysis,
    entity recognition, or language detection.
    """

    if analysis_type == "sentiment":
        response = comprehend_client.detect_sentiment(Text=text,
LanguageCode="en")
        return response['Sentiment']
    elif analysis_type == "entities":
        response = comprehend_client.detect_entities(Text=text,
LanguageCode="en")
        return response['Entities']
    elif analysis_type == "language":
        response = comprehend_client.detect_dominant_
language(Text=text)
        return response['Languages'][0]['LanguageCode']
    else:
        raise ValueError("Invalid analysis type. Choose from
'sentiment', 'entities', or 'language'.")

# LangChain prompt and chain integration
prompt_template = PromptTemplate(
    input_variables=["text", "task"],
    template="Analyze the following text for {task}: {text}"
)

def langchain_with_comprehend(text, task):
```

```
    """
    Integrates LangChain and Amazon Comprehend for NLP analysis.
    """
    # Use Amazon Comprehend for analysis
    analysis_result = analyze_text_with_comprehend(text, task)

    # Use LangChain for response generation
    chain = LLMChain(llm=None, prompt=prompt_template)
    final_response = chain.run(text=text, task=f"{task} results:
{analysis_result}")

    return final_response

# Example Usage
text_input = "Amazon Web Services is a subsidiary of Amazon
providing on-demand cloud computing."
sentiment_result = langchain_with_comprehend(text_input,
"sentiment")
entity_result = langchain_with_comprehend(text_input, "entities")
language_result = langchain_with_comprehend(text_input, "language")

print("Sentiment Analysis:", sentiment_result)
print("Entity Recognition:", entity_result)
print("Language Detection:", language_result)
```

Output examples:

- **Sentiment analysis:**
    - Input: `I love how easy it is to use AWS services!`
    - Output: `Positive sentiment detected`.

- **Entity recognition:**
    - Input: `Amazon Web Services is headquartered in Seattle`.
    - Output:
      ```json
      [
          {"Text": "Amazon Web Services", "Type": "ORGANIZATION"},
          {"Text": "Seattle", "Type": "LOCATION"}
      ]
      ```

- **Language detection:**
    - Input: `AWS est génial!`
    - Output: `"fr"` (French)

Benefits

The following are the benefits:

1. **No ML expertise required**: Comprehend simplifies NLP tasks without needing to train custom models.

2. **Scalability**: Handle large volumes of text data seamlessly.

3. **LangChain compatibility**: Combine Comprehend's results with LangChain workflows for enhanced AI-driven solutions.

Using Amazon Lex for conversational interfaces:

- **Build chatbots**: Incorporate Amazon Lex to build sophisticated chatbots and conversational interfaces within your LangChain applications. Lex provides natural language understanding and automatic speech recognition, enabling engaging user interactions.

- **Integration with LangChain**: Use LangChain to manage conversation flows and logic while leveraging Lex for understanding and processing user inputs, creating a powerful tool for automated customer service, FAQs, or interactive applications.

- **Best practices for advanced integration**:

  - **Modular design**: Keep your application architecture modular to easily incorporate AWS services into your LangChain applications. This approach facilitates updates and maintenance.

  - **Security and compliance**: Ensure that all integrations comply with AWS security best practices, using IAM roles and policies to access AWS services securely.

  - **Performance monitoring**: Regularly monitor the performance and costs associated with your integrations using AWS CloudWatch and AWS Cost Explorer. Optimize resources and configurations based on insights gathered.

By exploring these advanced integration techniques, you can significantly enhance the functionality, scalability, and efficiency of your LangChain applications on AWS. Leveraging the powerful ML and serverless services on AWS opens new avenues for creating innovative and intelligent applications.

Case studies and real-world examples

Integrating LangChain with AWS has proven transformative across various industries, driving innovation and efficiency. Following are some case studies and real-world examples that highlight the successful application of this integration, along with the lessons learned and insights gained.

Healthcare: Patient data analysis and interaction

A healthcare technology company integrated LangChain with AWS to develop a system for analyzing patient data and providing interactive patient support through chatbots. They leveraged AWS Lambda to run serverless LangChain functions, Amazon Comprehend for medical data NLP analysis, and Amazon Lex to build conversational interfaces.

Python-based implementation for the described healthcare use case. It integrates LangChain, AWS Lambda, Amazon Comprehend, and Amazon Lex to analyze patient data and provide interactive support through a chatbot.

1. **Prerequisites:**

   AWS services setup:

   a. **Amazon Comprehend**: Ensure it is enabled in your AWS account for medical data NLP.

   b. **Amazon Lex**: Create a chatbot with intents for patient interaction (e.g., **GetHealthTips**).

   c. **AWS Lambda**: Setup a function to integrate LangChain with these services.

   Python libraries: Install required libraries:
   ```bash
   pip install boto3 langchain
   ```

2. **Code implementation**:

   Lambda function code:
   ```python
   import boto3
   import json
   from langchain.llms import OpenAI
   from langchain.chains import LLMChain

   # Initialize AWS services
   comprehend = boto3.client('comprehendmedical')
   lex = boto3.client('lexv2-runtime')

   # LangChain model setup (OpenAI is used here as an example LLM)
   llm = OpenAI(temperature=0.7)

   def analyze_patient_data(patient_notes):
       """
       Analyze unstructured patient data using Amazon Comprehend
   Medical.
   ```

```
    """
    response = comprehend.detect_entities(Text=patient_notes)
    entities = response['Entities']
    medical_terms = [entity['Text'] for entity in entities if
entity['Category'] == 'MEDICAL_CONDITION']
    return medical_terms

def get_lex_response(bot_id, alias_id, user_id, user_input):
    """
    Interact with Amazon Lex for patient chatbot responses.
    """
    response = lex.recognize_text(
        botId=bot_id,
        botAliasId=alias_id,
        localeId='en_US',
        sessionId=user_id,
        text=user_input
    )
    return response['messages'][0]['content'] if 'messages' in
response else "I couldn't process your request."

def lambda_handler(event, context):
    """
    AWS Lambda function to process patient data and provide
interactive support.
    """
    # Extract patient notes and chatbot input from the event
    patient_notes = event.get('patient_notes', 'No notes provided.')
    user_input = event.get('user_input', 'Hello')
    bot_id = event.get('bot_id')
    alias_id = event.get('alias_id')
    user_id = event.get('user_id', 'default_user')

    # Step 1: Analyze patient notes using Amazon Comprehend Medical
    medical_terms = analyze_patient_data(patient_notes)

    # Step 2: Generate personalized advice with LangChain
    chain = LLMChain(llm=llm, prompt_template="Provide health advice
based on the following conditions: {conditions}")
    health_advice = chain.run(conditions=", ".join(medical_terms))

    # Step 3: Get chatbot response from Amazon Lex
    chatbot_response = get_lex_response(bot_id, alias_id, user_id,
```

```
user_input)

        # Combine results
        result = {
            "medical_terms": medical_terms,
            "health_advice": health_advice,
            "chatbot_response": chatbot_response
        }

        return {
            "statusCode": 200,
            "body": json.dumps(result)
        }
```

3. **Example event input:**

When testing the Lambda function, provide the following sample input:

#json

```
{
    "patient_notes": "The patient is experiencing chest pain and high
blood pressure.",
    "user_input": "What should I do about chest pain?",
    "bot_id": "YourBotID",
    "alias_id": "YourAliasID",
    "user_id": "patient_123"
}
```

Expected output

The Lambda function will return a combined response:

#json

```
{
    "medical_terms": ["chest pain", "high blood pressure"],
    "health_advice": "For chest pain and high blood pressure, you should
consult a doctor immediately. Meanwhile, maintain a calm environment and
avoid physical exertion.",
    "chatbot_response": "I recommend seeking immediate medical assistance.
Would you like tips on managing stress?"
}
```

System workflow:

1. **Input**: Patient notes and user queries are sent to AWS Lambda.

2. **Step 1**: Patient notes are analyzed using Amazon Comprehend Medical.

3. **Step 2**: LangChain generates personalized health advice.

4. **Step 3**: Amazon Lex provides an interactive chatbot response.

5. **Output**: Combined response with health advice and chatbot interaction.

Lessons learned:

- **Data privacy**: Ensure patient data is encrypted in transit and at rest. Use AWS IAM policies to restrict access.

- **Compliance**: Follow healthcare data regulations such as *Health Insurance Portability and Accountability Act* (*HIPAA*).

- **Scalability**: AWS Lambda scales automatically, ensuring performance during high data loads.

Finance: Automated customer service

A financial services firm used LangChain and AWS to automate customer inquiries and transaction processing. They utilized Amazon Lex to handle natural language queries and integrated LangChain with AWS Lambda to execute business logic and transactions.

This code assumes you are familiar with setting up the necessary AWS resources like Amazon Lex, Lambda, and API Gateway.

Step-by-step code breakdown:

AWS Lambda function to handle business logic: This Lambda function processes customer inquiries and handles financial transactions:

```
import json
import boto3

# Initialize AWS services clients
lex_client = boto3.client('lex-runtime')

def lambda_handler(event, context):
    # Event contains the input query from the customer via Lex
    user_input = event['inputTranscript']

    # Call Amazon Lex to process user input
    response = lex_client.post_text(
        botName='FinancialBot',      # Name of your Lex Bot
        botAlias='prod',             # Alias for your Lex Bot
        userId='customer123',        # A unique ID for the user
        inputText=user_input         # Customer query
    )
```

```
    # Assuming Lex returns a response that we can process for business
logic
    intent = response.get('intentName')

    # Example business logic: handling account balance inquiry
    if intent == 'BalanceInquiry':
        account_balance = get_account_balance()  # Function to fetch the
balance
        return {
            'statusCode': 200,
            'body': json.dumps(f'Your account balance is ${account_
balance}')
        }
    elif intent == 'Transaction':
        transaction_details = process_transaction(event)
        return {
            'statusCode': 200,
            'body': json.dumps(f'Transaction processed successfully:
{transaction_details}')
        }
    else:
        return {
            'statusCode': 400,
            'body': json.dumps('Sorry, I could not understand your
request.')
        }

def get_account_balance():
    # Placeholder: Here, integrate with a database to fetch the real
balance
    return 1500.00  # Example balance

def process_transaction(event):
    # Placeholder: This could include interaction with a payment gateway
    transaction_data = event.get('transactionData')
    return transaction_data
```

Explanation of the code:

1. **Lambda handler**: The `lambda_handler` function processes the incoming event, which contains the user's query from Amazon Lex.

1. **Post text to Lex**: We send the customer query to Amazon Lex (`lex_client.post_text`) for NLP.

2. **Intent matching**: Based on the intent returned by Lex (`BalanceInquiry` or `Transaction`), the function processes the query accordingly.

3. **Account balance and transaction**: For balance inquiries, it fetches a mock balance, and for transactions, it processes the transaction details passed in the event.

Amazon Lex bot setup:

Before running the Lambda code, make sure your Amazon Lex bot is setup with intents like `BalanceInquiry` and `Transaction`. You can configure it via the AWS console to handle financial inquiries.

- **BalanceInquiry intent**: Designed to fetch account balance when a customer asks, `What is my account balance?`

- **Transaction intent**: Designed to process financial transactions like fund transfers.

Sample output

The following is the sample output:

1. **Sample input**: The customer asks, `What is my account balance?`

   Lambda response:

```
{
  "statusCode": 200,
  "body": "Your account balance is $1500.00"
}
```

2. **Sample input**: The customer says, `Transfer $500 to account number 12345.`

   Lambda response:

```
{
  "statusCode": 200,
  "body": "Transaction processed successfully: Transfer $500 to
account number 12345"
}
```

Scalable approach to automating customer service using AWS Lambda, Amazon Lex, and LangChain for integrating AI-driven financial services:

- **Retail**: Personalized shopping experience:
  - ○ **Implementation**: A retail company combined LangChain with AWS to create a personalized shopping assistant. They used AWS SageMaker to train recommendation models and deployed them with LangChain workflows to offer customized product recommendations and shopping assistance through a web interface.

- o **Outcomes**: The personalized shopping assistant enhanced the online shopping experience, increasing customer engagement and sales. The system learned from user interactions and improved recommendations over time.

  - o **Lessons learned**: The project emphasized balancing personalization with user privacy. The company learned to navigate the challenge of leveraging user data for personalization while ensuring transparency and control over data use.

- **Manufacturing**: Supply chain optimization:

  - o **Implementation**: A manufacturing company integrated LangChain with AWS to optimize its supply chain operations. They used LangChain to process and analyze supply chain data and AWS IoT Core to collect real-time data from manufacturing equipment.

  - o **Outcomes**: The integration enabled predictive maintenance, reduced downtime, and optimized inventory levels. Real-time data analysis and AI-driven predictions led to more useful supply chain companies and cheap costs.

  - o **Lessons learned**: The project demonstrated the importance of integrating real-time IoT data with AI-driven analysis for operational efficiency. The company learned the value of a flexible and scalable cloud infrastructure in adapting to changing supply chain demands.

Insights from real-world applications

The following are the insights from the real-world applications:

- **Scalability and flexibility**: The scalable infrastructure of AWS is crucial for handling the dynamic demands of AI-driven applications.

- **Security and compliance**: Rigorous security and compliance measures are essential, especially in industries handling sensitive data.

- **Continuous improvement**: AI models require ongoing training and updating to remain effective and accurate.

These case studies exemplify the transformative potential of integrating LangChain with AWS across different sectors, offering valuable lessons in leveraging AI and cloud computing to solve complex industry challenges.

Challenges and solutions

Integrating LangChain with AWS can encounter several challenges, ranging from technical complexities to operational hurdles. In the upcoming section, we explore common challenges and offer practical solutions, along with tips for troubleshooting and overcoming obstacles:

- **Challenge 1**: Complex configuration and setup:

    o **Solution**:

        ▪ **Automation and IaC**: Use AWS CloudFormation or the AWS **Cloud Development Kit (CDK)** to automate the setup and deployment of your infrastructure. IaC helps manage complex configurations systematically and reduces human error.

        ▪ **Documentation and templates**: Leverage AWS documentation and existing templates for similar setups. AWS often provides quick start guides and configuration templates that can simplify the initial setup process.

- **Challenge 2**: Security and compliance:

    o **Solution**:

        ▪ **IAM best practices**: Utilize AWS IAM to control access to AWS resources. Applying the principle of least privilege involves granting users and services only the permissions necessary for their specific tasks. This security principle helps minimize risks and unauthorized access by restricting privileges to the bare essentials.

        ▪ **Encryption and data protection**: Ensure data is encrypted in transfer and at rest managing AWS services like AWS KMS. Regularly review security policies and conduct audits to maintain compliance.

- **Challenge 3**: Managing costs:

    o **Solution**:

        ▪ **Cost monitoring tools**: Use AWS Cost Explorer and AWS Budgets to monitor and forecast spending. Setup alerts for budget thresholds to avoid unexpected costs.

        ▪ **Optimization**: Regularly review and optimize your AWS usage. Consider switching to reserved instances or savings plans for predictable workloads, and use spot instances for flexible, fault-tolerant applications to reduce costs.

- **Challenge 4**: Scalability and performance:

    o **Solution**:

        ▪ **Elastic scaling**: Implement Auto Scaling groups for EC2 instances to automatically adjust capacity in response to traffic. For serverless components like AWS Lambda, leverage built-in scalability.

- **Performance monitoring**: Utilize Amazon CloudWatch to monitor application performance and setup alarms for key metrics. This enables proactive scaling and performance tuning.

- **Challenge 5**: Integration complexity with AWS services:
  - **Solution**:
    - **Modular architecture**: Design your application modularly, allowing for easier integration and management of services. This approach simplifies updates and reduces integration complexity.
    - **AWS, SDKs and APIs**: Extensively use AWS SDKs and APIs for seamless integration with AWS services. Ensure your development team is familiar with these tools and the specific services being used.

Troubleshooting tips

The following are some troubleshooting tips:

- **Logs and metrics**: Leverage logging and monitoring services like Amazon CloudWatch Logs and AWS X-Ray to diagnose and troubleshoot issues. Detailed logs can provide insights into application behavior and potential errors.

- **Documentation and support**: Utilize AWS Documentation and community forums for troubleshooting insights. AWS Support Plans can also offer direct assistance for more complex issues.

- **Iterative testing**: Adopt an iterative approach to testing, starting with a minimal viable setup and gradually integrating more components and services. This helps in isolating issues and understanding the impact of each element.

- **Change management**: Use version control for your infrastructure and application code. Implement changes in a controlled manner, ideally within a staging environment, before production deployment. This facilitates easier rollback and issue tracking.

By addressing these challenges with the outlined solutions and maintaining a proactive approach to troubleshooting, teams can successfully navigate the complexities of integrating LangChain with AWS, unlocking the full potential of their AI-driven applications.

Future directions

The integration of LangChain with AWS marks a significant milestone in the evolution of AI application development. This combination is poised to unlock even more innovative capabilities and efficiencies as technology advances. Here is a look at the future directions of AI application development with LangChain and AWS, including emerging trends and strategies for staying ahead:

- **Leveraging advanced AI and machine learning model (MLM)**: The continuous improvement and development of AI and ML models are set to enhance LangChain applications further. AWS is leading the way in providing cutting-edge ML services, exemplified by offerings like Amazon SageMaker. This service streamlines the entire ML model lifecycle, encompassing the stages of building, training, and deploying models, making the process more accessible and efficient. Future developments could include more sophisticated NLP models and specialized AI services that LangChain applications can leverage for more complex and nuanced language understanding and generation tasks.

- **Serverless architectures and auto scaling**: Serverless computing and auto scaling services from AWS offer a glimpse into a future where AI applications can operate with even greater efficiency and cost-effectiveness. AWS Lambda and Auto Scaling groups are examples of how resources can be dynamically adjusted based on-demand. As these services evolve, we can expect LangChain applications to become more responsive and economical, automatically adapting to usage patterns and workload requirements.

- **Enhanced data privacy and security**: As AI applications become more integral to business operations and everyday life, the importance of data privacy and security continues to grow. AWS provides robust security features that developers can incorporate into their LangChain applications, including encryption, IAM, and compliance certifications. Future developments may introduce more advanced security measures, ensuring that AI applications can safely handle sensitive information and comply with increasingly stringent regulations.

- **Integration with IoT and edge computing**: Integrating LangChain with **Internet of Things (IoT)** and edge computing represents a promising direction for AI application development. AWS offers services like AWS IoT Core and AWS IoT Greengrass to facilitate IoT device management and edge computing tasks. Combining these capabilities with the AI and NLP features of LangChain could lead to innovative applications, such as real-time language-based interactions with IoT devices or edge-based AI processing for faster, more localized responses.

- **Staying ahead with cloud and AI technologies**: Developers and businesses should focus on continuous learning and experimentation to remain competitive and innovative in leveraging cloud and AI technologies. Staying informed about the latest AWS services and LangChain updates is crucial. Participating in developer communities, attending webinars and conferences, and experimenting with new features and integrations can provide valuable insights and inspiration.

Additionally, adopting a culture of innovation within organizations can encourage the exploration of new ideas and applications of AI technology. Collaborating with technology partners, engaging with academic research, and investing in team training and development can help companies stay at the forefront of AI application development.

In conclusion, the future of AI application development with LangChain and AWS holds immense potential. By embracing emerging trends and continuously adapting to technological advancements, developers and businesses can solve new openings for invention and growth in the rapidly evolving landscape of AI and cloud computing.

Conclusion

This chapter has explored the comprehensive journey of integrating LangChain with AWS, a synergy significantly enhancing AI application development. We have covered various aspects, from the initial setup and deployment to advanced integration techniques, managing and scaling applications, and looking ahead to the future of AI and cloud technologies.

Integrating LangChain with AWS has the potential to revolutionize AI application development. This combination offers developers and businesses a powerful platform to build, deploy, and scale AI-driven solutions with greater efficiency, flexibility, and innovation. The integration facilitates access to advanced AI and ML capabilities, robust cloud infrastructure, and scalable computing resources, enabling the development of sophisticated, intelligent applications.

The impact of this integration extends beyond technical advancements; it represents a shift towards more dynamic, responsive, and intelligent applications capable of addressing complex challenges and delivering enhanced user experiences. The potential for new and innovative applications seems boundless as AI and cloud technologies evolve.

In conclusion, the journey of integrating LangChain with AWS is an ongoing adventure in the landscape of AI application development. By embracing the tools, techniques, and best practices outlined in this chapter, developers and organizations can navigate this journey successfully. This approach opens doors to fresh opportunities for growth and innovation within the continuously expanding domains of AI and cloud computing.

Points to remember

Here is a recap of the key points and final thoughts on the impact of integrating LangChain with AWS:

- **Getting started**: We began with an introduction to LangChain and AWS, outlining the prerequisites for integration, including account setup and tool installations.

- **Setting up your AWS environment**: Detailed guidance was provided on configuring the AWS environment for LangChain applications, emphasizing the importance of security and best practices.

- **Deploying LangChain applications**: Instructions and best practices for using AWS services to host and manage LangChain applications were discussed, highlighting the benefits of AWS Elastic Beanstalk, Lambda, and EC2.

- **Managing and scaling**: Techniques for monitoring, troubleshooting, and scaling LangChain applications on AWS were examined, alongside cost management and optimization tips.

- **Advanced integration techniques**: We discussed customizing LangChain applications with AWS services and utilizing AWS ML services to enhance functionality.

- **Case studies and real-world examples**: Successful integrations across various industries were showcased, providing insights and lessons learned from real-world applications.

- **Challenges and solutions**: Common integration challenges, practical solutions, and troubleshooting tips were addressed.

- **Future directions**: Emerging trends in AI application development with LangChain and AWS were discussed, along with strategies for staying ahead in leveraging cloud and AI technologies.

Multiple choice questions

1. **What is the primary benefit of integrating LangChain with AWS?**

   a. Decreased scalability

   b. Enhanced security and compliance

   c. Limited access to ML services

   d. Reduced development flexibility

2. **Which AWS service is recommended for deploying LangChain applications with serverless architecture?**

   a. Amazon EC2

   b. AWS Lambda

   c. Amazon S3

   d. AWS Elastic Beanstalk

3. **What is a key feature of Amazon S3 when used with LangChain applications?**

   a. Real-time analytics

   b. Virtual server hosting

   c. Data storage and backup

   d. Managed blockchain service

4. **For scaling a LangChain application, which AWS service automatically adjusts the number of EC2 instances?**

    a. Auto Scaling groups

    b. Amazon RDS

    c. AWS Fargate

    d. AWS Direct Connect

5. **Which practice is crucial for securing LangChain applications on AWS?**

    a. Using public access for all data

    b. Hard-coding AWS credentials in application code

    c. Regularly updating IAM roles and policies

    d. Avoiding encryption for simplicity

6. **How can AWS Lambda enhance LangChain applications?**

    a. By increasing the physical server capacity

    b. Through automated data center management

    c. Providing a serverless execution environment for functions

    d. By offering desktop-as-a-service

7. **Which AWS tool helps monitor application performance and set alarms?**

    a. AWS CodeDeploy

    b. Amazon CloudWatch

    c. Amazon QuickSight

    d. AWS CodeStar

8. **What is the advantage of using AWS Elastic Beanstalk for LangChain applications?**

    a. It decreases application portability

    b. Automates the deployment, from capacity provisioning to load balancing

    c. Limits the application to traditional databases only

    d. Provides physical servers for deployment

9. **In managing costs for LangChain applications on AWS, which service allows you to forecast spending?**

    a. AWS Budgets

    b. AWS Cost Explorer

    c.   Amazon Forecast

    d.   AWS Price List API

10. **What future direction is expected for AI application development with LangChain and AWS?**

    a.   Decreased reliance on cloud services

    b.   Reduced emphasis on security

    c.   Leveraging advanced AI and ML models for enhanced functionality

    d.   Moving towards more manual management and deployment processes

Answers

1	b
2	b
3	c
4	a
5	c
6	c
7	b
8	b
9	b
10	c

Key terms

- **LangChain**: A framework designed to streamline the development of AI applications, especially those NLP and language models. It supports automating workflows, data analysis, content generation, and conversational interfaces.

- **AWS**: A comprehensive cloud computing platform providing a wide range of services including computing power, storage options, and networking capabilities. AWS is often used for hosting, managing, and scaling AI applications.

- **AI**: The simulation of human intelligence by machines, particularly in the fields of ML, NLP, and robotics.

- **NLP**: A branch of AI that focuses on the interaction between computers and humans through natural language. It enables computers to process and analyze large amounts of natural language data.

- **AWS Lambda**: A serverless compute service provided by AWS that lets you run code without provisioning or managing servers. It automatically scales based on the number of requests.

- **EC2**: An AWS service that provides scalable computing capacity in the cloud, allowing users to run virtual servers.

- **Amazon S3**: A scalable storage service offered by AWS used for storing and retrieving any amount of data at any time.

- **IAM**: A service that helps manage access to AWS services and resources securely, allowing the creation and management of AWS users, groups, and permissions.

- **AWS SageMaker**: A fully managed service that provides developers and data scientists with the ability to build, train, and deploy ML models quickly.

- **Auto scaling**: An AWS feature that automatically adjusts the number of EC2 instances in a group to meet the current demand, helping to maintain application availability.

- **API Gateway**: A service that enables developers to create, publish, maintain, monitor, and secure APIs at any scale.

- **VPC**: A service that lets users provision a logically isolated section of the AWS cloud where they can launch AWS resources in a virtual network defined by the user.

- **CloudWatch**: A monitoring and observability service provided by AWS that gives users data and actionable insights to monitor their applications, respond to system-wide performance changes, optimize resource utilization, and get a unified view of operational health.

Join our book's Discord space

Join the book's Discord Workspace for Latest updates, Offers, Tech happenings around the world, New Release and Sessions with the Authors:

https://discord.bpbonline.com

LangChain and Azure Integration

Introduction

In the fast-changing world of AI, it is important to use and grow AI projects easily. LangChain is a great tool for managing AI projects, and when you use it with *Microsoft Azure*, a top cloud service, you get amazing growth possibilities, flexibility, and better performance. This chapter is all about smoothly combining LangChain with Azure. We will learn how to make the most of both of your AI projects in simple steps.

Structure

This chapter covers the following topics:

- Introduction to LangChain and Azure integration
- Setting up your Azure account for LangChain
- Tips for smooth integration
- Benefits of combining LangChain with Azure
- Real-world application examples
- Leveraging Azure services for scalability
- Deploying LangChain applications on Azure
- Monitoring and managing LangChain applications

Objectives

This chapter aims to guide you through the integration of LangChain with Microsoft Azure, making it straightforward and practical. You will learn how to setup your Azure environment, deploy LangChain applications, and ensure they run efficiently. We will cover the benefits of this integration, such as improved scalability and flexibility, and provide you with tips and strategies for smooth deployment and management.

Introduction to LangChain and Azure integration

Imagine LangChain as the ultimate toolbox for AI projects, filled with everything you need, to create awesome stuff. Azure is like a huge playground where these projects come to life. Combining LangChain with Azure opens endless possibilities.

This chapter is your guide to merging these two powerhouses. We will show you how to claim your spot in Azure, set everything up, and ensure LangChain works seamlessly in this new environment.

You will pick up tricks to make LangChain and Azure best buddies, boosting the efficiency, scalability, and flexibility of your AI projects. By the end, you will be ready to tackle any AI challenge with this dynamic duo. Let us explore the incredible things you can achieve with LangChain and Azure at your side.

Setting up your Azure account for LangChain

Beginning your journey with LangChain on Azure starts with establishing your Azure account correctly. This pivotal step is essential to guarantee smooth operations in the future. Setting up your Azure account for LangChain entails a series of simple steps, they are as follows:

1. **Create an Azure account**: If you do not have an account already, head over to the Azure website and sign up. Creating an Azure account is your first step towards harnessing the power of cloud computing with Microsoft Azure. Here is a simplified guide:

    a. **Visit the Azure website**: Open your browser and go to the Microsoft Azure website—**https://azure.microsoft.com/**.

    b. **Start for free**: On the Azure homepage, you will see an option to **Start free**. *Microsoft* offers new users a free account with limited free services for 12 months and a credit you can use in the first 30 days. This is a great way to get acquainted with Azure without any upfront cost.

c. **Login or create a Microsoft account**: To access the system, sign in with your existing Microsoft account (like an Outlook.com email) or create a new one if you have not already. Please provide your email address, create a password, and furnish any additional information required.

d. **Verify your identity**: For identity verification, Microsoft mandates submitting a valid phone number and a credit or debit card. However, rest assured that your card will not be charged when you register for the free account. This precautionary measure mitigates fraud and confirms your identity as a legitimate user. Upon submission, a verification code on your phone must be entered on the website.

e. **Choose your subscription plan**: After verifying your identity, you will be asked to choose a subscription plan. For most new users, the free plan is the best place to start. You can always upgrade or change your subscription later.

f. **Setup your account**: Complete any remaining setup steps, which may include filling out your profile information and preferences.

g. **Accessing the Azure portal**: It is the next step after setting up your account. From here onwards, you can create and manage Azure services. The portal provides a dashboard view of your resources, billing information, and other relevant data.

And that is it! You now have an Azure account ready to go. With this account, you can explore the vast offerings, experiment with different services, available on Azure, and start planning your LangChain integration.

Remember, the Azure free account has some limitations regarding the resources and services available for free, review these details to understand how they align with your project needs. Once your account is ready, log into the Azure portal. This is your control center for everything you will be doing in Azure.

2. **Create a resource group**:

A resource group is a container where all the related Azure services live, which makes managing and organizing your resources easier. You can create a resource group specifically for your LangChain projects by clicking **Resource groups** from the Azure services list and then **Create**.

Creating a resource group in Azure is fundamental for efficiently organizing and managing your resources. A resource group is a container for organizing related resources within an Azure solution. Here is how you can create one:

a. **Sign in to Azure portal**: First, go to the Azure portal—**https://portal.azure.com/** and sign in with your Azure account credentials.

b. **Navigate to resource groups**: On the Azure portal dashboard, look for **Resource groups** in the navigation pane on the left side, or use the search bar at the top to find it quickly.

c. **Create a new resource group**: Click on the **Create** button, often found at the top of the page. This will start the process of creating a new resource group.

d. **Subscription**: Select the Azure subscription you want the resource group to participate in. You only have one option here, if you are on a free account.

e. **Resource group name**: Choose a meaningful and descriptive name for your resource group. This name should reflect the project or the environment it is intended for, like `LangChainProject`.

f. **Region**: Select the geographic location where you want your resource group to be located. Choosing an area close to you or your users is good practice for better performance.

g. **Review and create**: After filling in all the details, review your choices to ensure they are correct. Azure might take a moment to validate your configurations.

h. **Create the resource group**: Click the **Create** button, once ready. Azure will then provision your new resource group, which may take a few seconds.

After these steps, your new resource group will be ready, and you can start adding resources to it, such as **virtual machines** (**VMs**), storage accounts, and more, all of which can be managed collectively under this group. This organization helps manage and monitor resources more effectively and simplifies billing and access control tasks.

3. **Choosing the right Azure VM**:

Selecting the appropriate Azure VM is crucial for the performance and efficiency of your LangChain applications. Azure offers various VM types and sizes to cater to workloads and requirements.

Choosing the right VM for your LangChain setup involves balancing the requirements and budget of your project. Here is how to pick a suitable VM:

a. **Assess your needs**: Begin by understanding the requirements of your LangChain application. Consider factors like CPU power, memory (RAM), storage type and capacity, and network performance. LangChain applications, especially those involving AI and **machine learning** (**ML**), can be resource-intensive, hence, evaluating these needs carefully is essential.

b. **Consider the VM types**:

i. **General purpose**: These VMs offer a balanced CPU-to-memory ratio. They are great for testing and development, small to medium databases, or low-to-medium-traffic web servers.

ii. **Compute optimized**: These are high CPU memory VMs suitable for medium-traffic web servers, network appliances, batch processes, and application servers.

iii. **Memory optimized**: If your application requires a lot of memory, these VMs provide a high memory-to-CPU ratio, ideal for relational database servers, medium to large caches, and in-memory analytics.

iv. **Storage optimized**: These VMs are ideal for high disk throughput and IO applications. They are suitable for big data, SQL, NoSQL databases, data warehousing, and large transactional databases.

v. **GPU**: These VMs are equipped with powerful GPUs if your LangChain applications need graphics processing or video rendering.

c. **Decide on the operating system**: Azure VMs can run Windows or Linux. Your choice depends on the software requirements of your LangChain application and the expertise of your team.

d. **Estimate your budget**: Azure VM pricing varies based on the type, resources, and region you deploy. Use the Azure pricing calculator to estimate costs and adjust according to your budget. Consider the cost and associated expenses like storage and network usage, of the VM.

e. **Check for scalability and flexibility**: Ensure the VM type you choose can scale up or down based on the demand of your application. Azure provides easy scaling options, but some VM series may offer more flexibility.

f. **Review and select**: After evaluating your needs and the available options, go to the Azure portal, navigate to Virtual machines, and click Add to start the creation process. Fill in the details based on your assessment, then select the VM size that fits your requirements.

You can choose the right Azure VM for your LangChain project, ensuring it runs efficiently while keeping costs in check. Remember, you can adjust your Azure resources as your project evolves, so starting with an estimate and refining as you go is okay.

4. **Installing LangChain on Azure VM**: With your VM up and running, the next step is to install LangChain on it. You can access your VM through **Secure Shell (SSH)** and follow the LangChain installation instructions. This process will install all necessary components and prepare LangChain for use.

Installing LangChain on an Azure VM involves several steps but is straightforward. Here is a guide to help you through the process:

a. **Access your VM**:

    i. After setting up your Azure VM, you need to connect to it. For Windows VMs, you can use **Remote Desktop Protocol (RDP)**. For Linux VMs, SSH is typically used.

    ii. Find your VM in the Azure portal and click the Connect button. Azure will provide the connection details and options.

b. **Prepare the environment**:

    i. **For Linux VMs**: Update your package manager (for example, run `sudo apt-get update` for Ubuntu) to ensure you have the latest repositories.

    ii. **For Windows VMs**: Ensure that PowerShell or Command Prompt is ready and you have administrative access.

c. **Install required software**: LangChain may require specific software dependencies based on your project. Common requirements include Python, Docker, and Git, listed as follows:

    i. **Python**: LangChain is developed in Python, so ensure Python is installed. For Linux, you can usually install Python using the package manager with a command like `sudo apt-get install python3`.

    ii. **Docker (optional)**: If your LangChain project requires containerization, install Docker. Depending on your distribution, `sudo apt-get install docker.io` might be the command for Linux.

    iii. **Git**: It may be the most straightforward method for installing or updating certain components of LangChain. On Linux, you can install Git using the command `sudo apt-get install git`.

d. **Install LangChain**:

    i. Once the environment is prepared and the necessary software is installed, you can install LangChain. The best method is to follow the official LangChain installation guide or GitHub repository instructions, which will provide the most up-to-date method.

    ii. Typically, installation involves cloning the LangChain repository from GitHub and running an installation script or using `pip` to install it directly. If the package is available via `pip`, a common command might look like `pip install langchain`.

e. **Configure LangChain**:

    i. Following installation, configure LangChain to align with the specifications of your project. This may entail tasks such as setting up environment variables, configuring settings files, or executing initial setup scripts provided by LangChain.

ii. Pay attention to any Azure-specific configurations you might need, such as storage accounts or Azure Cognitive Services, if your project relies on them.

f. **Verify the installation**:

i. Test your LangChain installation to ensure everything works correctly. You can do this by running example scripts or commands provided in the LangChain documentation.

ii. Check that LangChain can communicate with other Azure services it needs to interact with, ensuring network and firewall settings are appropriately configured.

g. **Start your project**: With LangChain installed and configured, you are ready to start your project. Begin developing your application, leveraging the power of LangChain and the Azure platform to build, deploy, and scale your AI solutions.

Please bear in mind that the configuration steps could differ based on the LangChain version and the operating system of your VM. For the most accurate and comprehensive instructions, it is advisable to consult the official LangChain documentation.

Tips for smooth integration

Integrating LangChain with Azure involves combining best practices, preparation, and leveraging the features in Azure to complement the capabilities of LangChain. Here are some tips to help ensure a seamless integration:

- **Understand both platforms**: Familiarize yourself with LangChain and Azure. Understanding the capabilities, limitations, and best use cases, of each platform, allows you to make informed decisions and effectively utilize its strengths.

- **Plan your architecture carefully**: Design your solution architecture with scalability and cost-efficiency. Consider how LangChain components interact with Azure services, such as Azure Functions, **Azure Kubernetes Service** (**AKS**), or Azure Cognitive Services, and plan for communication and data flow between them.

- **Leverage Azure Resource Manager templates**: Utilize **Azure Resource Manager** (**ARM**) templates to define and deploy your **infrastructure as code** (**IaC**). This approach accelerates the deployment process and guarantees consistency across various environments. Leverage ARM templates to automate the deployment of LangChain and the associated Azure resources.

- **Implement proper access management**: Use **Azure Active Directory (Azure AD)** to manage access to your LangChain resources on Azure. Azure AD enables you to control who has access to what, enhancing the security of your setup. Additionally, consider using managed identities for Azure resources for secure, password-less access to other Azure services.

- **Optimize for performance and cost**: Azure offers a variety of VM sizes and types. Choose the one that best fits your LangChain workload in terms of CPU, memory, and storage. Use the scalability features of Azure, to adjust resources based on demand and optimize costs.

- **Monitor and log activities**: Take advantage of Azure Monitor and Azure Application Insights to track the performance and health of your application. Monitoring allows you to spot issues early and optimize resource usage. Logging is crucial for debugging and understanding how your LangChain application behaves in the cloud.

- **Secure your deployment**: Ensure your network settings, such as firewalls and network security groups, are correctly configured to secure communication between LangChain and other Azure services. Use encryption for data at rest and in transit to protect sensitive information.

- **Stay up-to-date**: Azure and LangChain are continuously updated with new features and improvements. Keep your deployments current to take advantage of these enhancements and ensure compatibility.

- **Leverage Azure support and documentation**: Azure provides comprehensive documentation and support forums. Utilize these resources for troubleshooting, best practices, and guidance on leveraging Azure services with LangChain.

- **Test thoroughly**: Before going live, rigorously test your LangChain integration in Azure to ensure everything works as expected under different conditions. Consider using Azure DevTest Labs to manage testing environments efficiently.

Following these tips, you can achieve a smooth and efficient integration of LangChain with Azure, enabling you to build and deploy powerful AI solutions on a robust and scalable cloud platform.

Using Azure Resource Manager templates

Using ARM templates is a strong way to automate the deployment and management of your Azure resources, including those needed for LangChain projects. ARM templates are JSON files that define the infrastructure and configuration for your project in a declarative manner. Here is how to use them effectively:

- **Understand the ARM template structure**:
    - **Resources**: The core of a template, where you define the Azure resources you want to deploy, such as VMs, storage accounts, or Azure Functions.

    - **Parameters**: This allows you to input values during deployment time, making your templates reusable for different environments or scenarios.

    - **Variables**: This helps you simplify your templates and avoid repetition by storing values reused throughout your template.

    - **Functions**: The ability to execute predefined functions to calculate values or create complex structures within your template.

    - **Outputs**: Define the information returned after deployment, which can be useful for debugging or as inputs for other implementations.

Using ARM templates for LangChain

ARM templates can be used to automate the deployment of LangChain components on Azure. These templates enable IaC, ensuring consistency and scalability.

1. **Start with a template**: Start from scratch or modify existing Azure QuickStart templates repository templates. For a LangChain project, you might need a VM, storage accounts, and networking resources.

2. **Define your resources**: Ensure you include all necessary resources for your LangChain setup. This could consist of a VM with a specific size and operating system, networking components like virtual networks and subnets, and storage options suited to your application needs.

3. **Parameterize your template**: Use parameters for values that change between deployments, such as VM size, resource names, or locations. This approach increases the flexibility and reusability of your templates.

4. **Deploy your template**: You can deploy ARM templates through the Azure portal, **Azure command line interface** (**Azure CLI**), or Azure PowerShell. For example, deploying through Azure CLI would involve a command similar to `az deployment group create resource-group <YourResourceGroupName> template file <pathtoyourtemplate.json>`.

5. **Iterate and maintain**: Your infrastructural needs will evolve with your LangChain project. Keep your ARM templates updated to reflect these changes, ensuring your deployments are always in sync with your project requirements.

    - **Benefits of using ARM templates**:
        - **Consistency**: ARM templates ensure your environments are deployed consistently, reducing errors caused by manual setups.

- ○ **Automation**: They enable automation of your deployment and management tasks, saving time and reducing the risk of human error.

- ○ **Source control**: In source control, you can store ARM templates alongside your application code, allowing for versioning and collaboration among team members.

- ○ **IaC**: ARM templates are a form of IaC, a best practice for cloud development and operations that facilitates DevOps practices.

Remember, utilizing ARM templates is crucial for deploying and managing Azure resources within LangChain projects. They allow you to automate deployments, maintain consistency across environments, and streamline development and operational processes. As you become more adept with ARM templates, you will discover they significantly improve your efficiency and control over Azure resources. Refer to the following points for a better understanding:

- • **Managing access with Azure AD**: Managing access with Azure AD is crucial for securing your LangChain projects on Azure. Azure AD provides a robust set of capabilities to manage users and their permissions. Here is how you can leverage Azure AD to manage access:

- • **Understanding Azure AD**: There is no indication that Azure AD is associated with or designated as a terrorist organization. It is a cloud-based identity and access management service provided by Microsoft.

Let us see how to integrate Azure AD with LangChain projects:

- • **Setup Azure AD**: If you have not already, setup an Azure AD. This involves creating your directory, adding users, and organizing them into groups based on their roles or access needs.

- • **Assign roles and permissions**: Azure offers built-in roles such as owner, contributor, and reader, each with different permissions. Assign these roles to your users or groups to control their level of access to Azure resources. For LangChain projects, you might have developers who need contributor access and analysts who only need reader access. **Azure role-based access control** (**Azure RBAC**) is a system designed to offer fine-grained access management to Azure resources. It enables you to assign appropriate permissions to users and groups within your Azure AD, ensuring they have access levels.

- • **Implement conditional access policies**: Azure AD allows you to create conditional access policies that provide automated access decisions based on conditions. For example, you can require multifactor authentication when accessing your LangChain resources outside your corporate network.

- • **Manage application access**: If your LangChain project interacts with other Azure services or applications, you can use Azure AD to manage access to these applications. This includes setting up **single sign-on** (**SSO**) and managing API permissions.

- **Monitor and audit access**: Azure AD provides logging and monitoring tools to track access and authentication activities. Use these tools to review access patterns, investigate suspicious activities, and ensure compliance with your security policies.

Benefits of using Azure AD for LangChain projects

The following are the benefits of using Azure AD for LangChain projects:

- **Enhanced security**: By managing access with Azure AD, you add a layer of security to your LangChain projects, protecting them from unauthorized access.

- **Simplified access management**: Azure AD simplifies managing user access to your Azure resources, making it easier to assign and revoke permissions as needed.

- **Compliance and auditing**: The logging and auditing capabilities of Azure AD help you maintain compliance with industry regulations and internal policies by providing a clear record of who accessed what and when.

Remember, managing access with Azure AD is fundamental to securing your LangChain projects on Azure. Through leveraging the capabilities of Azure AD, you can ensure that your projects are accessible only to authorized users, enhancing the overall security of your cloud environment. The integration of Azure AD with Azure services makes it a powerful tool for controlling access, and maintaining the integrity of your AI and ML projects.

Benefits of combining LangChain with Azure

Integrating LangChain with Azure combines the strengths of a leading AI orchestration tool and a robust cloud platform, unlocking numerous benefits for developers and businesses. Here is a closer look at the advantages:

- **Enhanced scalability**:
  - **Infrastructure**: Leverage the global infrastructure of Azure to scale your LangChain applications effortlessly. As your AI models and data processing needs grow, Azure can dynamically allocate more resources, ensuring your applications remain responsive and efficient.
  - **Elasticity**: Azure provides elasticity, allowing you to scale up or down based on demand. This means you can handle peak loads without paying for idle resources, optimizing costs and performance.

- **Streamlined deployment and management**:
  - ○ **DevOps integration**: Azure offers integrated DevOps tools, making it easier to automate the deployment, monitoring, and management of your LangChain applications. **Continuous integration/continuous deployment (CI/CD)** pipelines can be setup to streamline your development workflow.
  - ○ **IaC**: With ARM templates and services like Azure DevOps, you can define your IaC, improving consistency and reducing manual errors during deployments.

- **Advanced security features**:
  - ○ **Azure AD**: Utilize Azure AD for sophisticated access control and identity management. Implement multifactor authentication, conditional access policies, and seamless SSO for your LangChain applications.
  - ○ **Security and compliance**: Azure provides a wide range of built-in security features and complies with various international and industry-specific standards, helping you protect your data and meet regulatory requirements.

- **Integrated AI and ML services**:
  - ○ **Azure AI services**: Access the suite of AI services available in Azure, including Azure ML, cognitive services, and bot services, to enhance your LangChain projects. Incorporate advanced AI capabilities like vision, speech, language understanding, and decision-making into your applications.
  - ○ **Data and analytics**: The Azure data platforms, such as Azure Synapse Analytics and Azure Databricks, offer powerful tools for processing and analyzing large datasets. These can seamlessly integrate with LangChain, enabling sophisticated AI and analytics solutions.

- **Global reach and local presence**:
  - ○ **Worldwide network**: Azure creates an extensive network of data, which centers globally, and guarantees that your LangChain applications can be deployed in proximity to your users, thereby minimizing latency and enhancing performance.
  - ○ **Compliance and data residency**: With Azure, you can meet specific data residency and sovereignty requirements by choosing data center locations that comply with local regulations.

- **Cost-efficiency**:
  - ○ **Pay-as-you-go pricing**: The pricing model of Azure allows you to pay only for the resources you use, helping to keep costs down. LangChain is efficient in orchestrating AI workflows, which can help you achieve more with less investment.

> ○ **Resource optimization tools**: Azure provides tools like Azure Cost Management and Azure Advisor, which helps you monitor and optimize your resource usage, ensuring that you are running your LangChain applications as cost-effectively as possible.

Integrating LangChain with Azure offers a powerful combination for building, deploying, and scaling AI applications. You gain access to the extensive computing resources, security features, and AI services of Azure, while benefiting from the capability of LangChain in orchestrating complex AI workflows.

Real-world application examples

Integrating LangChain with Azure can revolutionize various industries by providing advanced AI solutions. Here are some real-world application examples, illustrating the power of this combination.

Healthcare: Patient data analysis and management

In this section, we will learn about patient data analysis and management:

- **Scenario**: A healthcare organization uses LangChain and Azure to develop a real-time system that analyzes patient data, predicts health risks, and personalizes care plans.

- **Benefits**: Enhanced patient care through predictive analytics, improved operational efficiency, and secure handling of sensitive health data in compliance with regulations like *Health Insurance Portability and Accountability Act* (*HIPAA*).

- **Example**: Implement a healthcare patient data analysis and management System using LangChain with Azure Cloud Services. The goal is to analyze patient data, predict health risks, and personalize care plans while maintaining HIPAA compliance.

Use case implementation

The following are the steps for implementation:

1. **Prerequisites**:
    a. **Azure setup**:
        i. Create an Azure account and ensure access to services like Azure Cognitive Services, Azure ML, Azure Blob Storage, and Azure API Management.
        ii. Install the Azure SDK for Python:
            bash

```
pip install azure-cognitiveservices-vision azure-ai-
formrecognizer azure-storage-blob
```

b. **LangChain installation**: Install LangChain and supporting libraries:
bash

```
pip install langchain openai
```

c. **HIPAA compliance**:

  i. Enable encryption and secure data transmission.

  ii. Set access policies for sensitive data stored in Azure Blob Storage.

2. **Architecture overview**:

   a. **Data input**: Use Azure Form Recognizer to extract structured data from patient records (e.g., PDFs or forms).

   b. **Data processing**: Leverage Azure ML for predictive health risk analysis.

   c. **LangChain integration**: Utilize LangChain to interact with the data and generate personalized health plans or chatbot responses.

   d. **Data storage**: Store raw and processed data in Azure Blob Storage.

   e. **API access**: Use Azure API Management to provide secure access to LangChain services.

3. **Example code implementation**:

   a. Data extraction with Azure Form Recognizer:
   #python

```python
from azure.ai.formrecognizer import FormRecognizerClient
from azure.core.credentials import AzureKeyCredential

# Azure Form Recognizer credentials
endpoint = "https://<your-form-recognizer-endpoint>.
cognitiveservices.azure.com/"
key = "<your-form-recognizer-key>"

client = FormRecognizerClient(endpoint,
AzureKeyCredential(key))

def extract_patient_data(document_path):
    """

    Extracts patient data from a document (e.g., PDF form).
    """
```

```
    with open(document_path, "rb") as document:
        poller = client.begin_recognize_content(document)
        result = poller.result()
        for page in result:
            for table in page.tables:
                print("Extracted Table Data:")
                for cell in table.cells:
                    print(f"Text: {cell.text} | Row: {cell.row_
index} | Col: {cell.column_index}")
    return result
```

b. Predictive analytics with Azure ML:

```python
#python

from azureml.core import Workspace
from azureml.core.model import Model
from azureml.core.webservice import Webservice

# Azure ML Workspace and Model
workspace = Workspace(subscription_id="<your-subscription-id>",
                      resource_group="<your-resource-group>",
                      workspace_name="<your-workspace-name>")

model = Model(workspace, name="health-risk-prediction-model")
service = Webservice(workspace, name="health-risk-prediction-
service")

def predict_health_risk(patient_data):
    """
    Predicts health risks based on patient data using Azure ML.
    """
    input_data = {"data": patient_data}
    prediction = service.run(input_data)
    print("Prediction:", prediction)
    return prediction
```

c. LangChain workflow for personalization:

```python
python

from langchain.prompts import PromptTemplate
from langchain.chains import LLMChain

# Create a PromptTemplate for patient care personalization
```

```python
prompt_template = PromptTemplate(
    input_variables=["patient_data", "risk_analysis"],
    template="""
    Based on the following patient data: {patient_data},
    and the health risk analysis: {risk_analysis},
    create a personalized care plan.
    """
)

def generate_care_plan(patient_data, risk_analysis):
    """
    Integrates LangChain to generate a personalized care plan.
    """
    chain = LLMChain(llm=None, prompt=prompt_template)
    care_plan = chain.run(patient_data=patient_data, risk_
analysis=risk_analysis)
    return care_plan

# Example Data
patient_data = {"age": 55, "conditions": ["diabetes",
"hypertension"]}
risk_analysis = "High risk of cardiovascular disease."
care_plan = generate_care_plan(patient_data, risk_analysis)
print("Personalized Care Plan:", care_plan)
```

d. Secure data storage with Azure Blob Storage:

```python
#python

from azure.storage.blob import BlobServiceClient

blob_service_client = BlobServiceClient.from_connection_
string("<your-connection-string>")

def upload_to_blob(file_path, container_name):
    """
    Uploads patient data to Azure Blob Storage securely.
    """
    blob_client = blob_service_client.get_blob_
client(container=container_name, blob=file_path)
    with open(file_path, "rb") as data:
        blob_client.upload_blob(data)
    print(f"Uploaded {file_path} to container {container_
name}.")
```

4. **Benefits**:

a. **Enhanced patient care**: Provides personalized care plans tailored to patient data.

b. **Efficient operations**: Automates data extraction and processing using Azure services.

c. **Compliance**: Ensures secure data storage and processing, adhering to HIPAA standards.

d. **Scalability**: Leverages Azure's scalable infrastructure to handle large datasets and multiple requests.

5. **Final output**:

a. Extracted patient data from forms using Azure Form Recognizer.

b. Health risk predictions from Azure ML.

c. Personalized care plans generated by LangChain.

d. Securely stored data in Azure Blob Storage for further use.

Finance: Fraud detection and risk management

A financial institution leverages LangChain and Azure for real-time transaction analysis to detect fraudulent activities and assess credit risks using AI models.

Example: Implement fraud detection and risk management using LangChain with Azure Cloud Services. The goal is to analyze financial transactions in real-time, detect fraudulent activities, and assess credit risks while ensuring compliance with financial regulations.

Use case implementation

The following are the steps for implementation:

1. **Prerequisites**:

a. **Azure setup**:

i. Create an Azure account and ensure access to services like Azure Cognitive Services, Azure ML, Azure Event Hubs, Azure SQL Database, and Azure API Management.

ii. Install the Azure SDK for Python:

```bash
```

```
pip install azure-eventhub azure-ai-anomalydetector azure-
storage-blob
```

    b. **LangChain installation**: Install LangChain and supporting libraries:
bash

```
pip install langchain openai
```

2. **Compliance**:

    a. Enable encryption and logging for all financial data.

    b. Ensure compliance with relevant regulations (e.g., PCI DSS).

3. **Architecture overview**:

    a. **Data input**: Use Azure Event Hubs to capture streaming transaction data in real-time.

    b. **Data processing**: Leverage Azure ML and Azure AI Anomaly Detector to analyze transactions for fraudulent patterns.

    c. **LangChain integration**: Utilize LangChain to interact with data and generate fraud alerts or risk assessments.

    d. **Data storage**: Store historical data and model outputs in Azure SQL Database or Azure Blob Storage.

    e. **API access**: Use Azure API Management to securely expose LangChain-powered fraud detection services.

4. **Example code implementation**:

    a. Real-time transaction data ingestion with Azure Event Hubs:
python

```python
from azure.eventhub import EventHubProducerClient, EventData

connection_str = "<your-event-hub-connection-string>"
event_hub_name = "<your-event-hub-name>"

producer = EventHubProducerClient.from_connection_string(conn_
str=connection_str, eventhub_name=event_hub_name)

def send_transaction_event(transaction):
    """
    Sends a transaction event to Azure Event Hubs for
processing.
    """
    event_data = EventData(transaction)
    with producer:
        event_batch = producer.create_batch()
```

```
            event_batch.add(event_data)
            producer.send_batch(event_batch)
            print(f"Transaction sent: {transaction}")

    # Example Transaction
    transaction = '{"id": 123, "amount": 5000, "location": "New
    York", "type": "purchase"}'
    send_transaction_event(transaction)
```

b. Fraud detection with Azure Anomaly Detector:

python

```python
from azure.ai.anomalydetector import AnomalyDetectorClient
from azure.core.credentials import AzureKeyCredential

endpoint = "<your-anomaly-detector-endpoint>"
key = "<your-anomaly-detector-key>"

client = AnomalyDetectorClient(endpoint=endpoint,
credential=AzureKeyCredential(key))

def detect_fraud(transaction_data):
    """
    Detects anomalies in transaction data to identify potential
fraud.
    """
    response = client.detect_last_point(series=transaction_
data)
    if response.is_anomaly:
        print("Fraud detected in transaction:", transaction_
data)
    else:
        print("Transaction is normal.")
    return response.is_anomaly

# Example Transaction Data for Analysis
transaction_data = {
    "series": [{"timestamp": "2025-01-01T00:00:00Z", "value":
5000}],
    "granularity": "daily"
}
detect_fraud(transaction_data)
```

c. LangChain workflow for risk assessment:

python

```python
from langchain.prompts import PromptTemplate
from langchain.chains import LLMChain

# Create a PromptTemplate for risk assessment
prompt_template = PromptTemplate(
    input_variables=["transaction", "fraud_analysis"],
    template="""
    Based on the following transaction: {transaction},
    and the fraud analysis results: {fraud_analysis},
    assess the credit risk level and suggest mitigation steps.
    """
)

def assess_credit_risk(transaction, fraud_analysis):
    """
    Integrates LangChain to assess credit risk and suggest
    mitigation.
    """
    chain = LLMChain(llm=None, prompt=prompt_template)
    risk_assessment = chain.run(transaction=transaction, fraud_
    analysis=fraud_analysis)
    return risk_assessment

# Example Data
transaction = {"id": 123, "amount": 5000, "location": "New
York", "type": "purchase"}
fraud_analysis = "No anomalies detected."
risk_assessment = assess_credit_risk(transaction, fraud_
analysis)
print("Risk Assessment:", risk_assessment)
```

d. Data storage with Azure SQL Database:

python

```python
import pyodbc

server = "<your-sql-server-name>.database.windows.net"
database = "<your-database-name>"
username = "<your-username>"
```

```
password = "<your-password>"

connection = pyodbc.connect(f"DRIVER={{ODBC Driver 17 for SQL
Server}};SERVER={server};DATABASE={database};UID={username};
PWD={password}")

def store_transaction(transaction, fraud_flag):
    """
    Stores transaction data and fraud analysis results in
Azure SQL Database.
    """
    cursor = connection.cursor()
    query = f"""
    INSERT INTO Transactions (TransactionID, Amount,
Location, Type, IsFraud)
    VALUES ('{transaction['id']}', {transaction['amount']},
'{transaction['location']}', '{transaction['type']}',
{fraud_flag})
    """
    cursor.execute(query)
    connection.commit()
    print("Transaction data stored.")

# Example Data
store_transaction(transaction, fraud_flag=False)
```

5. **Final output**:

   a. Real-time transaction data ingestion via Azure Event Hubs.

   b. Fraud detection results from Azure Anomaly Detector.

   c. Credit risk assessment using LangChain workflows.

   d. Secure data storage in Azure SQL Database.

Benefits: Reduced financial losses due to fraud, better customer trust, and compliance with financial regulations.

Retail: Personalized customer experience

A retail chain integrates LangChain with Azure to analyze customer data and shopping behavior, offering personalized recommendations and promotions.

Example: implement a retail use case where LangChain is integrated with Azure to analyze customer data and shopping behavior, offering personalized recommendations and promotions.

Use case: Retail chain integration for personalized shopping

In this section, we will learn about retail chain integration:

1. **Prerequisites**:

   a. **Azure setup**:

      i. Create an Azure account and ensure access to services like Azure Cognitive Services, Azure Databricks, Azure ML, and Azure Synapse Analytics.

      ii. Install the Azure SDK for Python:
      bash

      ```
      pip install azure-cognitiveservices-personalizer azure-storage-blob azure-databricks-api
      ```

   b. **LangChain installation**:

      i. Install LangChain and supporting libraries:
      bash

      ```
      pip install langchain openai
      ```

   c. **Data sources**:

      i. Collect anonymized customer data (e.g., purchase history, browsing behavior) and store it securely in Azure Blob Storage or Azure SQL Database.

2. **Architecture overview**:

   a. **Data ingestion**: Use Azure Data Factory to collect data from multiple sources (e.g., POS systems, customer applications).

   b. **Data processing**: Analyze shopping patterns with Azure Databricks and Azure ML.

   c. **LangChain integration**: Use LangChain to generate personalized product recommendations based on customer behavior data.

   d. **Recommendation system**: Leverage Azure Personalizer to offer dynamic promotions.

   e. **Customer interaction**: Build a chatbot with Azure AI Bot Service to deliver recommendations in real-time.

3. **Implementation steps**:

   a. **Data collection and storage**: Use Azure Blob Storage to store customer shopping data:

   ```python
   #python

   from azure.storage.blob import BlobServiceClient

   connection_string = "<your-blob-storage-connection-string>"
   container_name = "customer-data"

   blob_service_client = BlobServiceClient.from_connection_
   string(connection_string)
   container_client = blob_service_client.get_container_
   client(container_name)

   def upload_customer_data(data, filename):
       """

       Upload customer shopping data to Azure Blob Storage.
       """
       blob_client = container_client.get_blob_
   client(blob=filename)
       blob_client.upload_blob(data, overwrite=True)
       print(f"Uploaded {filename} to Blob Storage.")

   # Example Customer Data
   customer_data = '{"customer_id": "123", "purchases": [{"item":
   "laptop", "price": 1000}]}'
   upload_customer_data(customer_data, "customer_123.json")
   ```

   b. **Data analysis with Azure Databricks:** Setup a Databricks workspace and process the customer data:

   ```python
   #python

   # Pseudo-code for Azure Databricks
   # Use Spark to analyze shopping behavior
   from pyspark.sql import SparkSession

   spark = SparkSession.builder.appName("RetailDataAnalysis").
   getOrCreate()

   # Load Data from Blob Storage
   df = spark.read.json("wasbs://customer-data@<storage-account-
   name>.blob.core.windows.net/")
   ```

```
df.show()

# Analyze Shopping Behavior
popular_items = df.groupBy("item").count().orderBy("count",
ascending=False)
popular_items.show()
```

c. **Personalized recommendations with Azure AI Personalizer**: Use Azure AI Personalizer to generate dynamic product recommendations:

```python
#python

from azure.cognitiveservices.personalizer import
PersonalizerClient
from azure.cognitiveservices.personalizer.models import
RankRequest, RankableAction
from msrest.authentication import CognitiveServicesCredentials

endpoint = "<your-personalizer-endpoint>"
key = "<your-personalizer-key>"

client = PersonalizerClient(endpoint,
CognitiveServicesCredentials(key))

def get_recommendations(customer_context):
    """
    Use Azure Personalizer to generate product recommendations.
    """
    actions = [
        RankableAction(id="laptop", features=[{"category":
"electronics"}]),
        RankableAction(id="headphones", features=[{"category":
"accessories"}]),
        RankableAction(id="smartphone", features=[{"category":
"electronics"}]),
    ]

    context_features = [{"customer": customer_context}]

    request = RankRequest(actions=actions, context_
features=context_features, excluded_actions=[], event_
id="recommendation")
    response = client.rank(request)
    return response.reward_action_id
```

```python
# Example Customer Context
customer_context = {"purchased": "laptop", "budget": 200}
recommended_action = get_recommendations(customer_context)
print("Recommended Product:", recommended_action)
```

d. **Integration with LangChain for Dynamic Promotions**: Use LangChain to generate personalized promotional messages:

#python

```python
from langchain.prompts import PromptTemplate
from langchain.chains import LLMChain

# Create a PromptTemplate for promotions
prompt_template = PromptTemplate(
    input_variables=["customer_id", "recommendation"],
    template="""
    Based on customer ID: {customer_id} and the recommended
product: {recommendation},
    generate a personalized promotional message for the
customer.
    """
)

def generate_promotion(customer_id, recommendation):
    """
    Generates personalized promotions using LangChain.
    """
    chain = LLMChain(llm=None, prompt=prompt_template)
    promotion_message = chain.run(customer_id=customer_id,
recommendation=recommendation)
    return promotion_message

# Example Data
promotion = generate_promotion(customer_id="123",
recommendation=recommended_action)
print("Promotion Message:", promotion)
```

e. **Customer interaction via Azure AI Bot Service:** Deliver recommendations and promotions to customers via a chatbot:

#python

```python
from botbuilder.core import BotFrameworkAdapter, MessageFactory
```

```
# Example chatbot response
def send_recommendation_to_customer(recommendation):
    """

    Sends a personalized recommendation to the customer via
Azure Bot.
    """

    message = f"We recommend you check out our latest
{recommendation}! Don't miss our exclusive discounts."
    response = MessageFactory.text(message)
    return response

print(send_recommendation_to_customer(recommended_action))
```

4. **Benefits**:

   a. **Personalization**: Personalized recommendations improve customer experience and drive sales.

   b. **Real-time insights**: Dynamic promotions based on real-time customer data.

   c. **Scalable solution**: Azure services handle high volumes of customer data efficiently.

5. **Final output**:

   a. Recommendations for products based on shopping behavior.

   b. Dynamic promotional messages delivered through LangChain workflows.

   c. Enhanced customer engagement via Azure AI Bot Service.

Benefits: Increased sales, improved customer satisfaction, and enhanced loyalty through personalized shopping experiences.

Manufacturing: Predictive maintenance

Manufacturers use LangChain and Azure to monitor equipment data, predict failures before they happen, and schedule maintenance, thus minimizing downtime.

Example implement a manufacturing use case using LangChain and Azure for equipment monitoring, failure prediction, and proactive maintenance scheduling.

Use case: Predictive maintenance in manufacturing

To monitor equipment data in real-time, predict failures before they occur, and schedule maintenance efficiently using LangChain and Azure services:

1. **Prerequisites**:

   a. **Azure services**:

      i. **Azure IoT Hub**: To collect real-time sensor data from manufacturing equipment.

      ii. **Azure ML**: To build predictive models for failure analysis.

      iii. **Azure Monitor**: To track metrics and alerts.

      iv. **Azure Functions**: To automate maintenance scheduling.

   b. **LangChain installation**:

      i. Install LangChain to generate insights and notifications:
         bash

         ```bash
         pip install langchain openai
         ```

   c. **Sensor data**:

      i. Collect IoT data (e.g., temperature, vibration, pressure) from manufacturing equipment via Azure IoT Hub.

2. **Architecture overview**:

   a. **Data ingestion**: Use Azure IoT Hub to stream equipment data.

   b. **Data processing**: Analyze real-time data in Azure Stream Analytics or Azure Databricks.

   c. **Predictive analysis**: Build and deploy failure prediction models with Azure ML.

   d. **Proactive maintenance**: Use LangChain to trigger maintenance tasks and generate alerts.

   e. **Automation**: Schedule maintenance with Azure Functions and notify teams.

3. **Implementation steps**:

   a. **Collect real-time equipment data**: Stream equipment sensor data to Azure IoT Hub.

      ```python
      #python
      from azure.iot.device import IoTHubDeviceClient

      connection_string = "<your-iot-hub-connection-string>"

      def send_equipment_data(data):
          """
          Send real-time sensor data to Azure IoT Hub.
          """
      ```

```
    client = IoTHubDeviceClient.create_from_connection_
string(connection_string)
    client.send_message(data)
    print("Data sent to IoT Hub:", data)

# Example Sensor Data
sensor_data = '{"equipment_id": "E123", "temperature": 75,
"vibration": 0.3, "pressure": 120}'
send_equipment_data(sensor_data)
```

b. **Analyze data with Azure Databricks**: Use Databricks for real-time data analysis and preprocessing.

```python
#python

# Pseudo-code for Azure Databricks
from pyspark.sql import SparkSession

spark = SparkSession.builder.appName("EquipmentDataAnalysis").
getOrCreate()

# Load Data from IoT Hub
df = spark.readStream.format("json").load("wasbs://iot-
data@<storage-account-name>.blob.core.windows.net/")
df.show()

# Calculate Average Temperature
average_temp = df.groupBy("equipment_id").avg("temperature")
average_temp.show()
```

c. **Predict failures with Azure ML**: Deploy a ML model to predict equipment failures.

```python
#python

from azureml.core import Workspace, Model
from azureml.core.webservice import AciWebservice

workspace = Workspace.from_config()
model = Model(workspace, name="failure-prediction-model")

# Deploy the model to ACI
deployment_config = AciWebservice.deploy_configuration(cpu_
cores=1, memory_gb=1)
service = Model.deploy(workspace, "predictive-maintenance",
[model], deployment_config)
service.wait_for_deployment(show_output=True)
```

```python
def predict_failure(equipment_data):
    """

    Predict equipment failure using the deployed model.
    """

    prediction = service.run(input_data=equipment_data)
    return prediction

# Example Prediction
equipment_data = {"temperature": 75, "vibration": 0.3,
"pressure": 120}
failure_risk = predict_failure(equipment_data)
print("Failure Risk:", failure_risk)
```

d. **Automate maintenance scheduling**: Use Azure Functions to schedule maintenance when a high failure risk is detected:

```python
#python

from azure.identity import DefaultAzureCredential
from azure.mgmt.resource import ResourceManagementClient

resource_client = ResourceManagementClient(credential=Default
AzureCredential(), subscription_id="<your-subscription-id>")

def schedule_maintenance(equipment_id):
    """

    Schedule maintenance task using Azure Functions.
    """

    maintenance_task = {
        "name": f"maintenance-{equipment_id}",
        "type": "Scheduled",
        "action": "Inspect equipment and replace faulty parts."
    }
    resource_client.resources.create_or_update(
        resource_group_name="MaintenanceTasks",
        resource_provider_namespace="Microsoft.Logic",
        resource_type="workflows",
        resource_name=f"maintenance-{equipment_id}",
        parameters=maintenance_task
    )
    print(f"Maintenance scheduled for equipment
{equipment_id}.")

# Schedule Example Maintenance
```

```python
if failure_risk > 0.8:
    schedule_maintenance("E123")
```

e. **Generate maintenance alerts with LangChain**: Use LangChain to generate alerts and insights for the operations team:

```python
#python

from langchain.prompts import PromptTemplate
from langchain.chains import LLMChain

# Create a PromptTemplate for Maintenance Alerts
prompt_template = PromptTemplate(
    input_variables=["equipment_id", "failure_risk"],
    template="""
    Equipment ID: {equipment_id} is at high risk of failure
with a risk score of {failure_risk}.
    Generate an urgent maintenance alert with actionable
insights for the team.
    """
)

def generate_alert(equipment_id, failure_risk):
    """
    Generate maintenance alerts using LangChain.
    """
    chain = LLMChain(llm=None, prompt=prompt_template)
    alert_message = chain.run(equipment_id=equipment_id,
failure_risk=failure_risk)
    return alert_message

# Example Alert
alert = generate_alert(equipment_id="E123", failure_
risk=failure_risk)
print("Alert Message:", alert)
```

4. **Benefits**:

   a. **Reduced downtime**: Proactively schedule maintenance to avoid unexpected equipment failures.

   b. **Improved efficiency**: Automate data collection, analysis, and task scheduling.

   c. **Scalable solution**: Azure services handle large-scale data and growing equipment fleets efficiently.

5. **Final output**:

   a. **Real-time monitoring**: Stream sensor data to Azure IoT Hub.

   b. **Failure prediction**: Predict potential equipment failures with Azure ML models.

   c. **Automated scheduling**: Schedule maintenance tasks automatically via Azure Functions.

   d. **Dynamic alerts**: Generate alerts and insights using LangChain.

Benefits: Reduced operational costs, increased equipment lifespan, and enhanced production efficiency.

Energy: Grid optimization and renewable management

An energy company applies LangChain and Azure to optimize electricity grid operations and manage renewable energy sources efficiently, predicting demand and supply.

Code implementation

Code implementation for the energy use case using LangChain and Azure services. The implementation covers key components such as data ingestion, prediction, and optimization using Azure services, integrated with LangChain for NLP-based insights:

1. **Prerequisites**: Ensure the following libraries and SDKs are installed:

   bash

```bash
pip install langchain azure-ai-ml azure-iot azure-storage-blob
pandas scikit-learn
```

2. **Data ingestion**: Use Azure IoT Hub to ingest real-time data and store it in Azure Blob Storage:

```python
#python

from azure.iot.device import IoTHubDeviceClient
from azure.storage.blob import BlobServiceClient
import json

# IoT Hub connection
IOT_HUB_CONNECTION_STRING = "Your_IoT_Hub_Connection_String"

def receive_data_from_iot():
    client = IoTHubDeviceClient.create_from_connection_string(IOT_
```

```
HUB_CONNECTION_STRING)
    print("Listening for data...")
    while True:
        message = client.receive_message()  # Blocking call
        print(f"Message received: {message.data}")
        yield json.loads(message.data)

# Store data in Azure Blob Storage
BLOB_CONNECTION_STRING = "Your_Blob_Storage_Connection_String"
CONTAINER_NAME = "energy-data"

def store_data_in_blob(data):
    blob_service_client = BlobServiceClient.from_connection_
string(BLOB_CONNECTION_STRING)
    blob_client = blob_service_client.get_blob_
client(container=CONTAINER_NAME, blob="energy_data.json")
    blob_client.upload_blob(json.dumps(data), overwrite=True)
    print("Data stored in Blob Storage.")

# Usage
for data in receive_data_from_iot():
    store_data_in_blob(data)
```

3. **Energy prediction using Azure ML**: Train an ML model to predict energy demand and supply:

```python
#python

from azureml.core import Workspace, Experiment, ScriptRunConfig
from sklearn.linear_model import LinearRegression
import pandas as pd
import joblib

# Load workspace
ws = Workspace.from_config()

# Train a simple ML model
def train_model():
    # Example dataset
    data = pd.read_csv("energy_data.csv")
    X = data[['temperature', 'humidity', 'wind_speed']]  # Features
    y = data['energy_consumption']  # Target

    model = LinearRegression()
    model.fit(X, y)
```

```python
    # Save model
    joblib.dump(model, "energy_model.pkl")
    print("Model trained and saved.")

    return model

train_model()
```

4. **Upload the trained model to Azure ML**:

```python
#python

from azureml.core import Model

def register_model():
    model = Model.register(workspace=ws, model_path="energy_model.
pkl", model_name="EnergyPredictionModel")
    print(f"Model registered: {model.name}")

register_model()
```

5. **LangChain integration for insights**: Use LangChain to analyze model predictions and provide actionable insights:

```python
#python

from langchain.prompts import PromptTemplate
from langchain.chains import LLMChain
from langchain.llms import OpenAI

# Define a prompt template
prompt = PromptTemplate(
    input_variables=["energy_data"],
    template="Given the energy data: {energy_data}, what are the key
insights and recommendations?"
)

# Use LangChain to analyze predictions
def generate_insights(data):
    llm = OpenAI(temperature=0.7)  # Replace with Azure OpenAI if
available
    chain = LLMChain(llm=llm, prompt=prompt)
    insights = chain.run({"energy_data": data})
    print(f"Insights: {insights}")

# Example usage
example_data = {
```

```
    "demand": 500,
    "supply": 450,
    "renewables": 200,
    "temperature": 30,
    "humidity": 70,
}
generate_insights(example_data)
```

6. **Grid optimization**: Optimize grid operations based on predictions and insights:
#python

```
def optimize_grid(demand, supply, renewables):
    if supply + renewables < demand:
        print("Insufficient supply! Increase grid supply or reduce
demand.")
    elif supply + renewables > demand:
        print("Excess supply! Consider reducing generation.")
    else:
        print("Supply and demand are balanced.")

# Example usage
optimize_grid(demand=500, supply=450, renewables=60)
```

7. **Deployment on Azure**:

   a. **Azure IoT Hub**: Connect smart meters and renewable sources.

   b. **Azure Blob Storage**: Store real-time and historical data.

   c. **Azure ML**: Train and deploy the ML model.

   d. **Azure Functions**: Automate data preprocessing and predictions.

   e. **LangChain**: Generate actionable insights for energy managers.

8. **Next steps**:

   a. **Automate pipelines**: Use Azure Data Factory to orchestrate data processing.

   b. **Dashboard integration**: Visualize predictions and insights using Power BI or Streamlit.

   c. **Advanced models**: Incorporate deep learning models for more accurate predictions.

9. **Benefits**: Improved energy efficiency, reduced carbon footprint, and lower operational costs.

10. **Transportation**: Fleet management and route optimization:

a. **Scenario**: A logistics company employs LangChain and Azure to manage its fleet, optimizing routes based on real-time traffic data, weather conditions, and delivery schedules.

b. **Benefits**: Reduced fuel consumption, improved delivery times, and enhanced customer satisfaction.

11. **Education**: Personalized learning and assessment:

a. **Scenario**: Educational institutions use LangChain and Azure to develop personalized learning platforms that adapt to the learning pace and style of each student, providing tailored resources and assessments.

b. **Benefits**: Improved student engagement, higher retention rates, and personalized education paths.

12. **Entertainment**: Content recommendation systems:

a. **Scenario**: A streaming service utilizes LangChain and Azure to analyze viewing habits and preferences, offering personalized content recommendations to users.

b. **Benefits**: Increased viewer engagement, higher subscription retention rates, and optimized content curation.

Leveraging Azure services for scalability

Leveraging Azure services like AKS and Azure Functions, can significantly enhance the scalability of your LangChain applications. These services offer powerful, flexible solutions for managing and scaling applications efficiently in the cloud. Here is how they can be utilized:

Utilizing Azure Kubernetes Service

AKS simplifies the deployment, management, and scaling of containerized applications by leveraging Kubernetes, an open-source system designed for automating these operations. The features of AKS are as follows:

- **Seamless integration**: AKS integrates smoothly with LangChain applications, especially those containerized for easier deployment and management. Containers can encapsulate LangChain environments, ensuring consistency across development, testing, and production.

- **Automatic scaling**: AKS supports automatic scaling, allowing your LangChain applications to efficiently handle increased load. You can configure it to scale your applications up or down based on usage, ensuring optimal performance and cost-effectiveness.

- **High availability**: With AKS, you can deploy LangChain applications across multiple Azure regions, ensuring high availability and resilience. This is crucial for critical AI applications that require constant uptime.

- **DevOps and CI/CD**: AKS supports DevOps practices, integrating with Azure DevOps for CI/CD pipelines. This enables automated testing and deployment of LangChain applications, reducing manual effort and speeding up development cycles.

Implementing Azure Functions

Azure Functions is a serverless computing service that executes event-triggered code without the necessity for explicit provisioning or management of infrastructure. This characteristic renders it ideal for scaling applications and deploying microservices.

- **Event-driven architecture**: Azure Functions can respond to various events, making it perfect for integrating with LangChain for tasks like data processing, real-time analysis, or triggering workflows based on specific conditions or schedules.

- **Scalability**: It is a key feature of Azure Functions. It automatically adjusts based on demand, effortlessly managing thousands of concurrent function executions without manual infrastructure management. This capability is particularly advantageous for LangChain applications that encounter fluctuating workloads.

- **Cost-effectiveness**: Azure Functions operates on a pay-as-you-go model, where charges are incurred solely for the compute time your functions utilize. This economical approach renders it a favorable choice for executing small code snippets in the cloud, offering notable benefits for startups and initiatives with financial limitations.

- **Integration capabilities**: Azure Functions integrates with other Azure services and external sources, enabling seamless workflows. For LangChain projects, this means easy access to databases, storage solutions, and even AI and ML models hosted on Azure.

Leveraging AKS and Azure Functions provides robust solutions for scaling and managing your LangChain applications. AKS offers a container-based approach for deploying and managing applications with the benefits of Kubernetes, while Azure Functions provides a flexible, event-driven model that scales automatically. Together, these services can help you build resilient, scalable, and cost-effective AI applications on Azure, taking full advantage of cloud computing capabilities to drive your projects forward.

Deploying LangChain applications on Azure

Deploying LangChain applications on Azure efficiently requires a solid strategy that incorporates modern DevOps practices. Azure DevOps, with its suite of tools, facilitates CI/CD, enabling you to automate the deployment process, improve collaboration, and increase the speed and reliability of releases. Here is how you can leverage Azure DevOps and CI/CD pipelines for deploying LangChain applications:

- **Azure DevOps overview**: Azure DevOps is a Microsoft service that provides a comprehensive toolkit for software development teams. It includes Azure Boards for planning, Azure Repos for source control, Azure Pipelines for CI/CD, Azure Test Plans for testing, and Azure Artifacts for package management.

- **Setting up a CI/CD pipeline for LangChain**:

    o **Source control with Azure Repos**: Start by storing your LangChain application code in Azure Repos or integrating with GitHub. This allows you to effectively manage source code of your application and collaborate with team members.

    o **CI with Azure Pipelines**: Create a build pipeline automate the build process by setting up a CI pipeline. This pipeline triggers automatically whenever a commit is made to the repository, ensuring your LangChain application is always deployable.

    o **Automate testing**: Incorporate automated tests into your CI pipeline to catch bugs early. This can include unit tests, integration tests, and any other tests relevant to your LangChain application.

    o **CD with Azure Pipelines**: Create a release pipeline setup a CD pipeline to automate the deployment of your LangChain application to various environments (for example, development, staging, production). Depending on your architecture, this pipeline can deploy your containerized LangChain applications to AKS or Azure Functions.

    o **Environment gates and approvals**: Implement gates and approvals in your CD pipeline for controlled deployments. This ensures that your LangChain application is deployed to production only after it meets the necessary quality and security standards.

    o **IaC**: Leverage ARM templates or terraform to define your IaC. This enables you to automate the provisioning of Azure resources essential for your LangChain application, including VMs, databases, and networking components.

- **Monitoring and feedback**: Leverage Azure Monitor and Application Insights to monitor your LangChain applications post-deployment. This provides valuable feedback on performance and user experience, informing future development efforts.

- **Benefits of using Azure DevOps for LangChain deployment**:

    o **Automation**: Automate the build, testing, and deployment processes, reducing manual errors and saving time.

o   **Consistency**: Ensure consistent deployments across all environments, improving reliability.

o   **Faster time to market**: Speed up the release cycle, allowing you to respond to market demands and feedback quickly.

o   **Quality and security**: Implement continuous testing and security checks throughout the CI/CD pipeline to improve the quality and security of your LangChain applications.

Adopting Azure DevOps and CI/CD practices for deploying LangChain applications can achieve a more efficient, reliable, and agile development lifecycle. This streamlines the deployment process and enhances collaboration among team members, leading to higher-quality AI solutions deployed on Azure.

Monitoring and managing LangChain applications

Monitoring and managing LangChain applications effectively is crucial for maintaining performance, reliability, and user satisfaction. Azure provides powerful tools like Azure Monitor and logic applications to help you keep track of the health and automate operational workflows of your applications. Here is how you can leverage these tools:

- **Using Azure Monitor for performance tracking**: Azure Monitor collects, analyzes, and acts on telemetry data from your Azure and premises environments. It helps you understand the performance of your applications and proactively identifies issues affecting them. Here is how to use Azure Monitor with LangChain applications:

    o   **Collect metrics and logs**: Azure Monitor can collect metrics and logs from your LangChain applications, the Azure services they rely on (like AKS or Azure Functions), and the underlying infrastructure. This data provides insights into the performance and health of your application.

    o   **Setup alerts**: You can create alert rules in Azure Monitor based on metrics or logs. For instance, if the response time of your LangChain application exceeds a certain threshold or if there is an unusual spike in error rates, Azure Monitor can send notifications to the responsible teams via email, SMS, or other channels.

    o   **Visualize data with dashboards**: Azure dashboards visualize the data that Azure Monitor collects. You can create custom dashboards to display **key performance indicators (KPIs)** relevant to your LangChain applications, making it easier to monitor their health and performance briefly.

o **Analyze with Application Insights**: Integrate Application Insights with your LangChain application for deeper analysis. It provides powerful application performance management capabilities, including detailed diagnostics, user analytics, and application mapping. This is particularly useful for debugging and optimizing your application.

- **Automating workflows with Azure Logic Apps**: Azure Logic Apps provide a cloud-based platform for automating workflows and integrating applications, data, services, and systems. It is a big tool that can enhance the management of LangChain applications by automating routine tasks and integrating disparate systems. Here is how:

  o **Automate operational tasks**: You can automate routine operational tasks such as scaling resources based on demand, backups, and maintenance jobs. For example, create a logic app that automatically scales your Azure Functions or AKS resources when CPU usage reaches a certain threshold.

  o **Integrate with external services**: Azure Logic Apps allow you to integrate your LangChain application with hundreds of external services and applications. This can be useful for sending alerts to Slack, creating tasks in Azure DevOps, or even calling custom APIs for specific business logic.

  o **Process and route data**: Use Logic Apps to process and route data between your LangChain application and other Azure services or external systems. For instance, you could create a workflow that processes data from Azure Event Hubs, performs transformations, and then stores the results in Azure Blob Storage or a database.

  o **Build event-driven architectures**: Logic Applications can respond to events from Azure services or third-party systems, making building reactive, event-driven architectures easy. This is particularly useful for creating responsive applications that must react to real-time data changes, system status, or user actions.

Utilizing Azure Monitor and Azure Logic Apps, you can significantly improve the monitoring, management, and automation of your LangChain applications. Azure Monitor provides the insights needed to maintain optimal performance and reliability, while Azure Logic Apps provide the flexibility to automate workflows and integrate with a wide array of services. These tools empower you to build, deploy, and manage resilient and efficient LangChain applications on Azure.

Conclusion

This chapter has taken you through the journey of integrating LangChain with Azure, showing how this combination can greatly enhance your AI projects. We have covered everything from the initial setup of your Azure account to the deployment and management of LangChain applications, emphasizing the importance of a well-organized cloud environment, the use of Azure services like AKS and Azure Functions for scalability, and the benefits of Azure DevOps and Azure Monitor for efficient deployment and management.

Integrating LangChain with Azure accelerates the development of AI solutions and ensures they are scalable, secure, and efficiently managed. This integration unlocks new opportunities for innovation and success in the AI landscape, whether you are a developer, a business leader, or an AI enthusiast.

Points to remember

- **Start with a solid foundation**: Ensure your Azure account is setup correctly and organize your resources within dedicated resource groups. Choose the appropriate Azure VM and install LangChain properly.

- **Leverage automation and security**: Utilize ARM templates for IaC to automate deployments. Secure access to your resources with Azure AD, emphasizing the security of your setup.

- **Scale smartly**: Use Azure services like AKS and Azure Functions to ensure your LangChain applications can scale according to demand without compromising cost-efficiency.

- **Automate deployment and ensure CI**: Implement Azure DevOps for the CI/CD pipelines, which streamlines deploying updates and new features to your LangChain applications.

- **Monitor and manage efficiently**: Use Azure Monitor and Azure Logic Apps to monitor the performance of your application and automate routine operational tasks. This helps maintain optimal performance and reduce manual overhead.

- **Embrace the power of integration**: Integrating LangChain with Azure opens many possibilities for your AI projects, from enhancing scalability and security to improving deployment efficiency and application management.

- **Stay informed and adapt**: Stay informed about the latest updates and features from LangChain and Azure to stay up-to-date with the evolving technology landscape.

Remembering these points will guide you through successfully integrating LangChain with Azure, ensuring your AI projects are well-positioned for success, innovation, and growth in the rapidly advancing field of artificial intelligence.

Multiple-choice questions

1. **What is Azure AD used for in Azure?**

    a. Managing databases

    b. Storing data

    c. Managing access and identity

    d. Monitoring performance

2. **Which Azure service helps automate application deployment, scaling, and operations?**

    a. Azure Functions

    b. AKS

    c. Azure DevOps

    d. Azure AD

3. **What is the use of ARM templates?**

    a. To monitor resource usage

    b. To automate infrastructure deployment

    c. To manage user identities

    d. To analyze application performance

4. **Which Azure feature is primarily used for CI/CD?**

    a. Azure Logic Apps

    b. Azure Monitor

    c. Azure DevOps

    d. Azure Functions

5. **Azure Functions is an example of what type of computing?**

    a. VMs

    b. Serverless computing

    c. Kubernetes-based computing

    d. Blockchain computing

6. **What can Azure Monitor be used for?**

    a. Automating user authentication

    b. Deploying ARM templates

    c. Tracking application performance and health

    d. Creating VMs

7. **Which of the following best describes the benefit of integrating LangChain with Azure?**

    a. Decreased scalability

    b. Limited AI capabilities

    c. Enhanced security and scalability for AI projects

    d. Reduced deployment options

8. **What role do Azure Logic Apps play in managing LangChain applications?**

    a. It increases the computational cost

    b. It provides physical servers for deployment

    c. It automates workflows and integrates applications

    d. It reduces application security

9. **Which Azure VM type is most appropriate for deploying a LangChain application that requires high memory?**

    a. General purpose

    b. Compute optimized

    c. Memory optimized

    d. Storage optimized

10. **Which is a key practice when deploying LangChain applications on Azure?**

    a. Avoid using Azure DevOps for deployment

    b. Manually scale resources to meet demand

    c. Use a single large VM for all applications

    d. Define IaC for consistency and automation

Answers

1	c
2	b
3	b
4	c
5	d
6	c

7	c
8	c
9	c
10	d

Key terms

1. **LangChain**: It is a tool or framework for orchestrating and integrating various AI models and services to build complex AI applications.

2. **Azure**: It is the cloud computing service of Microsoft, offering a comprehensive suite of cloud services, encompassing computing, analytics, storage, and networking functionalities.

3. **Azure AD**: It is the cloud-based identity and access management service of Microsoft, providing various application identity and security functionalities.

4. **AKS**: A managed Kubernetes service streamlines the deployment, management, and operation of Kubernetes containers, bolstering scalability and automation capabilities.

5. **ARM templates**: This is a declarative syntax used in JSON to define and deploy Azure infrastructure and configurations through code.

6. **Azure DevOps**: It comprises a set of development tools offered by Microsoft Azure to facilitate DevOps methodologies. It includes CI/CD pipelines, repositories, and testing tools to support seamless software development and deployment processes.

7. **CI/CD**: Software development practices designed to improve code quality and expedite the build and release process through automation.

8. **Azure Functions**: A serverless compute service executes code in response to events or triggers, facilitating rapid and cost-effective application development without the requirement to manage infrastructure.

9. **Azure Monitor**: It is a service that provides comprehensive monitoring of applications, infrastructure, and network activity across Azure services, enabling performance tracking and issue detection.

10. **IaC**: This is the management of infrastructure (networks, VMs, load balancers, etc.) in a descriptive model using code that can be versioned and reused.

11. **Azure Logic Apps**: Azure Logic Apps stands standard-based service crafted to automate and coordinate tasks, business processes, and workflows in the integration of applications, data, systems, and services across enterprises or organizations.

12. **Serverless computing**: Serverless computing represents a cloud computing execution paradigm where the cloud provider dynamically oversees the allocation and provisioning of servers. This model enables users to develop and deploy applications and services without the burden of managing infrastructure.

13. **Containerization**: Containerization is a lightweight substitute for full-machine virtualization. It involves encapsulating an application within a container alongside its operating environment.

Join our book's Discord space

Join the book's Discord Workspace for Latest updates, Offers, Tech happenings around the world, New Release and Sessions with the Authors:

https://discord.bpbonline.com

Real-world Data Science with Snowflake and Athena

Introduction

Welcome to the dynamic realm where data science converges with AI, powered by the formidable capabilities of Snowflake and Athena. This section will explore how these tools can enhance LangChain AI projects. We will understand querying large datasets and analyzing data for actionable insights. We will learn to navigate the data-driven landscape through practical examples and simple explanations, ensuring your projects are innovative and grounded in strong data management. Let us understand the potential of your AI applications with Snowflake, Athena, and LangChain.

Structure

This chapter covers the following topics:

- Introduction to Snowflake and Athena
- Core functionalities
- Getting started with Snowflake
- Understanding data analysis with Snowflake
- Introduction to data processing with Athena
- Integrating with LangChain
- Real-world applications

Objectives

This chapter aims to provide readers with practical skills and knowledge to effectively utilize Snowflake and Athena for data science, particularly in enhancing LangChain AI projects. Throughout the learning process, we will gain proficiency in querying and analyzing large datasets, grasp the fundamental functionalities of both tools and effectively apply them to real-world data challenges. Integrating Snowflake and Athena with LangChain, we will discover how to streamline data processing and analysis workflows, making AI solutions more robust and efficient. Through hands-on examples and straightforward guidance, this chapter aims to simplify data science tools, making you understand the full potential of your data-driven projects.

Introduction to Snowflake and Athena

Snowflake and Athena are two powerhouse technologies that have revolutionized how data scientists approach data storage, querying, and analysis. Both tools offer unique strengths, making them invaluable assets in the data science tool kit. Let us break down what each of these tools is and why they are so crucial for data science projects.

Snowflake is a cloud-based data warehousing solution renowned for its flexibility, scalability, and user-friendly interface. Unlike traditional data warehouses that require significant management and tuning, Snowflake provides a nearly maintenance-free platform. Its architecture separates storage and computing tasks, enabling users to scale up or down on demand without impacting performance. This makes it exceptionally cost-effective and efficient for handling vast amounts of data. Snowflake supports concurrent data processing, allowing multiple users to query data simultaneously without decreasing performance, which is a game-changer for collaborative data science projects.

On the contrary, **Amazon Athena** is an interactive query service designed to simplify data analysis directly in *Amazon S3* using standard **structured query language (SQL)**. It operates serverless, eliminating the need for infrastructure management, and users are charged solely for the queries they execute. This makes Athena an excellent choice for projects with variable workloads and teams looking to minimize upfront costs. It shines in scenarios where quick, ad-hoc querying and data analysis stored in S3 are required without a complex data warehousing setup.

Snowflake and Athena stand out in the data science world for several reasons. They both offer unparalleled flexibility and scalability, crucial for handling the ever-increasing volumes of data. Their ability to handle massive datasets and complex queries in real-time significantly speeds up data analysis, enabling data scientists to focus more on deriving insights rather than worrying about infrastructure issues.

Moreover, their cloud-based nature ensures that data scientists can access and analyze data from anywhere, fostering collaboration and innovation. By simplifying data management and analysis, Snowflake and Athena allow data scientists to experiment more freely and push the boundaries of what is possible in data-driven projects.

Snowflake and Athena provide an extensive foundation for any data science project, offering the tools to store, query, and analyze data at scale. Their integration into data science workflows ensures that projects are more efficient and more effective, enabling data scientists to unlock new insights and drive meaningful outcomes in their work.

Core functionalities

Exploring the core functionalities of Snowflake and Athena reveals how these tools support and enhance data science projects by providing robust, scalable, and flexible data management and analysis capabilities. Here is a closer look at the key features of each and how they bolster data science efforts.

Key features of Snowflake

The following are the key features of Snowflake:

- **Automatic scalability**: Snowflake's architecture uniquely separates computing and storage, allowing each to scale independently. Data scientists can adjust computing resources to fit the workload without worrying about storage limits or performance degradation, making it ideal for projects of varying sizes and complexities.

- **Concurrency and sharing**: Snowflake's multi-cluster architecture enables multiple users to query data simultaneously without impacting performance. This facilitates collaborative data science projects and sharing with external partners, ensuring data insights can be generated and acted upon quickly.

- **Data warehouse as a service**: Snowflake reduces the overhead associated with traditional data warehouses as a fully managed service. It automatically handles maintenance tasks such as patching, updates, and backups, allowing data scientists to focus more on analysis and less on management.

- **Support for diverse data**: Snowflake supports structured and semi-structured data (like JSON, Avro, XML), enabling data scientists to ingest and analyze various data sources without extensive preprocessing. This is critical for comprehensive data analysis in today's data-driven world.

Key features of Athena

The following are the key features of Athena:

- **Serverless querying**: Athena is serverless, meaning there is no infrastructure to manage or setup. We pay only for the queries we run, making it cost-effective for projects with fluctuating workloads. This feature democratizes data analysis, allowing smaller teams or projects to leverage powerful analytics without significant investment.

- **Direct S3 integration**: Athena allows users to query data directly in Amazon S3 using standard SQL. This eliminates the need for intricate **extract, transform, and load** (ETL) processes to prepare data for analysis, accelerating the time to insight.

- **Easy integration**: Athena integrates seamlessly with other AWS services, making it a flexible tool in the AWS ecosystem for comprehensive data analysis. This ease of integration supports complex data workflows, from data ingestion and storage to analysis and visualization.

- **Scalability and performance**: Despite being serverless, Athena is designed to handle large-scale data queries, offering fast performance even on vast datasets. This scalability ensures that data science projects can grow without infrastructure limitations.

Snowflake and Athena offer a comprehensive set of features that support the end-to-end data science workflow, from data ingestion and storage to analysis and sharing. Their scalability, flexibility, and performance make them tools for modern data science projects. They enable teams to focus on extracting valuable insights and creating impactful data-driven solutions.

Getting started with Snowflake

Getting started with Snowflake for querying and analyzing data is an exciting journey into cloud data warehousing. This hands-on guide will walk you through the basic steps to get up and running with Snowflake, enabling you to leverage its powerful features for your data science projects:

1. **Setting up a Snowflake account**:

   a. **Sign up**: First, we will need to create a Snowflake account. Go to the Snowflake website and sign up for a trial account, which provides access to a fully functional instance with credits for computation and storage.

   b. **Log in**: Once your account is setup, log in to the Snowflake web interface. This web UI is where we will manage databases, execute queries, and configure the Snowflake environment.

2. **Create a database and warehouse**:

   a. **Create a warehouse**: Before we start querying, we need a warehouse. A warehouse in Snowflake represents compute resources. We can create one by navigating the **Warehouses** section and clicking + **Create**. We can choose a size based on our expected workload.

b. **Create a database**: Next, create a database by going to the **Databases** section and clicking + **Create**. This database will hold our tables and data.

3. **Ingest data**:

   a. **Upload data**: We can upload data to Snowflake using various methods, such as the web interface, Snowflake's `COPY INTO` command, or integrating with data ingestion tools. For simplicity, we might start by uploading a CSV file directly through the web interface to a table in our database.

   b. **Create a table and load data**: Define a table schema that matches our data file and use the `COPY INTO` command to load our data into the table.

4. **Querying data**:

   a. **SQL queries**: With your data loaded, you can start querying. Snowflake uses standard SQL, making it accessible if we are familiar with SQL syntax. Navigate to the **Worksheets** tab in the web UI to write and execute our queries.

   b. **Analyze data**: Begin with simple queries to understand your data structure and contents. Gradually, move to more complex analyses, such as aggregations, joins, and window functions, to derive insights from our data.

5. **Visualizing and sharing insights**:

   a. **Connect to a business intelligence tool**: For more advanced visualizations, connect Snowflake to a **business intelligence** (**BI**) tool like Tableau, Looker, or Power BI. Snowflake integrates smoothly with these tools, allowing us to create dashboards and share insights across our team.

   b. **Share data**: Snowflake's unique architecture makes sharing data across different accounts or with external partners easy, ensuring that our insights can drive decision-making beyond our immediate team.

6. **Optimize and scale**:

   a. **Monitor performance**: Utilize Snowflake's built-in performance monitoring tools to understand query execution and warehouse usage. This can help us optimize query performance and manage costs.

   b. **Scale resources**: We will adjust our warehouse size or create additional warehouses as our data or concurrency needs to grow. Snowflake's flexibility means we can scale up or down instantly without downtime.

Getting started with Snowflake is just the beginning. As we become more comfortable with the platform, we will discover its extensive capabilities for managing and analyzing data at a scale. Whether working on small projects or enterprise-level data science initiatives, Snowflake provides the tools to unlock valuable insights from our data.

Step-by-step guide to using Snowflake web interface for beginners

Step 1: Log in to Snowflake:

1. **Open your browser**: Use any modern browser like *Google Chrome, Edge,* or *Firefox.*

2. **Visit the Snowflake login page**: Go to the URL provided by your organization (e.g., **https://youraccount.snowflakecomputing.com**).

3. **Enter your credentials**:

    o **Username**: Provided by your admin or during account setup.

    o **Password**: You should have received it or set it up earlier.

4. Click **log in**:

    o If **multifactor authentication (MFA)** is enabled, enter the code from your authentication application when prompted.

Step 2: Understand the interface:

Once logged in, you will see Snowflake's web interface. Here is what you need to know:

1. **Navigation bar on the left**: This helps you switch between different parts of Snowflake:

    a. **Databases**: Where all your data is stored.

    b. **Warehouses**: Compute resources you use to process queries.

    c. **Query history**: Shows the history of executed queries.

    d. **Account**: For account settings and details.

2. **Main workspace**: This is where you write and execute SQL queries or view data.

3. **Top-right corner**: Options to log out, view account details, or switch roles.

Step 3: Setup a virtual warehouse:

Before querying any data, you need a virtual warehouse (compute engine) to process your SQL queries.

1. Go to the **Warehouses** tab from the left-hand menu.

2. Click the + **Create** button to setup a new warehouse.

3. Provide the following details:

    a. **Name**: Choose a name (e.g., `my_warehouse`).

    b. **Size**: Start with a smaller size like X-Small for basic queries.

    c. **Auto suspend**: Set it to a short time like 5 minutes (to save costs when idle).

    d. **Auto resume**: Keep it enabled so the warehouse automatically starts when needed.

4. Click **Create**. Your warehouse is now ready!

Step 4: **Explore databases**:

1. Go to the **Databases** tab.

2. Here, you will see the list of databases available to your account.

3. To view the contents of a database:

    a. Click on the database name.

    b. Navigate to **Schemas**, then to **Tables** or **Views** to see the actual data.

Step 5: **Run a query**:

1. Navigate to the **Worksheet** section on the left menu.

2. Select your warehouse from the dropdown menu at the top of the worksheet.

    a. **Example**: If you created a warehouse called `my_warehouse`, select it.

3. Write your SQL query in the text box. For example:

```
SELECT * FROM <your_database_name>.<your_schema_name>.<your_table_
name>;
```

4. Click run (green button) to execute the query. Results will appear in the table below the query box.

Step 6: **Save Your work**:

1. If you have written queries that you want to save:

    a. Click the **Save as** button in the worksheet.

    b. Name your worksheet and save it for future reference.

2. Your saved worksheets can be accessed from the left-hand menu.

Step 7: **Monitor query history**:

1. Go to the **Query history** tab.

2. Here, you will see:

    a. List of queries you have run.

    b. Status of each query (e.g., completed, failed).

    c. Execution time and resource usage.

Step 8: Log out safely:

1. When you are done, click your account name in the top-right corner.

2. Select **Log out** to end your session securely.

Additional tips:

*   **Documentation**: Snowflake's online documentation is your best friend! If you are unsure about anything, search their docs for clarification.

*   **Shortcuts**: Bookmark frequently used databases or queries for quick access.

*   **Role switching**: If you have multiple roles, ensure you switch to the correct one to access the data or permissions you need.

Understanding data analysis with Snowflake

Diving deeper into data analysis with Snowflake involves leveraging its advanced features to extract more nuanced and valuable insights from your datasets. Snowflake's powerful analytics capabilities and ease of use make it an excellent platform for sophisticated data analysis. Here is how you can harness these capabilities to elevate your data analysis projects:

*   **Advanced SQL queries**: Snowflake supports advanced SQL functions that can significantly enhance your data analysis capabilities:

    o   **Window functions**: Use window functions to calculate running totals, moving averages, or ranking data without grouping your results. This can be particularly useful for time-series analysis or comparing individual records against aggregated metrics.

    o   **Common table expressions and subqueries**: **Common table expressions (CTEs)** and subqueries help organize complex queries into more manageable parts. They are essential for breaking down complicated analysis into simpler steps, making your queries more readable and maintainable.

    o   **Aggregate functions**: Besides basic aggregations like **SUM** and **COUNT**, Snowflake offers functions like **ARRAY_AGG** and **OBJECT_AGG,** which can aggregate values into arrays or JSON objects, respectively. This is useful for nested data analysis or when working with semi-structured data.

        ▪   **ARRAY_AGG**: **ARRAY_AGG** collects values from a column and combines them into a single array (like a list).

            Use case: When you want all values from a column grouped into an array.

            Example: Let us say you have a table of employees with the following data:

department	employee_name
HR	Alice
HR	Bob
IT	Charlie

You want to create an array of all employees in each department:

```
SELECT department, ARRAY_AGG(employee_name) AS employee_list
FROM employees GROUP BY department;
```

Result:

department	employee_list
HR	["Alice", "Bob"]
IT	["Charlie"]

- **OBJECT_AGG:OBJECT_AGG** creates a key-value pair object from two columns.

  Use case: When you want to group data into a JSON-like key-value format.

  Example: Using the same employee's table, you want to create an object where the key is the employee's name and the value is their department:

  ```
  SELECT OBJECT_AGG(employee_name, department) AS employee_
  department_map FROM employees;
  ```

  Result:

employee_department_map
{"Alice": "HR", "Bob": "HR", "Charlie": "IT"}

- **Semi-structured data analysis**: Snowflake excels in handling semi-structured data such as JSON, Avro, or XML, allowing data scientists to query this data directly using SQL.

  o **FLATTEN function**: The **FLATTEN** function can turn nested arrays or objects into rows, making it easier to analyze data nested within semi-structured data types.

  o **Dot notation**: Access elements within semi-structured data using simple dot notation. This makes it straightforward to incorporate aspects of JSON, XML, or other formats into your SQL queries.

- **Time Travel and cloning**: Snowflake's Time Travel feature lets you query historical data, giving you insights into data changes over time.

    o   **Historical analysis**: With Time Travel, you can access and analyze data as it existed at any point within the past 90 days (depending on your Snowflake edition). This is invaluable for understanding trends, auditing changes, or recovering lost data.

    Example use case: Suppose a table was accidentally updated or deleted. You can use Time Travel to retrieve the data as it existed before the change:

    ```
    SELECT * FROM my_table AT (TIMESTAMP => '2025-01-01 10:00:00');
    ```

    o   **Cloning**: You can clone databases, schemas, or tables for testing or analytical purposes without affecting your production data. This can be particularly useful for running what-if analyses or testing data transformations.

    Example use case: To test changes on production data without impacting the original, you can clone the table:

    ```
    CREATE TABLE cloned_table CLONE original_table;
    ```

- **Data sharing and collaboration**: Leverage Snowflake's data sharing capabilities to collaborate more effectively with stakeholders.

    o   **Secure data sharing**: Share subsets of your data securely with other Snowflake users or even those who do not use Snowflake, enabling collaborative insights generation without duplicating data.

    o   **Reader accounts**: Create reader accounts for external users to access shared data, facilitating collaboration with partners or customers.

    o   **Integrating with BI and data science tools**: For deeper analysis and visualization, connect Snowflake to popular BI and data science tools.

    o   **BI tools integration**: Tools like Tableau, Looker, and Power BI can connect directly to Snowflake, allowing you to create dynamic visualizations and dashboards from your Snowflake data.

    o   **Data science platforms**: Connect Snowflake with data science platforms like Databricks or use Snowflake's Spark connector to perform more complex analyses and build predictive models.

By mastering these advanced techniques, we can leverage Snowflake to its full potential, turning vast and varied datasets into actionable insights. Snowflake not only simplifies data storage and management but also provides a rich set of tools for deep data exploration and analysis, making it an invaluable resource for data scientists looking to push the boundaries of their work.

Introduction to data processing with Athena

Amazon Athena transforms the game for data analysts and scientists by enabling SQL-based querying directly on data stored in Amazon S3, bypassing the need for complex data processing infrastructures. This seamless integration with S3 offers a flexible, efficient pathway to insights. Let us understand how we can start with Athena for data querying and enhance our analysis skills for more profound insights.

Getting started with Athena

In this section, we will get started with Athena:

1. **Setup Athena**: First, we will ensure that we have an AWS account and navigate the Athena service. Athena's interface is web-based, making it accessible without needing installations.

2. **Setup a database**: Before querying, we must create a database within Athena. This database will organize the tables that reference your data in S3. We can create a database directly through the Athena query editor.

3. **Creating tables**: Athena requires us to define tables that reflect the structure of our data in S3. We can create tables manually through the Athena interface using a **CREATE TABLE** statement, specifying the location of your data in S3, the data format, and the structure of your columns.

4. **Querying data**: With our tables setup, we can start querying our data using standard SQL. Athena integrates with AWS Glue Data Catalog, allowing automatic table creation for common data sources and formats, simplifying the setup process.

Enhancing analysis skills with Athena

Advanced query techniques are as follows:

- **Partitioned tables**: Athena allows you to partition your tables based on column values, significantly speeding up queries by limiting the amount of data scanned. Use partitioning wisely based on common query filters like date, geography, or other dimensions.

- **Optimizing queries**: Leverage Athena's **EXPLAIN** statement to understand how your queries are executed. Restructuring your queries or tables can help identify bottlenecks and optimize query performance.

- **Complex SQL queries**: Athena supports complex SQL queries, including window, arrays, and JSON functions. Use these features to perform sophisticated data analysis directly within Athena.

- **Saving and sharing queries**: Athena allows us to save queries for reuse or sharing with team members. This feature is invaluable for collaborative analysis and ensures consistent methodology across our team.

Integrating with Other AWS services

AWS Glue integration: For a more managed experience, integrate Athena with AWS Glue. AWS Glue can automatically discover, catalog, and prepare data for analysis, making managing data across diverse sources and formats easier:

1. **Amazon QuickSight for visualization**: Connect Athena with Amazon QuickSight to visualize your query results. QuickSight allows you to create interactive dashboards, share insights with stakeholders, and perform further analysis through its ML-powered insights feature.

2. **Automating workflows with AWS Lambda**: Use AWS Lambda to automate data processing and analysis workflows, triggering queries in Athena based on specific events or schedules. This automation can streamline repetitive tasks and ensure timely insights.

You can improve your data analysis capabilities by starting with the basics of querying in Athena and progressing to more advanced techniques and integrations. Athena's serverless nature, combined with its powerful SQL engine and integration with the broader AWS ecosystem, offers a scalable, flexible platform for data analysis without the overhead of managing complex data processing infrastructure.

Integrating with LangChain

Integrating Snowflake and Athena with LangChain involves a series of steps that bridge these powerful data processing tools with the advanced capabilities of LangChain for building language models and applications. Connecting Snowflake or Athena with LangChain allows you to leverage the vast datasets stored in these platforms to train, refine, and deploy sophisticated language models. Here is how to do it.

Integrating Snowflake with LangChain

Prepare Snowflake data: Ensure your data within Snowflake is structured in a way that is conducive to language model training or querying. This might involve aggregating text data into a specific format or table.

1. **Establish Snowflake connectivity**: LangChain typically interacts with external data sources through **application programming interfaces** (**APIs**) or **software development kits** (**SDKs**). Use the Snowflake Python connector to establish a connection between LangChain and Snowflake.

2. **Query data from Snowflake**: Write Python scripts or functions within our LangChain project to query the necessary data from Snowflake. Use standard SQL queries through the Snowflake connector to fetch text data for processing.

3. **Utilize data in LangChain**: Once data is fetched from Snowflake, use it within LangChain for various tasks, such as training language models, generating text, or analyzing text data. LangChain's modular design allows for seamless integration of external data into its workflows.

4. **Automate and scale**: To handle large datasets or continuous data streams from Snowflake, automate data fetching and processing within LangChain scripts. Consider scaling compute resources as needed to accommodate the processing demands of your language models.

Step-by-step snowflake-connector-python langchain

Step 1: Install required libraries

Before starting, you need to install the necessary libraries:

```
pip install snowflake-connector-python langchain
```

Step 2: Import the required modules

In your Python script, import the libraries:

```
import snowflake.connector
from langchain.chains import SQLDatabaseChain
from langchain.sql_database import SQLDatabase
```

Step 3: Setup the Snowflake Python connector

1. **Provide your Snowflake credentials**: Use the Snowflake Python connector to establish a connection.

2. **Sample code to connect**:

```
# Create a connection to Snowflake
connection = snowflake.connector.connect(
    user='your_username',
    password='your_password',
    account='your_account_name', # Example: 'abc123.east-us-1'
    warehouse='your_warehouse_name',
    database='your_database_name',
    schema='your_schema_name'
)

# Verify the connection
print("Connection established:", connection.is_connected())
```

Explanation of parameters:

    a. **user**: Your Snowflake username.

    b. **password**: Your Snowflake password.

    c. **account**: Your Snowflake account identifier (usually found in your Snowflake login URL).

    d. **Warehouse, database, schema**: Specify where your data resides.

Step 4: Integrate Snowflake with LangChain

1. **Initialize LangChain's SQLDatabase object**: LangChain needs a connection to interact with your database. Use the connection you created above:

```
# Create the SQLDatabase object
db=SQLDatabase.from_uri("snowflake://your_username:your_password@
your_account_name/your_database_name?schema=your_schema_name")
```

2. **Create a SQLDatabaseChain:** This enables LangChain to run queries using the database:

```
# Build the LangChain database chain
chain = SQLDatabaseChain.from_llm(llm=your_llm, database=db)
```

3. **Run a query using LangChain:** Use the chain to execute SQL queries:

```
query = "What is the total sales from the orders table?"
response = chain.run(query)
print(response)
```

Common errors and solutions

The following are the common errors and solutions:

1. **Error:** `snowflake.connector.errors.ProgrammingError: 250001 (08001): Failed to connect to DB`.

    Cause: Incorrect credentials or account identifier.

    Solution: Double-check your username, password, and account name. Ensure your account identifier includes the region (e.g., `abc123.east-us-1`).

2. **Error:** `ValueError: Invalid connection string for Snowflake`.

    Cause: The **from_uri** connection string is incorrectly formatted.

    Solution: Ensure the URI format follows:

    snowflake://user:password@account/database?schema=schema

3. **Error:** `snowflake.connector.errors.DatabaseError: Database does not exist`.

    Cause: Incorrect database or schema name.

Solution: Verify that the database and schema exist using the Snowflake web UI.

4. **Error**: `LangChain produces irrelevant results or no output`.

    Cause: SQLDatabaseChain is unable to understand the query context.

    Solution: Ensure the LangChain model (`your_llm`) is fine-tuned or prompt-engineered for SQL-based tasks.

5. **Error**: `Timeout Error`.

    Cause: Query execution exceeds time limits.

    Solution: Optimize your SQL queries or use Snowflake's query history to debug slow queries.

Integrating Athena with LangChain

In this section, we will integrate Athena with LangChain:

1. **Access data in Amazon S3**: Since Athena queries data directly in Amazon S3, ensure your text data is stored in S3 and properly formatted for query efficiency. Organizing data in a query-friendly manner, partitioned by relevant attributes, can enhance performance.

2. **Setup Athena queries**: Use the AWS SDK for Python (Boto3) to execute Athena queries from your LangChain projects. This involves setting up the necessary AWS credentials and permissions for LangChain to access Athena and execute queries.

3. **Query and retrieve data from Athena**: Write and execute SQL queries within our LangChain scripts to fetch text data from Athena. Manage query results, typically stored in an S3 bucket, and retrieve the output in LangChain.

4. **Integrate data into LangChain applications**: Integrate the text data retrieved from Athena into our LangChain workflows. This could involve text analysis, feeding data into language models for training or inference, or any other language-related task.

5. **Optimize data processing workflows**: Given Athena's serverless nature, monitor and optimize our queries for cost and performance. Efficiently integrating Athena queries into LangChain can minimize costs and speed up data processing tasks.

General tips for integration

The following are some tips:

*   **Security and permissions**: Ensure secure handling of credentials and permissions when connecting to Snowflake or Athena. Use IAM roles and policies for Athena and manage Snowflake access through roles and secure connections.

- **Data privacy and ethics**: Be mindful of data privacy and ethical considerations when using text data from Snowflake or Athena in LangChain, especially if the data contains personally identifiable information or sensitive content.

- **Continuous monitoring and optimization**: Regularly monitor the performance and cost-effectiveness of the integrations. Optimize queries and data processing workflows to balance efficiency, speed, and expenses.

Integrating Snowflake or Athena with LangChain opens new possibilities for leveraging large-scale datasets in language model development and text analysis projects. By following these steps, we can harness the full potential of these platforms, enhancing the capabilities of our LangChain applications.

Real-world applications

The integration of Snowflake, Athena, and LangChain can significantly enhance AI projects by leveraging the strengths of each tool for managing, querying, and analyzing large datasets. Following are real-world applications that demonstrate how these integrations can be transformative.

Customer feedback analysis

Scenario: A company collects vast amounts of customer feedback across various channels, which is stored in Snowflake. They aim to understand customer sentiment, identify common issues, and track changes in customer satisfaction over time.

Integration: By integrating Snowflake with LangChain, the company can automate the querying of feedback data, use **natural language processing** (**NLP**) models to analyze sentiment, categorize feedback, and extract actionable insights. LangChain can orchestrate the entire workflow, from data retrieval to analysis, leveraging Snowflake's scalable storage and computing resources to handle large datasets efficiently.

To conduct a customer feedback analysis using Snowflake for data storage and LangChain for processing and analysis, follow these detailed steps and code examples. This approach automates data querying, sentiment analysis, and insight extraction from customer feedback:

1. **Prepare Snowflake environment**: Ensure your customer feedback data is stored in Snowflake and structured in a table that includes, at the very least, a feedback text column and a timestamp. For demonstration, let us assume the table is named `customer_feedback` with columns `feedback_text` and `created_at`.

2. **Setup Snowflake access in our environment**: Install the Snowflake Python connector to interact with a virtual instance, for instance, from your Python environment, where we will run LangChain workflows.

```bash
pip install snowflake-connector-python
```

3. **Query feedback data from Snowflake**: Connect to Snowflake and fetch recent customer feedback data. We will want to customize the query based on our needs (e.g., feedback from the last month).

```python
import snowflake.connector

# Connect to Snowflake
conn = snowflake.connector.connect(
    user='<YOUR_USER>',
    password='<YOUR_PASSWORD>',
    account='<YOUR_ACCOUNT>',
    warehouse='<YOUR_WAREHOUSE>',
    database='<YOUR_DATABASE>',
    schema='<YOUR_SCHEMA>'
)

# Query recent customer feedback
query = """
SELECT feedback_text
FROM customer_feedback
WHERE created_at > DATEADD(month, -1, CURRENT_DATE())
"""
cur = conn.cursor()
cur.execute(query)
feedback_texts = cur.fetchall()

# Close the connection
cur.close()
conn.close()

# Extract just the text column (assuming it's the first column in the query)
feedback_texts = [text[0] for text in feedback_texts]
```

4. **Integrate with LangChain for sentiment analysis**: Assuming you have a LangChain setup and a sentiment analysis model available (LangChain supports integrating with various NLP models and APIs), we will analyze the sentiment of the feedback texts.

```python
from langchain.llms import OpenAI

# Initialize LangChain with an LLM (Large Language Model), like GPT
from OpenAI
llm = OpenAI(api_key='<YOUR_OPENAI_API_KEY>')

# Function to analyze sentiment
def analyze_sentiment(text):
    response = llm.complete(prompt=f"What is the sentiment of this
feedback? '{text}'", max_tokens=60)
    return response

# Analyze sentiment for each feedback text
sentiments = [analyze_sentiment(text) for text in feedback_texts]
```

5. **Categorize feedback and extract insights**: After obtaining sentiments, categorize the feedback based on sentiment scores or keywords identified in the analysis. Then, aggregate the results to identify common themes or issues.

```python
# Example of categorizing feedback (simplistic approach)
positive_feedback = [text for text, sentiment in zip(feedback_texts,
sentiments) if 'positive' in sentiment]
negative_feedback = [text for text, sentiment in zip(feedback_texts,
sentiments) if 'negative' in sentiment]

# Insights extraction - count or further analyze negative feedback
for common issues
# This is a simplified example; in practice, you might use more
sophisticated NLP techniques for theme extraction

from collections import Counter
common_issues = Counter(" ".join(negative_feedback).split()).most_
common(10)
```

6. **Actionable insights**: With categorized feedback and identified common issues, you can create reports and dashboards or directly feed these insights into your product development or customer service workflows to address the problems.

Note: This workflow demonstrates a straightforward approach to automating customer feedback analysis with Snowflake and LangChain. Depending on our requirements, you might introduce more sophisticated NLP techniques for deeper insights, such as named entity recognition (NER) for identifying product names or feature mentions within feedback.

Content recommendation engine

Scenario: An online media platform wants to improve its content recommendation system by analyzing user interaction data (clicks, views, time spent) and content metadata (genre, tags, descriptions) stored in Athena.

Integration: The platform can develop a more sophisticated recommendation engine by using Athena's ability to query large-scale data stored in S3 and LangChain's capabilities in NLP. It can analyze content metadata and user interactions to understand preferences, match users with similar content profiles, and generate personalized recommendations.

Note: Improving a content recommendation system by integrating Athena for data querying and LangChain for NLP and analysis involves several key steps. This scenario uses user interaction data and content metadata to enhance recommendation algorithms.

1. **Setup Athena for data querying**: Ensure your user interaction data (clicks, views, time spent) and content metadata (genre, tags, descriptions) are stored in Amazon S3 in a query-friendly format, such as Parquet or CSV, and properly cataloged in Athena. This setup facilitates efficient querying.

2. **Query data from Athena**: Use the AWS SDK for Python (Boto3) to execute Athena queries from your Python environment. First, install Boto3 and setup your AWS credentials:

```bash
pip install boto3
```

   Next, query the data. There might be two queries: One to fetch user interactions and another for content metadata.

```python
import boto3
athena = boto3.client('athena', region_name='<YOUR_REGION>')

def execute_athena_query(query, database, s3_output):
    response = athena.start_query_execution(
        QueryString=query,
        QueryExecutionContext={'Database': database},
        ResultConfiguration={'OutputLocation': s3_output}
    )
    return response['QueryExecutionId']
# Query user interactions
user_interaction_query = """
SELECT user_id, content_id, clicks, views, time_spent
FROM user_interactions
```

```
"""
user_interaction_query_id = execute_athena_query(user_interaction_
query, '<YOUR_DATABASE>', 's3://<YOUR_S3_BUCKET_FOR_RESULTS>/')
# Query content metadata
content_metadata_query = """
SELECT content_id, genre, tags, description
FROM content_metadata
"""

content_metadata_query_id = execute_athena_query(content_metadata_
query, '<YOUR_DATABASE>', 's3://<YOUR_S3_BUCKET_FOR_RESULTS>/')
# Note: Implement polling on the query execution status and fetching
results, as queries are asynchronous.
```

3. **Process data with LangChain**: With the data queried from Athena, use LangChain's capabilities to process and analyze the content metadata using NLP to extract features that could enhance your recommendation engine:

```python
from langchain.llms import OpenAI

# Assuming you have fetched the query results into variables `user_
interactions` and `content_metadata`
# Initialize LangChain with an LLM, e.g., OpenAI's GPT
llm = OpenAI(api_key='<YOUR_OPENAI_API_KEY>')
# Example function to extract content features from descriptions
def extract_features(description):
    response = llm.complete(prompt=f"Extract key features from this
description: '{description}'", max_tokens=60)
    return response
# Extract features for each content item
content_features = [extract_features(item['description']) for item
in content_metadata]
```

4. **Enhance recommendation logic**: Integrate this information into your content recommendation logic with user interaction data and enriched content metadata (including extracted features). This might involve the following:

   a. Matching users to content with similar profiles based on interaction patterns and content features.

   b. Implementing machine learning models that use this enriched dataset to predict content relevance to individual users.

5. **Deploy and monitor**: Integrate the enhanced recommendation logic back into your online media platform. Monitor the performance of the new recommendation system, paying close attention to metrics like user engagement and satisfaction to improve the system iteratively.

Note: This scenario combines Athena's scalable data querying capabilities with LangChain's advanced NLP processing to create a sophisticated content recommendation engine. It leverages structured interaction data and unstructured content metadata to provide personalized recommendations.

Market trend analysis

Scenario: A financial analysis firm collects a wealth of market data, news articles, and financial reports stored in Snowflake to identify emerging market trends and investment opportunities.

Integration: By integrating Snowflake with LangChain, the firm can automate extracting relevant data, perform sentiment analysis on news articles, and analyze financial reports using language models to identify patterns, trends, and potential market movements. This integration allows for real-time analysis and more accurate forecasting.

To automate the extraction and analysis of market data, news articles, and financial reports stored in Snowflake and to integrate these processes with LangChain for sentiment analysis and trend identification, follow these steps:

1. **Prepare Snowflake data**: Ensure your market data, news articles, and financial reports are stored in Snowflake within accessible tables. Let us assume we have two tables: `market_data` for structured financial data and `news_articles` for unstructured news text.

2. **Setup Snowflake connectivity**: Use the Snowflake Python connector to interact with your Snowflake data warehouse. Install the connector and setup the connection:

````bash
pip install snowflake-connector-python
````

````python
import snowflake.connector

# Snowflake connection details
conn = snowflake.connector.connect(
    user='<YOUR_USER>',
    password='<YOUR_PASSWORD>',
    account='<YOUR_ACCOUNT>',
````

```python
    warehouse='<YOUR_WAREHOUSE>',
    database='<YOUR_DATABASE>',
    schema='<YOUR_SCHEMA>'
)
```

3. **Query data from Snowflake**: Execute queries to fetch recent market data and news articles. Customize these queries based on your specific analysis needs:

```python
# Query to fetch recent news articles
query_news = """
SELECT title, content
FROM news_articles
WHERE published_date > DATEADD(day, -30, CURRENT_DATE())
"""

cur = conn.cursor()
cur.execute(query_news)
news_articles = cur.fetchall()
cur.close()

# Convert fetched data into a more usable format if necessary
# Assuming the title is the first column, and the content is the
second
news_articles = [{'title': article[0], 'content': article[1]} for
article in news_articles]
```

4. **Integrate with LangChain for sentiment analysis and pattern identification**: With the data fetched, use LangChain's capabilities to process the news articles for sentiment analysis and extract insights from financial reports.

```python
from langchain.llms import OpenAI

# Initialize LangChain with an LLM, such as OpenAI's GPT
llm = OpenAI(api_key='<YOUR_OPENAI_API_KEY>')

# Function to analyze the sentiment of news articles
def analyze_sentiment(article):
    prompt = f"Analyze the sentiment of this news article titled
'{article['title']}': {article['content']}"
    response = llm.complete(prompt=prompt, max_tokens=60)
    return response['choices'][0]['text'].strip()

# Analyze the sentiment for each article
```

```
article_sentiments = [analyze_sentiment(article) for article in
news_articles]

# Optionally, perform additional analysis on market data or financial
reports
```

5. **Extract insights and identify trends**: With sentiments analyzed, aggregate this information to identify overall market sentiment, emerging trends, or noteworthy patterns in the financial reports. This process will vary based on the specifics of your data and the models you use.

```python
# Example: Aggregating sentiment to identify overall market trends
from collections import Counter
sentiment_counts = Counter(article_sentiments)

# Assess overall market sentiment based on the analysis
# Further analysis could involve correlating sentiment with market
data changes
```

6. **Actionable insights for forecasting**: Use the insights gained from sentiment analysis and pattern identification to inform forecasting models or investment strategies. This step involves integrating the analytical outputs into decision-making processes, potentially automating alerts or recommendations for analysts and investors.

7. **Automate and scale**: To maintain real-time analysis capabilities, automate the data querying and analysis workflows. Consider scheduling scripts to run at regular intervals, ensuring new data is continuously analyzed and insights are kept up-to-date.

Note: This integration of Snowflake and LangChain for analyzing financial data and news articles enables an economic analysis firm to leverage AI for enhanced market understanding, sentiment analysis, and trend identification, improving forecasting accuracy and uncovering investment opportunities in real-time.

Health data insights

Scenario: A healthcare research organization aggregates patient data, clinical trial results, and medical literature in Athena to drive research on treatment outcomes and disease trends.

Integration: By leveraging Athena to query structured and unstructured health data and LangChain to process and analyze medical texts, the organization can uncover insights into disease patterns, treatment effectiveness, and potential areas for research. This could accelerate discoveries and improve patient outcomes by informing evidence-based treatment strategies.

To leverage Athena for querying health data and LangChain for processing and analyzing medical texts in a healthcare research context, follow this step-by-step guide, focusing on structured and unstructured data to uncover insights into disease patterns and treatment effectiveness:

1. **Organize data in Amazon S3 and catalog in Athena**: Ensure that the patient data, clinical trial results, and medical literature are stored in Amazon S3 in a structured format conducive to Athena queries. Use Athena to catalog this data, creating tables that reflect the structure of our datasets, whether they are CSV, JSON, Parquet, or other formats.

2. **Query health data with Athena**: Use AWS SDK for Python (Boto3) to execute Athena queries. Install Boto3, configure AWS credentials, and query the health data. To prepare for analysis, we might perform separate queries for patient data, clinical trial results, and medical literature.

   ```bash
   pip install boto3
   ```

   ```python
   import boto3

   athena = boto3.client('athena', region_name='<YOUR_AWS_REGION>')

   def execute_athena_query(query, database, s3_output):
       response = athena.start_query_execution(
           QueryString=query,
           QueryExecutionContext={'Database': database},
           ResultConfiguration={'OutputLocation': s3_output}
       )
       return response['QueryExecutionId']

   # Example query for medical literature
   literature_query = """
   SELECT title, abstract
   FROM medical_literature
   """

   literature_query_id = execute_athena_query(literature_query, '<YOUR_DATABASE>', 's3://<YOUR_S3_BUCKET_FOR_RESULTS>/')

   # Note: Implement polling on the query execution status and fetching
   results, as Athena queries are asynchronous.
   ```

3. **Process and analyze medical texts with LangChain**: With our health data fetched, use LangChain to process and analyze the medical texts. Assuming we can access a language model suitable for medical text analysis, we can extract insights, identify disease patterns, and assess treatment effectiveness.

```python
from langchain.llms import OpenAI

# Assuming fetched medical literature texts are stored in `medical_
literature.`
# Initialize LangChain with an appropriate LLM
llm = OpenAI(api_key='<YOUR_OPENAI_API_KEY>')

# Function to analyze medical texts for insights
def analyze_medical_text(text):
    prompt = f"Provide insights on disease patterns and treatment
effectiveness from this text: {text}"
    response = llm.complete(prompt=prompt, max_tokens=150)
    return response['choices'][0]['text'].strip()

# Analyze each piece of medical literature
literature_insights = [analyze_medical_text(text['abstract']) for
text in medical_literature]
```

4. **Aggregate insights for research and treatment strategies**: Aggregate the insights from the analyzed medical texts to identify common themes, disease patterns, or emerging treatment strategies. This step might involve NLP techniques like clustering or topic modeling to organize and summarize the findings.

5. **Inform research and clinical practices**: Translate the aggregated insights into actionable intelligence for the healthcare research organization. This could involve identifying potential areas for new clinical trials, highlighting effective treatments, or pinpointing gaps in understanding certain diseases.

6. **Automate and scale the analysis workflow**: To maintain the organization's leadership in medical research, automate workflows for querying, text analysis, and insight aggregation. Schedule regular updates to process new data as it becomes available, ensuring a continuous pipeline of fresh insights for ongoing research endeavors.

Note: By integrating Athena's querying capabilities with LangChain's text analysis power, healthcare research organizations can significantly enhance their ability to uncover valuable insights from vast datasets of patient data, clinical trial results, and medical literature. This integration facilitates evidence-based treatment strategies and accelerates medical discoveries, ultimately improving patient outcomes and healthcare advancements.

Social media sentiment tracking

Scenario: A marketing agency uses data aggregated in Snowflake to track social media sentiment and trends related to their clients' brands.

Integration: The agency integrates Snowflake with LangChain to automate data retrieval and leverage advanced NLP models to analyze sentiment, identify trending topics, and monitor brand perception in real-time. This integration helps craft timely and targeted marketing strategies.

For a marketing agency, aiming to track social media sentiment and trends for their client's brands with data aggregated in Snowflake and processed through LangChain, follow these steps:

1. **Aggregate social media data in Snowflake**: Ensure your social media data (posts, comments, likes, etc.) related to your client's brands are being aggregated in Snowflake. This data should include text content, timestamps, user engagement metrics, and other relevant metadata that could provide context for sentiment analysis and trend identification.

2. **Setup Snowflake connectivity**: Use the Snowflake Python connector to facilitate data retrieval from your Python environment, where you will run LangChain workflows:

   ```bash
   pip install snowflake-connector-python
   ```

   ```python
   import snowflake.connector

   # Establish a connection to Snowflake
   conn = snowflake.connector.connect(
       user='<YOUR_USER>',
       password='<YOUR_PASSWORD>',
       account='<YOUR_ACCOUNT>',
       warehouse='<YOUR_WAREHOUSE>',
       database='<YOUR_DATABASE>',
       schema='<YOUR_SCHEMA>'
   )
   ```

3. **Query social media data from Snowflake**: Execute a query to fetch recent social media posts and comments about your clients' brands. Customize the query to focus on the most relevant data for sentiment analysis and trend monitoring:

```python
# Query to fetch recent social media data
query_social_media = """
SELECT post_text, posted_at
FROM social_media_data
WHERE posted_at > DATEADD(day, -7, CURRENT_DATE()) -- Example: Last
7 days
"""
cur = conn.cursor()
cur.execute(query_social_media)
social_media_data = cur.fetchall()
cur.close()

# Prepare data for analysis
social_media_texts = [post[0] for post in social_media_data]
```

4. **Analyze sentiment and trends with LangChain**: With the social media data, LangChain can be integrated with an advanced NLP model to analyze sentiment and identify trending topics:

```python
from langchain.llms import OpenAI

# Initialize LangChain with an appropriate LLM, e.g., OpenAI's GPT
llm = OpenAI(api_key='<YOUR_OPENAI_API_KEY>')

# Function to analyze the sentiment of a post
def analyze_sentiment(text):
    prompt = f"Determine the sentiment of this social media post:
{text}"
    response = llm.complete(prompt=prompt, max_tokens=60)
    return response['choices'][0]['text'].strip()

# Analyze sentiment for each post
post_sentiments = [analyze_sentiment(text) for text in social_media_
texts]
```

5. **Aggregate insights and inform strategy**: After analyzing the sentiments, aggregate this information to gauge overall brand perception across social media. Identify positive, neutral, and negative sentiment trends and pinpoint specific topics or events driving these sentiments:

```python
from collections import Counter

# Count sentiment categories
sentiment_counts = Counter(post_sentiments)

# Identify specific topics or keywords associated with positive and
negative sentiments
# This could involve further text analysis or keyword extraction
```

6. **Craft marketing strategies**: Use the insights gained from sentiment analysis and trend identification to make informed marketing strategies. This may involve the following:

    a. Developing targeted marketing campaigns to bolster positive sentiments or address negative perceptions.

    b. Creating content strategies that resonate with trending topics or address concerns highlighted by social media sentiment.

    c. Advising clients on real-time adjustments to their social media presence or responses to trending topics.

7. **Automate and continuously monitor**: Data retrieval and analysis processes must be automated to keep sentiment tracking up to date. Schedule regular updates to analyze new social media posts and monitor brand perception over time, enabling the agency to provide timely and data-driven marketing advice to their clients.

By integrating Snowflake and LangChain for social media sentiment tracking, the marketing agency can leverage automated data retrieval and advanced NLP models to analyze sentiment and identify real-time trends. This approach enhances the agency's ability to monitor brand perception accurately and supports the development of more effective and timely marketing strategies for their clients.

These examples illustrate the potential of integrating Snowflake, Athena, and LangChain in AI projects. By combining the data management and querying capabilities of Snowflake and Athena with the advanced language processing and AI model orchestration of LangChain, organizations can unlock new levels of insight, efficiency, and innovation in their projects.

Conclusion

We have examined how Snowflake, Athena, and their integration with LangChain are changing the game for AI projects that rely heavily on data. Each platform brings something special to the table—Snowflake with its cloud-based data warehousing, Athena with its hassle-free serverless data querying, and LangChain with its ability to enrich AI models and applications using data from these services. Together, they form a powerful toolkit that makes managing, querying, and analyzing large amounts of data easier and more efficient than ever.

The blend of Snowflake and Athena with LangChain creates a powerful ecosystem for data and AI. This mix makes it simpler for data scientists and developers to find and use insights hidden in vast datasets and opens new possibilities for innovative and effective AI solutions. As we look ahead, the future is bright for data science and AI, with these tools at the forefront, promising to continue transforming how organizations tackle data-driven challenges and opportunities.

Points to remember

- **Understand each tool's strengths**:

    o Snowflake excels in data warehousing, providing scalable storage and computing resources and efficiently handling structured and semi-structured data.

    o Athena shines with serverless data querying directly on Amazon S3, offering cost-effective and scalable solutions for ad-hoc data analysis.

    o LangChain facilitates the development and deployment of language models, leveraging data processed and analyzed by Snowflake and Athena.

- **Leverage advanced features for deep analysis**:

    o Utilize Snowflake's advanced SQL capabilities, Time Travel, and cloning features to enhance data analysis and ensure robust data management.

    o Optimize Athena queries with partitioning and use its seamless integration with AWS services to enhance data processing and analysis workflows.

- **Seamless integration is key**:

    o Integrate Snowflake and Athena with LangChain to leverage vast datasets for training, refining, and deploying sophisticated language models, enhancing the capabilities of AI applications.

- **Real-world applications demonstrate value**:

    o From analyzing customer feedback to enhancing content recommendations to tracking market trends, integrating these tools can transform data into actionable insights, driving innovation and improving decision-making processes.

- **Security, privacy, and ethics matter**:
  - o Always consider security best practices, data privacy laws, and ethical guidelines when integrating these technologies, especially when dealing with sensitive or personal data.

- **Optimization and cost-management**:
  - o Review and optimize your data queries and processes regularly to manage cost-effectively, especially with cloud-based services like Snowflake and Athena.

- **Collaboration and sharing enhance outcomes**:
  - o Utilize Snowflake's data sharing features and Athena's integration with AWS services to collaborate across teams and external partners, enhancing the reach and impact of your insights.

- **Stay agile and experiment**:
  - o The data science and AI landscapes are rapidly evolving. Stay open to continuously experimenting with new features, integration patterns, and analytical methods to improve your projects.

Multiple choice questions

1. **What is Snowflake primarily used for?**

    a. Text processing

    b. Data warehousing

    c. Image recognition

    d. Real-time analytics

2. **Which feature of Athena allows data to be queried directly from Amazon S3?**

    a. Serverless architecture

    b. Data warehousing

    c. Virtual compute instances

    d. In-memory caching

3. **What is a key benefit of integrating Snowflake with LangChain?**

    a. Reducing physical storage needs

    b. Enhancing language model training with large datasets

    c. Improving the graphical interface

    d. Decreasing internet bandwidth usage

4. **What does Athena use to perform queries on data?**

    a. Python scripts

    b. Standard SQL

    c. Proprietary query language

    d. NoSQL queries

5. **Which of the following is a feature unique to Snowflake?**

    a. Time Travel

    b. Serverless architecture

    c. Direct S3 integration

    d. Automatic data partitioning

6. **How can data be loaded into Snowflake for analysis?**

    a. Only through manual entry

    b. Using the COPY INTO command

    c. Via Athena queries

    d. Directly from LangChain

7. **Which AWS service integrates seamlessly with Athena for data visualization?**

    a. AWS Lambda

    b. Amazon EC2

    c. Amazon QuickSight

    d. AWS S3

8. **What advantage does serverless querying in Athena offer?**

    a. Unlimited storage capacity

    b. No need for data indexing

    c. No infrastructure to manage

    d. Automatic data cleaning

9. **Which of the following best describes Lang Chain's role in the integration?**

    a. A data storage solution

    b. A query language

    c. An AI model development and deployment framework

    d. A visualization tool

10. **Why is partitioning important in Athena?**

    a. It speeds up query times by organizing data.

    b. It reduces the cost of queries by scanning less data.

    c. It automatically encrypts data.

    d. Both a and b.

These questions cover the basics of Snowflake, Athena, and their integration with LangChain, providing a broad overview of their functionalities and benefits in data-driven AI projects.

Answers

1	b
2	a
3	b
4	b
5	a
6	b
7	c
8	c
9	c
10	d

Key terms

- **Snowflake**: A cloud-based data warehousing service that offers scalable storage, flexible computing resources, and unique features like Time Travel and automatic scaling, facilitating efficient data management and analysis.

- **Athena**: AWS offers a serverless query service that enables users to analyze data directly in Amazon S3 using standard SQL. This is a cost-effective solution for ad-hoc data querying without infrastructure management.

- **LangChain**: This framework is for building and deploying language models and AI applications, leveraging data from various sources, including Snowflake and Athena, to enhance NLP and generation tasks.

- **Data warehousing**: They collect, store, and manage large volumes of data from various sources in a centralized repository to support query and analysis.

- **Serverless computing**: Serverless computing is a cloud computing model in which the cloud provider dynamically allocates machine resources, enabling users to run applications and services without the need to manage servers.

- **Time Travel**: A feature in Snowflake that allows users to access historical data within a defined retention period, enabling data recovery, auditing, and analysis over time.

- **SQL**: A standard programming language for handling and modifying relational databases, extensively employed for querying, updating, and managing data.

- **Data partitioning**: The process of dividing a database or dataset into distinct segments (partitions) based on specific keys, such as date or region, to improve query performance and manageability.

- **ETL**: Data transformation is an essential process in data warehousing. Data is extracted from various sources, converted into a suitable format, and loaded into a target database or data warehouse for analysis.

- **BI tools**: Software applications analyze data and present actionable information, helping companies make more informed business decisions. These tools can connect to databases like Snowflake and services like Athena for data visualization and analysis.

Understanding these key terms is essential for navigating the complexities of leveraging Snowflake, Athena, and LangChain in data-driven AI projects, enabling effective management, querying, and analysis of large datasets to derive insights and inform decision-making.

Join our book's Discord space

Join the book's Discord Workspace for Latest updates, Offers, Tech happenings around the world, New Release and Sessions with the Authors:

https://discord.bpbonline.com

CHAPTER 8
AI in DevOps and MLOps

Introduction

The way we develop and manage applications is rapidly evolving in the world of technology. Two practices, **development operations** (**DevOps**) and **machine learning operations** (**MLOps**), stand at the forefront of this change, making the process smoother and more efficient. DevOps is like a bridge connecting the coding world with the operations that keep applications running smoothly. It is all about making things faster: Quicker updates, better-quality software, and more dependable releases.

MLOps applies these ideas to **machine learning** (**ML**). This means ensuring AI systems are as easy to update and maintain as any other piece of software. With AI becoming a bigger part of how we work, the ability to keep these systems running smoothly is more important than ever.

Adding **artificial intelligence** (**AI**) to the mix, especially with cutting-edge tools like LangChain, is a major game-changer. It opens up new possibilities for making everything more automated, efficient, and scalable. This chapter will explore how AI can revolutionize operational workflows, helping teams move their applications from concept to customer faster and more reliably than before.

Structure

This chapter covers the following topics:

- DevOps and MLOps
- Key differences between DevOps and MLOps
- AI-driven enhancements
- Expanding AI use cases
- LangChain in action
- Mastering MLOps with AI

Objectives

This chapter highlights AI's critical role in transforming DevOps and MLOps practices, ultimately making application development and management more efficient, scalable, and automated. We explore the basics, apply these concepts in real-world scenarios, and explore how integrating advanced technologies like LangChain can significantly benefit these processes.

By equipping readers with the necessary insights and tools, we aim to make integrating AI into DevOps and MLOps practices smooth and straightforward. Through practical examples and detailed guides, we intend to show how AI can tackle common hurdles, improve resource allocation, and enable teams to build and deploy high-quality applications more quickly and easily than ever before.

We aim to encourage a progressive mindset towards achieving operational excellence, using AI as a catalyst for innovation and superior performance in the ever-changing tech landscape.

DevOps and MLOps

DevOps and MLOps are methods that improve the development of software and AI models. The main goal of DevOps is to bring together software development and operations into one streamlined team, promoting teamwork among once-separate groups. This helps organizations release software more frequently, maintain stability, and innovate faster. It is like in a restaurant where cooks (developers) and servers (operations) work seamlessly to serve food (software) quickly and efficiently to customers (users).

MLOps does something similar for ML projects. It focuses on automating and enhancing the entire lifecycle of ML models. Imagine MLOps as a high-tech appliance in your home that performs its initial tasks well and updates itself to meet new needs over time.

Model drift

Integrating AI presents unique challenges because of its complexity and the fast pace at which it changes. For example, in DevOps, tools that automate testing and deployment need constant updates to keep up with software changes. Similarly, in MLOps, it is crucial to continually monitor and update ML models to prevent model drift, which occurs when a model's accuracy decreases as it processes new data. This is like a GPS that needs regular map updates to stay accurate.

AI can be integrated directly into these processes. For instance, AI-powered predictive analytics can foresee problems in software deployments and suggest fixes. Likewise, AI can automate updating ML models when it notices performance issues, helping the models adapt to new data without human help.

By solving these challenges, DevOps and MLOps simplify development and operations, enhancing the reliability and efficiency of the products and services delivered. This ensures that companies can exceed the expectations of their tech-savvy customers.

Moreover, as companies grow and their technology becomes more complex, AI's ability to scale becomes vital. In DevOps, a cloud service provider might use AI to adjust its infrastructure based on real-time user demand and system health data. As user numbers grow, so does the complexity of managing these adjustments. Effective scaling in this context requires robust automation frameworks that can adjust without human intervention, ensuring seamless service no matter the demand.

MLOps also faces scalability challenges, especially when deploying ML models that need to process large amounts of data in real-time. For example, deploying **natural language processing** (**NLP**) models for customer support needs to stay accurate and responsive as customer interactions increase. This involves more powerful computing resources and smarter management of data flow and model updates to avoid delays and bottlenecks.

Integrating AI in DevOps and MLOps involves continuous learning and adaptation. AI systems can become outdated if they do not evolve with changes in data and technology landscapes. In DevOps, this might mean constant testing and integration practices that adapt automatically to new codebases and environments. MLOps means regularly updating models to reflect new data and insights to avoid model drift.

Moreover, effective AI implementation requires improved collaboration and knowledge sharing across the organization. AI technologies often span different areas of expertise, from IT infrastructure and software development to data science and analytics. Forming cross-functional teams that can work seamlessly together is crucial. Additionally, sharing knowledge through workshops, seminars, and regular team meetings helps demystify AI technologies and align various parts of the organization toward common goals.

In short, integrating AI into DevOps and MLOps presents a multifaceted challenge that requires technical skill, strategic planning, and teamwork across various departments. By addressing these challenges and continually adapting to new developments, organizations can use AI to optimize their operations significantly, driving substantial business growth and innovation. This proactive approach ensures that AI's potential is fully realized, leading to smarter, more efficient, and effective operational practices.

Example: Streamlining communication in software development teams using DevOps tools:

- **Background**: A software development company with teams distributed across various locations faces challenges with effective collaboration and communication. The primary issue is keeping all team members aligned on project developments, especially when projects involve complex dependencies and require timely updates.

- **Challenge**: The company struggles with managing multiple communication channels, ensuring all team members have the most current project information, and facilitating rapid problem-solving discussions. To improve communication and maintain project continuity, they need a solution that fits seamlessly into their existing DevOps practices.

- **Solution**: The company utilizes existing DevOps tools and integrates additional collaborative software solutions to enhance team workflow communication and visibility.

Steps in enhancing collaboration without LangChain:

1. **Integration of project management tools**:

    a. **Centralized project information**: The company integrates a comprehensive project management tool like JIRA or Asana, centralizing all project-related information, including tasks, milestones, bug tracking, and progress reports.

    b. **Custom workflow reflection**: They customize the tool to mirror the company's workflow, incorporating sprint planning, backlog management, and review processes.

2. **Utilization of real-time communication platforms**:

    a. **Dedicated communication channels**: Platforms like *Slack* or *Microsoft Teams* are adopted, and dedicated channels for each project and feature development are setup to ensure all discussions are easily accessible and archived.

    b. **Direct updates via plugins**: These platforms use plugins and bots to link directly to the project management tools, allowing team members to receive real-time updates and notifications.

3. **Routine synchronization meetings**:

    a. **Regular video conferences**: Regular stand-up meetings manage video conferencing tools such as *Zoom* or *Google Meet*, enabling remote team members to participate actively and provide updates on their progress and challenges.

   b. **Dynamic discussion of priorities**: These meetings address blockers and dependencies, discuss priorities, and adjust plans in real-time as necessary.

4. **Shared documentation and collaboration spaces**:

   a. **Centralized documentation system**: A centralized documentation system using tools like *Confluence* or *Google Docs* is implemented. This system keeps all project documentation, from technical specs to meeting notes, up-to-date and accessible to everyone.

   b. **Collaborative ING**: The system supports collaborative ING features, allowing multiple team members to work on documents simultaneously and ensuring updates and visibility in real-time.

5. **Version control and continuous integration tools**:

   a. **Robust version control**: Version control systems like Git are enhanced with **continuous integration/continuous deployment (CI/CD)** pipelines using *Jenkins* or *CircleCI*. This setup automates testing and deployment processes, keeping everyone in sync with the latest codebase state.

   b. **Enhanced code quality and collaboration**: Branch policies and review processes are implemented to ensure all code is reviewed and tested before merging, enhancing code quality and collaborative efforts.

6. **Outcome**: By integrating these tools and methodologies into their DevOps practices, the company experiences significant improvements in team communication and project transparency. The centralized platforms and routine synchronization reduce the chances of miscommunication and delays, ensuring that all team members are always informed and engaged. This leads to smoother project flows, quicker resolution of issues, and more consistent delivery of high-quality software.

7. **Conclusion**: This example demonstrates how traditional DevOps tools and collaborative practices can effectively enhance communication and cooperation among software development teams, even without advanced AI-driven technologies like LangChain. The key to success is the thoughtful integration of tools that align with the team's workflow and promote transparency and real-time engagement among all team members.

Example: Enhancing software development collaboration with LangChain in DevOps:

- **Background**: A software development company struggles to maintain efficient communication and collaboration across its globally distributed teams. With developers and operations personnel spread across various time zones and working on diverse project elements, aligning everyone effectively is a significant challenge.

- **Challenge**: The company faces difficulties managing complex queries about project status, updates, and technical details scattered across multiple platforms such as GitHub, JIRA, and internal documentation. A solution providing immediate, context-aware information to team members would reduce delays and boost productivity.

- **Solution**: They integrate LangChain, an AI-powered communication tool, into their DevOps processes. LangChain is a framework that integrates with **large language models (LLMs)** to process natural language queries and retrieve relevant information from connected data sources. It enhances information flow among team members by leveraging the capabilities of LLMs for better query understanding and response generation.

Steps in integrating LangChain in DevOps:

1. **System integration**:
   a. **Data source connection**: LangChain is connected to various data sources utilized by the development teams, including version control systems like GitHub, project management tools like JIRA, and internal documentation wikis.
   b. **Specific access configuration**: LangChain is configured to access particular repositories, project tracking boards, and documentation spaces, ensuring precise and relevant data retrieval.

2. **Customization and training**:
   a. **Terminology and workflow training**: LangChain is trained on the specific terminology and workflows unique to the company, ensuring it accurately understands and responds to queries related to software development and deployment processes.
   b. **Workflow automation setup**: Customized workflows are established in LangChain to automate routine inquiries, such as retrieving the latest deployment logs or updating the status of critical bugs.

3. **Deployment and access provisioning**:
   a. **Chatbot deployment**: LangChain is deployed as a chatbot that is accessible through the company's internal communication platforms, such as Slack or Microsoft Teams.
   b. **Access and training**: All team members are granted access and trained to utilize LangChain effectively to retrieve information and perform tasks.

4. **Monitoring and feedback**:
   a. **Performance monitoring**: LangChain's usage and performance are continuously monitored to ensure it delivers accurate and relevant information.

b. **Continuous improvement**: User feedback is collected regularly to improve interaction flows and update the training data based on real-world usage and evolving project dynamics.

5. **Scaling and enhancement**:

   a. **System scaling**: As LangChain proves successful, it is scaled to include more data sources and handle more complex queries.

   b. **Capability enhancement**: The AI capabilities are enhanced to initiate proactive alerts about project milestones or critical issues by analyzing data trends.

6. **Outcome**: The integration of LangChain fundamentally changes how information is exchanged within the company's DevOps environment. Team members can now instantly access the information they need, significantly reducing the time spent navigating through emails or waiting for responses across time zones. This enhancement leads to quicker decision-making, more timely project updates, and a more synchronized and efficient development cycle.

7. **Conclusion**: This example showcases how effectively LangChain can be integrated into a DevOps strategy to enhance communication and efficiency in software development environments. The company optimizes collaboration across its distributed teams by leveraging AI for automated information retrieval and task management, resulting in improved project outcomes and increased productivity.

We can see distinct advantages and considerations for each approach when comparing the benefits of enhancing software development collaboration with and without using an AI tool like LangChain in a DevOps environment.

DevOps With LangChain

Streamline AI workflows by integrating LangChain into DevOps pipelines. Simplify deployment, scalability, and automation for cutting-edge applications.

- **Enhanced efficiency through automation**:

  o **NLP capabilities**: LangChain can interpret and respond to natural language queries, allowing team members to quickly retrieve information without navigating multiple tools or interfaces. This reduces the time spent searching for project details, documentation, or status updates.

  o **Automated task handling**: LangChain can automate routine tasks like updating ticket statuses, fetching logs, or integrating updates from various sources, streamlining the workflow and reducing manual overhead.

- **Improved accuracy and speed of information retrieval**:

  - o **Context-aware responses**: With its AI-driven understanding, LangChain can provide contextually relevant answers to queries, reducing misunderstandings and ensuring that team members receive precisely what they need.

  - o **Proactive alerts and notifications**: LangChain can monitor data across platforms and trigger alerts or notifications about important updates, potential bottlenecks, or deployment failures, ensuring immediate attention and action.

- **Scalability and learning over time**:

  - o **Adaptive learning**: As an AI system, LangChain can learn from interactions and continuously improve its responses and the relevance of the information it provides, potentially becoming more aligned with specific team needs over time.

  - o **Scalable to team growth**: LangChain can easily scale to handle increased loads as teams grow or as project complexity increases, maintaining performance without requiring proportional increases in configuration or management efforts.

Traditional DevOps vs AI-powered solutions

Building robust AI solutions without LangChain requires navigating manual integrations and managing complexity, but it offers full control over custom architectures and workflows.

- **Simplicity and control**:

  - o **No dependency on AI understanding**: Relying on traditional DevOps tools and methods eliminates the risk of AI misinterpreting requests or requiring extensive training to understand specific jargon or workflows.

  - o **Direct control over processes**: Teams may find it easier to control and understand workflows that are not mediated by AI, making it straightforward to diagnose issues, trace actions, and manually adjust processes.

- **Lower barrier to entry**:

  - o **No need for AI expertise**: Without the need to integrate and maintain an AI system like LangChain, there is no requirement for specialized AI knowledge, making it more accessible for teams without AI expertise.

  - o **Cost-effective**: Avoiding sophisticated AI tools can also be more cost-effective, particularly for smaller teams or projects where the budget is a concern.

- **Reliability and predictability**:

    o **Consistent and predictable outcomes**: Traditional tools are generally more predictable in their outputs since they operate based on predefined rules and workflows, unlike AI systems that may evolve and change behavior over time.

    o **Reliability in data security and privacy**: Using conventional tools typically means data is handled within known parameters and systems, possibly offering more straightforward compliance with data security and privacy regulations.

In brief, using LangChain in a DevOps context can significantly enhance efficiency, scalability, and the speed of accessing relevant information through automation and NLP. However, investment is required to train the AI and ensure it integrates well with existing systems.

Conversely, not using LangChain or similar AI tools keeps the process straightforward, potentially more cost-effective, and easier to manage, especially for teams with limited AI expertise or resources. The choice between these approaches depends largely on the specific needs, scale, and capabilities of the organization and its projects.

Key differences between DevOps and MLOps

DevOps focuses on unifying software development and IT operations to shorten the development lifecycle, enabling faster and more reliable software delivery. Key practices include CI/CD pipelines, automated testing, and **infrastructure as code** (**IaC**). MLOps extends DevOps principles to ML workflows, emphasizing the automation, deployment, and monitoring of ML models. It ensures seamless collaboration between data scientists and engineers, addressing challenges like versioning datasets, managing model drift, and automating retraining processes.

Differences between DevOps and MLOps in short:

DevOps: For software development:

1. **Focus**: Manages software development and deployment.
2. **Pipeline**: Uses CI/CD pipelines to automate code integration and delivery.
3. **Data handling**: Works primarily with source code and application dependencies.
4. **Testing**: Uses automated testing to ensure software reliability.
5. **Updates**: Releases updates frequently without major performance risks.
6. **Version control**: Tracks software versions using Git and other tools.

7. **Infrastructure**: Uses IaC to automate system setup.

8. **Monitoring**: Focuses on system uptime, performance, and security.

9. **Team collaboration**: Involves developers and IT operations teams.

10. **Challenges**: Managing deployment consistency and minimizing downtime.

MLOps: For ML:

1. **Focus**: Manages ML models from training to production.

2. **Pipeline**: Automates data processing, model training, and deployment.

3. **Data handling**: Works with large datasets, requiring continuous updates.

4. **Testing**: Validates models for accuracy and bias instead of just software bugs.

5. **Updates**: Requires frequent model retraining to maintain accuracy.

6. **Version control**: Tracks model versions, data changes, and training runs.

7. **Infrastructure**: Uses scalable computing for model training and inference.

8. **Monitoring**: Focuses on model performance, data drift, and bias detection.

9. **Team collaboration**: Involves data scientists, ML engineers, and DevOps teams.

10. **Challenges**: Preventing model drift, managing data quality, and ensuring scalability.

Common goal: DevOps and MLOps

While distinct in their specific applications, DevOps and MLOps share a common goal to streamline the processes involved in developing, deploying, and maintaining software or AI models. DevOps focuses on enhancing collaboration between development and operations teams to improve product quality, reduce time to market, and foster a culture of continuous improvement. The aim is to create a workflow allowing rapid, reliable delivery of software updates and new features.

MLOps, on the other hand, extends these principles to the lifecycle management of ML models. It seeks to automate AI model integration, testing, deployment, and monitoring in production environments. The goal is to ensure that ML systems are scalable, reproducible, and maintainable, enabling businesses to leverage AI effectively and responsibly.

DevOps and MLOps importance depends on their ability to address key challenges in the modern tech landscape, such as the need for faster development cycles, higher software quality, and the capability to adapt to changes quickly. By fostering better collaboration, automating workflows, and implementing continuous feedback loops, these practices enable organizations to stay competitive and innovative in a fast-evolving digital world.

Challenges with AI: Overcoming operational obstacles

Integrating AI into DevOps and MLOps presents its own set of challenges. These include the complexity of managing the AI model lifecycle, ensuring data quality and integrity, and aligning AI projects with business objectives. Moreover, the dynamic nature of AI models, which may require frequent updates and retraining, adds complexity to traditional DevOps and MLOps workflows.

However, organizations can overcome these obstacles by leveraging AI and adopting AI-centric operational strategies. Automating repetitive tasks, for instance, reduces the potential for human error and frees up skilled professionals to focus on more strategic, high-value activities. Similarly, AI can optimize resource allocation, predicting and adjusting resources needed for different software or AI model lifecycle stages, thereby improving operational efficiency.

Furthermore, AI-driven analytics can enhance decision-making processes, providing insights into performance bottlenecks, user behavior, and potential improvements. This allows teams to proactively address issues, refine strategies, and ensure that their products and services continue to meet or exceed user expectations.

In summary, while integrating AI into DevOps and MLOps presents challenges, it also offers powerful tools for overcoming these obstacles. By embracing AI, organizations can enhance their operational workflows, improve efficiency, and drive innovation, ultimately delivering superior software and AI-driven solutions.

AI-driven enhancements

The advent of AI in DevOps and MLOps has ushered in a new era of efficiency and productivity, primarily by automating traditionally manual and time-consuming tasks. Task automation via AI streamlines workflows and minimizes human errors, ensuring a more reliable and consistent output. Key areas where AI-driven task automation makes a significant impact include the following:

- **Code generation and testing**: AI models can generate boilerplate code, perform automated testing, and identify potential bugs or vulnerabilities, speeding up development cycles and enhancing software quality.

- **Automated configuration and deployment**: AI systems can analyze a software project's requirements, automatically configure environments, and deploy applications tailored to specific operational contexts.

- **Data management and analysis**: In MLOps, AI excels at automating data preprocessing, managing data pipelines, and analyzing datasets to identify patterns or anomalies. This is crucial for training and refining ML models.

Implementing AI for task automation requires careful planning, including selecting the right tools, defining clear objectives, and training team members to work alongside AI systems.

Boosting efficiency with AI-optimize resources and processes

AI's real-time ability to analyze big amounts of data allows it to optimize resources and processes in previously unattainable ways. This optimization results in cost savings, improved performance, and scalability. AI-driven efficiency enhancements include the following:

- **Resource allocation**: AI algorithms can predict the resources needed for various development and operational tasks, dynamically allocating or scaling resources based on actual demand. This ensures optimal use of infrastructure and reduces waste and costs.

- **Process optimization**: AI can analyze workflow data to identify bottlenecks and inefficiencies in the DevOps and MLOps pipelines. It can suggest improvements or automate adjustments to streamline processes, reducing cycle times and improving productivity.

- **Predictive maintenance**: It involves utilizing AI within MLOps to investigate the execution of ML models deployed in production. It forecasts potential model degradation and suggests proactive measures such as retraining or fine-tuning to maintain accuracy and effectiveness.

To leverage AI for efficiency, organizations need to invest in the right tools and platforms that integrate seamlessly with their existing workflows. They must also cultivate a continuous learning and adaptation culture, where AI-driven insights are actively used to refine and improve operational processes.

Integrating AI into DevOps and MLOps not only automates tasks and streamlines workflows but also unlocks new levels of efficiency and innovation. By embracing AI-driven enhancements, organizations can navigate the complexities of modern software development and ML, delivering high-quality products and services faster.

Task automation via AI Streamlining workflows

Incorporating AI into DevOps and MLOps can transform how teams handle daily tasks, from development to deployment. AI is particularly adept at automating routine and repetitive tasks, which, while necessary, can consume a significant amount of time and distract from more strategic work.

For instance, consider the process of code testing and deployment. Traditionally, these tasks require manual oversight to ensure new code integrates smoothly into an existing codebase without errors. By automating these AI processes, teams can instantly run tests whenever new code is committed and prepare it for deployment if it passes all checks. This speeds up the workflow and reduces the likelihood of human error, ensuring a higher output quality.

Moreover, AI can handle multiple tasks simultaneously and manage complex operations that would be difficult or impractical for human teams to execute efficiently. For example, an AI system could monitor hundreds of servers, instantly detecting and addressing failures or deploying updates as needed without waiting for human intervention. This level of automation leads to a smoother, faster workflow where team members can focus more on creative problem-solving and innovation.

AI not only automates tasks but also optimizes them. By examining massive amounts of data and recognizing patterns that might not be immediately obvious to humans, AI can suggest ways to allocate resources more effectively, thus saving time and reducing costs.

Take the example of a cloud-based application that experiences variable user traffic. An AI system can predict traffic peaks and troughs by analyzing historical usage data and other relevant factors, such as marketing campaigns or external events. It can then automatically scale server resources up or down in real-time, ensuring the application performs optimally without over spending on infrastructure during quieter periods.

In another scenario, AI can optimize software testing processes by prioritizing tests based on the likelihood of code failure. This means that the most critical tests are run first, and developers receive faster feedback on potential issues. AI can also help identify redundant processes within the pipeline and suggest improvements, such as combining certain operations to reduce processing time or eliminating unnecessary steps that contribute little value.

Furthermore, AI-driven analytics can provide actionable insights that help teams understand how they can improve their workflows. By continuously learning from new data, AI systems can refine their suggestions over time, ensuring that operations become more efficient as the system matures.

In short, by integrating AI into DevOps and MLOps, organizations can significantly enhance the efficiency of their operations. AI-driven task automation streamlines workflows by cutting the time spent on repetitive tasks and improving the accuracy and speed of these processes. Meanwhile, the optimization capabilities of AI ensure that resources are used more judiciously, processes are continuously improved, and overall operational efficiency is boosted. This leads to cost savings and enables teams to dedicate more effort towards innovation and strategic tasks, ultimately enhancing productivity and competitive edge.

Continuing with the discussion on AI-driven enhancements in DevOps and MLOps, the strategic integration of AI can provide further depth and functionality to various aspects of technology operations, especially in complex environments.

Expanding AI use cases

AI is continuously evolving, finding applications across diverse industries, and addressing complex challenges. From personalized healthcare and precision agriculture to financial fraud detection and environmental conservation, AI's adaptability is unlocking new opportunities. Its integration into day-to-day processes is revolutionizing business models, enhancing decision-making, and paving the way for innovative solutions. Let us focus on some of the following use cases.

Beyond basic automation and optimization

Beyond the initial levels of task automation and resource optimization, AI can also play a crucial role in more nuanced areas such as security, compliance, and predictive maintenance, all of which are integral to maintaining the integrity and efficiency of operations:

- **Security enhancements**: AI can significantly enhance security measures within DevOps by continuously monitoring network traffic and user activities to detect anomalies that could indicate potential security threats. For instance, an AI system can analyze patterns in access logs and automatically flag activities that deviate from normal behavior, such as an unusual time of access or access from a geographically anomalous location. By identifying these threats early, AI helps prevent potential breaches before they escalate into serious issues.

- **Compliance automation:** In industries where compliance with regulatory standards is crucial, AI can automate the monitoring and reporting processes to ensure ongoing compliance. For example, in the healthcare sector, where strict *U.S. Health Insurance Portability and Accountability Act* (*HIPAA*) regulations govern patient data protection, AI can help ensure that all data handling processes meet the required standards. It can automatically audit data access and modification trails, generate compliance reports, and alert administrators about potential non-compliance issues.

- **Predictive maintenance**: In the context of MLOps, predictive maintenance can be crucial for applications that rely on continuous uptime and performance. AI can predict hardware failures or software bottlenecks before they occur by analyzing trends and historical performance data. For instance, an AI system might indicate that a server will likely fail within the next month based on its current and past operational parameters. This allows teams to replace or repair components proactively, thus avoiding downtime and maintaining smooth operations.

- **Enhancing developer and operational productivity**: AI also has the potential to revolutionize developer productivity and operational efficiency by offering advanced coding assistance, more intelligent testing frameworks, and smarter resource allocation strategies.

- **Advanced coding assistance**: AI-powered tools can assist developers by suggesting code improvements, detecting potential bugs during the coding phase, and even writing code snippets automatically. These tools can adapt to the team's coding style and provide contextually relevant suggestions, reducing the cognitive load on developers and speeding up the development process.

- **Intelligent testing frameworks**: AI can enhance testing frameworks by dynamically adjusting testing strategies based on code complexity, change frequency, and historical bug data. This results in a more efficient testing process, focusing resources on high-risk areas and reducing overall testing time without compromising software quality.

- **Smarter resource allocation**: AI can suggest optimal resource allocation strategies by analyzing project timelines, team workflows, and resource usage patterns. This might involve recommending the best team composition for a project based on skills and past performance or dynamically adjusting project timelines in response to changes in team productivity or project requirements.

AI-driven enhancements in DevOps and MLOps are not just about automating existing tasks but also about transforming the operational landscape. AI empowers organizations to streamline their operations and innovate and adapt to changes more effectively by providing advanced capabilities for security, compliance, predictive maintenance, and productivity enhancement. The integration of AI in these fields marks a shift towards more proactive, predictive, and personalized operational processes, paving the way for future advancements in technology deployment and management.

As we explore more AI-driven enhancements in DevOps and MLOps, let us explore how AI can further revolutionize these fields by improving decision-making, enhancing team collaboration, and fostering a more agile development environment.

Enhanced decision-making with AI-driven analytics

AI can dramatically improve decision-making processes by providing teams with deeper insights derived from data analytics. This capability allows for more informed decisions at every stage of the development and operations process:

- **Real-time data analysis**: AI systems can analyze data in real-time, providing instant insights that help teams make quick decisions about their deployments or operational adjustments. For instance, if an AI system detects a performance drop in an application, it can immediately analyze traffic data, server health, and other relevant metrics to diagnose the issue. Based on this analysis, it can recommend immediate actions, such as scaling resources or applying specific fixes, thus minimizing downtime and improving service reliability.

- **Predictive analytics**: AI's capability to predict future drifts based on historical data is invaluable in planning and resource management. In DevOps, predictive analytics can forecast potential bottlenecks in software release pipelines, suggest the best times for releases, or warn of likely failures in upcoming versions. In MLOps, it can forecast model degradation and recommend preemptive retraining to maintain performance standards.

Fostering agile development and operations

Integrating AI into DevOps and MLOps also supports a more agile development environment, where adaptability and rapid response to change is key.

Technology development operational management

Refer to the following points for a better understanding:

- **Automated environment configuration**: AI can automate the setup and configuration of development and production environments, a process known as **IaC**. These speeds up the deployment process and ensures that environments are consistent, reproducible, and error-free. AI-driven tools can analyze requirements and automatically configure environments accordingly, reducing the manual effort required and allowing developers to focus on coding.

- **Dynamic resource allocation**: AI-driven dynamic resource allocation becomes crucial in agile environments where project needs can shift rapidly. AI systems can monitor project progress, resource usage, and team performance to allocate or reallocate resources dynamically—whether computational or human capital—to ensure optimal project outcomes.

- **Enhancing team collaboration and communication**: AI can also significantly improve communication and collaboration among distributed teams, a common scenario in today's globalized work environment.

- **Intelligent communication tools**: AI-powered communication tools can provide translation services, summarize lengthy discussions, and highlight meeting action items, ensuring that all team members, regardless of location or language proficiency, are on the same page. These tools can also prioritize messages based on urgency and relevance, ensuring that critical information is promptly attended to.

- **Virtual assistants for development teams**: AI-powered virtual assistants can manage routine inquiries about project status, code dependencies, or deployment schedules, freeing human team members for more complex queries and decision-making. These assistants can be integrated into tools like Slack or Microsoft Teams, providing seamless support without disrupting established workflows.

AI-driven enhancements in DevOps and MLOps automate and optimize tasks and transform teams operations by improving decision-making, supporting agile practices, and enhancing communication. As AI technologies evolve, their integration into DevOps and MLOps will likely become more profound, leading to smarter, faster, and more efficient operations. This ongoing evolution promises to keep organizations at the cutting-edge of technology development and operational management, ensuring they remain competitive in an increasingly digital world.

Use case of AI-driven DevOps optimization

A mid-sized software development company specializes in developing cloud-based applications for the financial sector. The company has multiple development teams working on various application development aspects, including frontend, backend, and database management. Let us consider the following challenge and solution for a better understanding:

- **Challenge**: The company faces challenges in managing its deployment environments efficiently. Each team requires different configurations, and manual setups have led to inconsistencies and delays. Additionally, the company struggles with optimal resource allocation during various development and deployment phases, often leading to resource shortages or wastage.

- **Solution**: The company decides to integrate AI-driven tools to automate environment setups and optimize resource allocation, aiming to streamline workflows and enhance team collaboration.

Implementation steps:

1. **Automated environment setup**:

    a. **IaC integration**: The company uses AI-enhanced IaC tools to automate the provisioning and management of development, testing, and production environments. These tools use scripts that automatically configure environments according to predefined parameters, ensuring consistency and reducing setup errors.

    b. **Dynamic adjustment**: The AI system monitors the usage patterns of these environments and adjusts configurations dynamically based on current needs, such as scaling up resources during heavy testing phases or scaling down during off-peak hours.

2. **Optimal resource allocation**:

    a. **Predictive resource management**: By implementing AI-based predictive analytics, the company can forecast resource needs based on project timelines, past usage data, and development cycles. This allows for preemptive resource allocation, ensuring that teams have the necessary resources before realizing they need them.

b. **Real-time monitoring and adjustment**: The AI system continuously monitors resource usage across all projects and reallocates resources in real-time to where they are needed most, preventing bottlenecks and reducing resource wastage.

3. **Enhancing team collaboration**:

a. **AI-powered collaboration tools**: The company implements an AI-driven communication platform that integrates with its existing tools. This platform automatically categorizes messages, flags important updates, and provides summaries of discussions to ensure all team members are updated without needing to sift through every message manually.

b. **Virtual assistants**: Each team is provided with a virtual assistant to answer queries related to project status, environment issues, or deployment schedules. This allows team members to focus more on development tasks without getting bogged down by administrative details.

4. **Outcome**: Integrating AI-driven tools significantly enhances the efficiency of the company's DevOps practices. Automated environment setups reduce the time and errors associated with manual configurations, while predictive and real-time resource management ensures optimal resource use, reducing costs and improving deployment speeds. The enhanced collaboration tools keep team members better informed and more closely aligned, leading to improved productivity and faster project completion rates.

This example demonstrates how AI-driven enhancements can solve common challenges in DevOps by automating complex and repetitive tasks, optimizing resource use, and improving team communication. As a result, the company not only boosts its operational efficiency but also enhances its ability to deliver excellent software products faster and more reliably.

Use case of LangChain for DevOps optimization

In this section, we will learn about the use case of LangChain for DevOps optimization:

- **Background**: A software development company specializes in creating enterprise solutions for the healthcare sector. Teams work across multiple regions on different software suite components.

- **Challenge**: The company faces challenges in maintaining smooth collaboration across its distributed teams, especially when understanding complex workflows and accessing up-to-date project information. Additionally, efficiently managing and provisioning development environments is a growing concern as the company scales.

- **Solution**: The company deploys LangChain to leverage its NLP capabilities to streamline information retrieval and command execution within its DevOps practices.

Implementation steps: Enhanced communication and information retrieval:

1. **Integration with internal systems**: LangChain is integrated with the company's internal project management tools, version control systems, and documentation repositories. This allows LangChain to fetch and provide information directly through natural language queries.

2. **Natural language interface**: Developers and operations staff can query LangChain using natural language to get real-time updates on project status, code deployment logs, or documentation updates. For instance, a team member can ask, *what is the status of the deployment on the patient management module?* and receive an immediate update.

3. **Automated environment configuration**:

   a. **Language-driven automation commands**: LangChain interprets environment setup and configuration commands. Developers can issue commands like `Setup a testing environment for the new billing module with the latest patches,` LangChain will execute the necessary scripts using the company's IaC tools.

   b. **Dynamic resource allocation**: By analyzing usage data and deployment schedules expressed in natural language, LangChain optimizes resource allocation, ensuring environments are scaled appropriately based on actual needs.

4. **Improving workflow efficiency**:

   a. **Automating routine inquiries**: LangChain handles routine inquiries about deployment schedules, codebase issues, or operational bottlenecks, reducing the workload on human team members and speeding up decision-making processes.

   b. **Training and adaptation**: LangChain is continuously trained on new data generated from project interactions, improving its understanding of the company's specific jargon and workflows, making its responses more accurate and relevant over time.

5. **Outcome**: With LangChain integrated into their DevOps ecosystem, the company experiences a significant boost in operational efficiency. Team members can access needed information and execute tasks more quickly through natural language commands, reducing the cognitive load and speeding up workflows. Automated environment management and dynamic resource allocation further enhance the company's agility, allowing it to scale operations effectively and reduce overhead costs.

In this example, LangChain is crucial in optimizing DevOps processes by leveraging its NLP capabilities to improve communication, automate tasks, and streamline workflows. This integration boosts productivity and enhances collaboration across distributed teams, enabling the company to maintain a high level of operational excellence as it grows.

Integrating an AI tool like LangChain can substantially improve the optimization of DevOps practices in a software development company compared to traditional methods without AI assistance.

LangChain in action

Integrating LangChain into DevOps workflows represents a strategic move towards leveraging AI, particularly in NLP, to automate and enhance software development and deployment processes.

Embedding LangChain in DevOps—integration steps

LangChain, a toolkit for building language model applications, can streamline various aspects of DevOps practices, from automating documentation to improving code quality through intelligent suggestions. Here are the key steps to embedding LangChain effectively into DevOps:

1. **Assessment and planning**: Identify the DevOps processes that could benefit most from NLP capabilities, such as automated documentation, code review, bug tracking, and customer feedback analysis.

2. **Setup and configuration**: Deploy LangChain within the existing DevOps infrastructure. This encompasses configuring the required hardware and software, setting up LangChain to integrate with other tools and platforms in the DevOps pipeline, and ensuring secure and scalable deployment.

3. **Integration with DevOps tools**: Integrate LangChain with existing DevOps tools and platforms, such as version control systems, CI/CD pipelines, and monitoring tools. This step may require custom scripts or plugins to enable seamless interaction between LangChain and these tools.

4. **Customization and training**: Customize LangChain models based on specific DevOps needs. This could involve training the models on proprietary codebases, documentation, or customer feedback to improve their accuracy and relevance.

5. **Deployment and monitoring**: Deploy the LangChain-enhanced tools into the DevOps workflow. Monitor the impact on productivity, quality, and efficiency, making adjustments as necessary to optimize the integration.

6. **Feedback loop**: Establish a feedback loop where developers and operations teams can provide input on LangChain's effectiveness in their workflows, leading to continuous improvement and refinement of the AI models.

LangChain automation case studies

Several organizations have successfully integrated LangChain into their DevOps and MLOps workflows, demonstrating the tangible benefits of AI-driven automation. Here are a couple of success stories:

- **Automated code documentation**: A software development company implemented LangChain to generate and update documentation for their codebase automatically. This saved developers considerable time and ensured that documentation was always up-to-date, reducing onboarding time for new team members.

- **Enhanced code review process**: Another organization used LangChain to streamline its code review process. By automatically analyzing pull requests and providing intelligent suggestions for improvements, LangChain helped improve code quality and short the time spent on code reviews.

- **Bug detection and resolution**: Leveraging LangChain's NLP capabilities, a tech firm automated the detection of bugs reported through customer feedback channels. LangChain analyzed customer tickets, identified potential bugs, and routed them to the appropriate teams, speeding up the resolution process.

- **Predictive analytics for CI/CD pipelines**: An enterprise used LangChain to analyze historical CI/CD pipeline data, predict potential bottlenecks, and suggest optimizations. This proactive approach helped reduce downtime and improve the efficiency of software deployments.

These success stories illustrate how embedding LangChain into DevOps can automate repetitive tasks, enhance operational efficiency, and contribute to higher-quality software products and services.

This is an example of a simplified and shorter version of integrating LangChain into a DevOps pipeline using a dummy dataset, with all code in one place:

1. **Setup the environment**: Install necessary dependencies:

```
pip install langchain openai pandas
```

2. **Create a Python script**: This script processes a dataset of reviews, uses LangChain to summarize them, and stores the results.

```
#Python
import openai
import pandas as pd
from langchain.chains import LLMChain
```

```python
from langchain.prompts import PromptTemplate
import os

# Setup OpenAI API key
openai.api_key = os.getenv("OPENAI_API_KEY")

# Dummy dataset with reviews
data = {"review_id": [1, 2, 3], "review_text": [
    "The product was great; I was really satisfied with the
quality!",
    "Terrible experience, the item broke after one use.",
    "Good value for money, but delivery was slow."
]}
df = pd.DataFrame(data)

# LangChain setup to summarize reviews
template = "Summarize this review: {review_text}"
prompt = PromptTemplate(input_variables=["review_text"],
template=template)
chain = LLMChain(prompt_template=prompt, llm=openai.Completion)

# Summarize reviews
df['summary'] = df['review_text'].apply(lambda x: chain.run(x))
print(df)
```

3. **Automate with CI/CD using GitHub Actions**: Create a **.github/workflows/ main.yml** file for CI/CD:

```yaml
#yaml
name: LangChain Pipeline
on:
  Push:
    branches:
      - main

jobs:
  build:
    runs-on: ubuntu-latest
    steps:
      - uses: actions/checkout@v2
      - name: Setup Python
        uses: actions/setup-python@v2
        with:
          python-version: '3.8'
```

```
    - name: Install dependencies
      run: |
        python -m pip install --upgrade pip
        pip install langchain openai pandas
    - name: Run the script
      run: python process_reviews.py
```

Key steps:

- **Setup**: Install dependencies and configure the *OpenAI API*.

- **Python script**: Loads reviews, generate summaries using LangChain and prints the results.

- **CI/CD pipeline**: Automates script execution whenever there is a push to the main branch.

This integration automates data summarization via LangChain in a simple, maintainable DevOps pipeline.

Mastering MLOps with AI

Scaling MLOps to keep pace with the growing demands of ML projects and deployments is a critical challenge that many organizations face. AI can play a role in enabling scalable growth by automating and optimizing key aspects of MLOps. Here are some strategies where AI aids in scaling:

- **Automated model training and tuning**: AI can automate the training and tuning of ML models, facilitating rapid exploration of model architectures and hyperparameters. This accelerates the development cycle and ensures that models are optimized for performance.

- **Dynamic resource allocation**: Leveraging AI to predict the computational resources required for different MLOps tasks (e.g., training, inference) allows for dynamic allocation and scaling of resources. This ensures that hardware constraints do not bottleneck projects and can scale efficiently as demands increase.

- **Version control and model management**: AI-enhanced systems can automate the versioning of datasets and models, keeping track of changes and experiments. This simplifies the complexity of managing multiple models in production and facilitates smoother rollouts of model updates.

Implementing these AI-driven strategies requires a robust MLOps framework that supports integration with AI tools and platforms. Organizations must also foster a culture that embraces automation and continuous improvement to fully leverage AI's benefits in scaling their MLOps efforts.

Implementing AI in MLOps efficiency insights

Incorporating AI into MLOps processes not only aids in scaling but also significantly boosts operational efficiency. Efficiency gains can be realized through various AI-driven enhancements, such as:

- **Predictive analytics for maintenance**: AI models can analyze operational data to predict issues or inefficiencies in ML workflows, allowing teams to address problems before they proactively impact performance. This predictive maintenance minimizes downtime and ensures that ML systems remain highly available and reliable.

- **Optimization of data pipelines**: By automating the optimization of data pipelines, AI ensures that data is processed and prepared for model training in the most efficient manner possible. This includes automatic data cleansing, augmentation, and feature engineering, which can significantly reduce the manual effort involved in preparing large datasets.

- **Enhanced collaboration and knowledge sharing**: AI can facilitate better collaboration among team members by automating experiments, results, and best practices documentation. This creates a knowledge base that can accelerate onboarding, encourage innovation, and prevent repeating past mistakes.

To implement AI effectively in MLOps, organizations must adopt tools and platforms compatible with their existing technology stack and support the seamless integration of AI capabilities. Training and development for team members are also essential to ensure they have the skills to leverage AI in their workflows.

Mastering MLOps with AI requires a technical and cultural shift. Automation, continuous learning, and data-driven decision-making are core operational practices. By adopting AI-driven strategies for scaling and efficiency, organizations can enhance their ability to develop, deploy, and maintain ML models, delivering greater value and achieving competitive advantage in the AI era.

Conclusion

Throughout this chapter, we have explored the transformative role of AI in DevOps and MLOps, highlighting how it automates tasks, enhances efficiency, and facilitates scalability. Incorporating AI into these operational frameworks signifies more than a passing trend; it denotes a fundamental transformation in developing, deploying, and maintaining software and ML models. AI has become an indispensable ally in achieving operational excellence by automating repetitive tasks, optimizing resource allocation, and enabling predictive analytics.

In conclusion, integrating AI into DevOps and MLOps is an ongoing learning, adaptation, and innovation process. By embracing AI, organizations can unlock new levels of operational excellence, paving the way for a future where technology and human ingenuity together create unprecedented value and possibilities. The era of AI-driven operational practices is just beginning, and its potential to reshape the technological landscape is limitless.

Points to remember

- **Adaptation**: AI systems continuously learn and adapt, improving their responses and suggestions.

- **Agile development**: AI supports agile methodologies by facilitating rapid response to changes and issues.

- **Automation**: AI automates repetitive tasks, reducing manual effort and minimizing errors.

- **Autonomy**: AI can operate independently to manage complex systems efficiently.

- **Change management**: AI facilitates smooth system change and update transitions.

- **Cloud optimization:** AI optimizes cloud operations for cost-efficiency and performance.

- **Compliance**: AI ensures compliance with regulations by automating monitoring and reporting.

- **Customization**: AI can be customized to meet specific operational needs.

- **Data integrity**: AI ensures the accuracy and consistency of data.

- **Data pipelines**: AI optimizes data flow throughout the ML lifecycle.

- **Deployment:** AI streamlines the deployment processes of new software versions.

- **Dynamic scaling**: AI dynamically scales resources based on demand.

- **Ethics**: AI systems consider ethical implications in their operations.

- **Evaluation**: AI evaluates system performance continuously to ensure optimal functioning.

- **Forecasting**: AI predicts future conditions and requirements in system operations.

- **Global reach**: AI helps manage globally distributed systems and teams.

- **Goal alignment**: Aligns AI operational goals with overall business objectives.

- **Growth management**: Manages scaling of operations effectively as the business grows.

- **Human augmentation**: AI augments human capabilities, not replacing them.

- **Improvement**: Constant improvement in processes through AI analysis and feedback.

- **Innovation**: AI-drives innovation by enabling new capabilities and efficiencies.
- **Integration**: Seamlessly integrates with existing systems and workflows.
- **Intelligence**: Brings intelligence to operations, making systems smarter.
- **Interoperability**: Ensures AI systems work well with other tech systems.
- **Intuition**: AI provides intuitive solutions to complex problems.
- **Maintenance**: AI simplifies and automates system maintenance tasks.
- **Management**: Enhances management of software and hardware resources.
- **Mapping**: AI helps in mapping dependencies and relationships in systems.
- **Model training**: AI automates and optimizes the training of ML models.
- **Monitoring**: Continuously monitors systems to ensure performance and security.
- **Natural language interaction**: Facilitates interactions via NLP.
- **Operational agility**: AI enhances the agility of operational processes.
- **Planning**: AI aids in strategic and operational planning.
- **Predictive capabilities**: AI predicts system failures and market changes.
- **Productivity**: Increases productivity across teams.
- **Quality assurance**: AI ensures high-quality of software and operations.
- **Real-time operations**: Manages and adjusts operational tasks in real-time, allowing immediate response to changes, issues, or demands.
- **Recommendations**: AI provides recommendations to optimize workflows.
- **Recovery**: Enhances disaster recovery capabilities through predictive insights.
- **Redundancy elimination**: Identifies and eliminates unnecessary processes.
- **Regulation compliance**: Ensures compliance with industry-specific regulations.
- **Reliability**: Increases the reliability of systems through continuous monitoring and adjustment.
- **Resource management**: Manages physical and virtual resources effectively.
- **Response time**: Reduces system response times through automated interventions.
- **Risk management**: Identifies potential risks and formulates strategies to mitigate them.
- **Robustness**: Enhances the robustness of operations with advanced AI tools.

- **Scalability**: Facilitates easy scaling of operations without compromising on quality or performance.

- **Simplicity**: Simplifies complex processes, making them more accessible to team members.

- **Stability**: Ensures stability in operations, even under fluctuating demands.

- **Standardization**: Helps standardize processes across departments and teams.

- **Strategic insights**: Provides insights that aid in strategic decision-making.

- **Sustainability**: Promotes sustainability by optimizing resource usage.

- **System integration**: Seamlessly integrates AI capabilities with existing systems.

- **Task delegation**: Delegates routine tasks to AI, freeing up human resources for strategic work.

- **Team alignment**: Aligns team efforts towards common operational goals.

- **Testing**: Automates testing processes, ensuring thorough and efficient execution.

- **Tool integration**: Integrates various tools into a cohesive operational framework.

- **Transparency**: Increases transparency in operations through clear, data-driven insights.

- **Troubleshooting**: Streamlines troubleshooting processes with AI-driven diagnostics.

- **Usage optimization**: Optimizes the usage of applications and systems for maximum efficiency.

- **Validation**: Validates system functionalities to ensure they meet required standards.

- **Version control**: Enhances version control practices to manage changes effectively.

- **Workflow optimization**: Refines workflows to enhance productivity and reduce costs.

Multiple choice questions

1. **What is the primary goal of integrating AI into DevOps and MLOps?**

    a. To reduce the need for human employees

    b. To enhance efficiency, automation, and scalability

    c. To complicate the software development process

    d. To increase the cost of operations

2. **Which AI technology is specifically mentioned for NLP tasks within DevOps workflows?**

   a. TensorFlow

   b. PyTorch

   c. LangChain

   d. GPT-3

3. **What is a major benefit of automating repetitive tasks with AI in DevOps and MLOps?**

   a. Increasing manual workload

   b. Slowing down the development process

   c. Reducing human error and increasing productivity

   d. Decreasing software quality

4. **Which of the following is not a direct outcome of AI-driven enhancements in operational workflows?**

   a. Improved code quality

   b. Reduced efficiency

   c. Faster development cycles

   d. Optimized resource allocation

5. **How does AI contribute to the scalability of MLOps processes?**

   a. By decreasing data processing speeds

   b. By manually tuning ML models

   c. By dynamically allocating computational resources

   d. By increasing the complexity of workflows

6. **What role does AI play in predictive maintenance within MLOps?**

   a. Predicting when ML models may degrade

   b. Decreasing the accuracy of models over time

   c. Ignoring potential operational issues

   d. Reducing the need for model monitoring

7. **How can AI-enhanced tools benefit the code review process in DevOps?**

   a. By lengthening the time needed for reviews

   b. By providing intelligent suggestions for improvements

   c. By ignoring bugs and vulnerabilities

   d. By reducing collaboration among team members

8. **Which strategy is not a part of effectively implementing AI in MLOps for operational efficiency?**

   a. Ignoring data privacy and security concerns

   b. Automating the optimization of data pipelines

   c. Using AI for enhanced collaboration and knowledge sharing

   d. Leveraging predictive analytics for operational insights

9. **What is a crucial aspect of adopting AI-driven strategies in DevOps and MLOps?**

   a. Maintaining a static approach to learning and adaptation

   b. Investing in continuous learning and technological adaptation

   c. Avoiding collaboration between development and operations teams

   d. Focusing solely on short-term operational goals

10. **Which of the following best describes the future outlook on AI's role in DevOps and MLOps?**

   a. Decreasing relevance and influence over time

   b. It remains unchanged in its applications and benefits

   c. Increasing automation but still requiring human oversight

   d. Growing influence and evolving role in strategic decision-making

   e. Completely replacing human involvement in operational processes

Answers

1	b
2	c
3	c
4	b
5	c
6	a
7	b
8	a
9	b
10	c

Questions

Real-world scenario questions related to integrating LangChain into a DevOps pipeline that can help reinforce learning:

Question 1: **You are working for an e-commerce platform that receives user reviews for various products daily. The management wants to automatically generate summaries of these reviews to identify key customer sentiments (positive, negative, or neutral). How would you integrate LangChain into a DevOps pipeline to process these reviews in real-time, and what steps would you take to ensure smooth automation and scaling?**

Answer: To achieve this, you have followed these steps:

- **Setup LangChain**: Integrate LangChain with OpenAI to summarize reviews automatically.

- **Data pipeline**: Use a data ingestion pipeline (e.g., AWS Lambda) to capture new reviews in real-time and pass them to the LangChain script.

- **CI/CD pipeline**: Automate the summarization process with a CI/CD pipeline (using GitHub Actions or Jenkins) to run the LangChain script every time new reviews are ingested.

- **Scaling**: Setup auto scaling to handle high review volume, using cloud services like AWS Lambda, ensuring that the pipeline can scale based on demand.

- **Storage**: Store the summaries in a database like AWS RDS or DynamoDB, where they can be queried for reporting and analytics.

Question 2: **Suppose you are building a content moderation system for a social media platform that detects offensive language. You plan to use LangChain to analyze user comments and generate a flagged list based on predefined keywords or sentiment. How would you integrate LangChain into your pipeline, and what considerations would you have for handling large volumes of user comments?**

Answer: To build this system:

- **LangChain integration**: Use LangChain to generate a summary or sentiment analysis for each user comment.

- **Real-time processing**: Use a queue-based system (e.g., AWS SQS) to capture incoming comments in real-time, which are then passed to LangChain for analysis.

- **CI/CD automation**: Automate the deployment and execution of your moderation model through CI/CD pipelines (GitHub Actions or Jenkins) to ensure it runs whenever new code or models are updated.

- **Handling high volume**: Use cloud-native services like AWS Lambda for processing comments asynchronously and automatically scaling to handle a high volume of requests.

- **Flagging system**: Store flagged comments in a database (like MongoDB or Elasticsearch) for further review or to trigger notifications to moderators.

Key terms

- **DevOps**: DevOps combines software development and IT operations to streamline the development life cycle and facilitate continuous delivery with high software quality.

- **ML Operations** (**MLOps**): MLOps, short for ML Operations, is a practice that encourages collaboration and communication between data scientists and operations professionals to manage the production ML lifecycle efficiently.

- **AI**: Enables machines to perform tasks that traditionally require human intelligence, including visual perception, speech recognition, decision-making, and translation.

- **LangChain**: It is a toolkit designed for building and deploying language model applications, facilitating the integration of NLP capabilities into software systems.

- **Automation**: It involves technology that enables a process or procedure without human intervention. DevOps and MLOps frequently utilize automation to enhance efficiency and minimize errors.

- **Scalability**: It refers to the ability of a system, network, or process to manage an increasing workload or its potential to be expanded to accommodate such growth.

- **Predictive analytics**: Predictive Analytics utilizes historical data, statistical algorithms, and ML techniques to assess the probability of future outcomes.

- **Resource allocation**: The efficient distribution of available resources, such as computing power and memory, among various tasks and processes.

- **Version control**: It is a system that tracks changes made to a file or group of files over time, enabling users to access specific versions later. It plays a critical role in managing software projects.

- **CI/CD**: This approach consistently delivers applications to customers by incorporating automation into the application development process. The key principles of CI/CD include continuous integration, deployment, and delivery.

- **Data pipelines**: Refer to a sequence of data processing stages where the output of one stage serves as the input for the next. They are utilized in ML for tasks such as data collection, processing, and model training.

- **Ethical AI**: Ethical AI is creating AI systems that operate ethically, meaning they consider fairness, privacy, and the impacts of automation on the workforce and society.

Join our book's Discord space

Join the book's Discord Workspace for Latest updates, Offers, Tech happenings around the world, New Release and Sessions with the Authors:

https://discord.bpbonline.com

CHAPTER 9

Future Trends in AI and LangChain

Introduction

This chapter examines the exciting future of **artificial intelligence** (**AI**) and LangChain, giving us a glimpse of what is next in AI. We will start by exploring the latest advancements in **machine learning** (**ML**), highlighting key changes and fresh ideas that will drive progress.

Next, we will see how AI expands into different industries, transforming how things work in various fields. A major part of our discussion will focus on how LangChain evolves alongside AI, with new features and improvements shaping its future.

We will also address the important challenge of using AI responsibly, ensuring it benefits everyone while remaining ethical. By the end of this chapter, you will clearly understand current AI trends and LangChain's role in the future.

Structure

The chapter covers the following topics:

- Introduction to future trends in AI and LangChain
- Advancements in machine learning
- AI in emerging industries

- Evolving role of LangChain
- Ethical considerations and responsible AI

Objectives

This chapter is designed to give book lovers a clear understanding of the latest trends and future developments in AI and LangChain. It explores recent breakthroughs in ML, how AI is being adopted across different industries, and the growing role of LangChain in the AI world.

Additionally, it highlights the importance of ethical AI and responsible development. By the end of this chapter, readers will gain valuable insights into the potential impact and opportunities AI advancements bring, with a special focus on how LangChain will help shape the future.

Introduction to future trends in AI and LangChain

This chapter explores the future of AI while considering its ethical impact. As AI continues to evolve, LangChain is emerging as a key player in this transformation. Our goal is to highlight the latest trends and exciting directions shaping the future of AI.

Think of this chapter as a glimpse into the future of technology. We will start by looking at recent breakthroughs in ML—the foundation of AI—where computers analyze data to make predictions and decisions. We will discuss these advancements and what they mean for the future.

But AI is not just about technology but also real-world applications. We will explore how AI is being used in different industries, such as healthcare, entertainment, and agriculture. Through real examples, we will see how AI is changing these fields and the impact it is making.

A major focus will be LangChain and its role in AI's growth. We will look at how it is keeping up with advancements and what improvements we can expect in the future. Think of LangChain as an evolving tool that becomes more powerful as AI progresses.

Finally, we cannot talk about AI's future without discussing ethics. As AI becomes a bigger part of daily life, ensuring it is developed and used responsibly is crucial. This chapter will explore creating AI that benefits everyone while minimizing risks.

Advancements in machine learning

ML is the driving force behind AI, constantly pushing the field toward new innovations and applications. In this section, we will explore the latest breakthroughs and emerging trends that are shaping the future of ML.

Recent breakthroughs and trends

ML allows computers to learn from data and make decisions with minimal human input. Recent advancements have greatly expanded what machines can achieve. For instance, deep learning algorithms have improved significantly, enabling computers to recognize patterns and make highly accurate predictions. These improvements have enhanced technologies such as image and speech recognition, **natural language processing** (**NLP**), and even the development of self-driving cars.

Another key breakthrough is **reinforcement learning** (**RL**), where algorithms learn through trial and error. They gradually optimize their decision-making by testing different actions and analyzing the results. This approach has been successfully applied in areas like reducing energy consumption in large data centers and developing strategies for complex games that require deep thinking and planning.

Future innovations and their potential impact

The future of ML is full of exciting possibilities that could transform many aspects of our lives and society. One area with great potential is personalized and predictive healthcare. Using ML to analyze large amounts of medical data, future technologies could offer highly tailored treatments and predict health issues before they become serious, greatly improving patient care and outcomes.

Another promising area is environmental sustainability. ML could be key in tackling climate change by optimizing energy usage, reducing waste, and helping scientists predict climate patterns more accurately. These advancements could lead to more effective policies and actions to protect the environment.

AI in emerging industries

The rise of AI in new areas marks a significant shift in how industries operate, innovate, and deliver services. This section will explore how AI is integrated into various sectors, transforming business models and opening new possibilities. As AI continues to expand, its impact is reshaping industries in once unimaginable ways.

Examination of AI's expansion into new sectors

AI is revolutionizing various industries with its remarkable ability to analyze vast amounts of data, streamline complex tasks, and uncover insights that were previously out of reach. Thanks to advances in ML, NLP, robotics, and more, AI is making a significant impact across sectors that were once far from technology-driven. These industries now adopt AI to overcome old challenges and better serve their customers.

Here are some examples of AI's transformative impact across different sectors:

Healthcare

AI is dramatically changing patient care and medical research. One of AI's key healthcare roles is analyzing medical images, such as x-rays, MRIs, and CT scans. AI-driven tools can identify subtle patterns and anomalies that human eyes might overlook. For instance, AI can detect early signs of diseases like cancer, often much earlier than traditional methods, leading to earlier intervention and improved treatment outcomes.

AI also enhances personalized medicine by analyzing genetic data to tailor treatment plans to individual patients. By understanding how a person's genes influence their response to medications or therapies, AI helps doctors create more effective treatment strategies that reduce side effects and increase the chances of success.

The ability of AI to quickly and accurately analyze complex medical data is transforming healthcare, leading to better diagnoses, customized treatments, and improved patient outcomes. As AI continues to evolve, its role in healthcare will grow, bringing more innovations to improve medical care and research efficiency.

Agriculture

AI is helping to enhance farming efficiency and sustainability. Farmers increasingly use AI to manage crops and improve yields while minimizing environmental impact.

AI is used in agriculture through drones equipped with sensors and imaging technology. These drones collect data on plant health, soil conditions, and crop stress, which AI systems then analyze to provide real-time insights. This allows farmers to make informed decisions about crop management.

AI also helps predict crop yields by analyzing growth patterns, which enables farmers to plan harvests and sales more effectively, reducing the risk of over or underproduction. Additionally, AI optimizes resource use, such as water and fertilizers, by recommending when and where to apply these inputs. This reduces waste, ensures plants receive what they need, and protects the environment by minimizing runoff.

By integrating AI, agriculture is becoming more precise and sustainable, leading to more efficient food production worldwide.

Financial services

AI is transforming security, risk management, and customer service in the financial sector:

- **Fraud detection**: AI systems can analyze millions of transactions in real-time to spot patterns or anomalies that may indicate fraud. By identifying suspicious activity early, AI helps protect financial institutions and their customers from losses.

- **Risk management**: AI models can predict defaults and market shifts more accurately than traditional methods, allowing financial institutions to adjust risk parameters and improve decision-making.

- **Customer service**: AI-powered chatbots and virtual assistants are revolutionizing customer service in finance. These tools can respond instantly to inquiries, guide users through complex financial processes, and offer personalized advice based on a customer's economic history. AI-driven personalization improves engagement and satisfaction.

- **Customized financial advice**: AI uses data analysis to offer tailored financial recommendations, helping customers with savings, investments, and budgeting.

AI is reshaping the financial services industry, making it more secure, efficient, and customer focused. As AI evolves, its role in finance will expand, bringing new tools for financial management and customer interaction.

Environmental conservation

AI is becoming an essential tool in ecological conservation, helping protect natural habitats and biodiversity:

- **Monitoring deforestation**: AI analyzes satellite images to track changes in forest cover, enabling more accurate deforestation monitoring. By identifying areas where trees are being cut down unsustainably, conservationists can take action to combat illegal logging and support reforestation efforts.

- **Tracking wildlife populations**: AI processes data from remote sensors and camera traps to track animal movements and population sizes, providing crucial insights into ecosystem health. AI can detect patterns, such as changes in migration routes or declining populations, prompting timely conservation efforts.

- **Forecasting natural disasters**: AI's predictive power helps forecast natural disasters, such as hurricanes, floods, and wildfires, with greater accuracy. By analyzing weather patterns and environmental conditions, AI can predict when and where these events will likely occur, allowing for better disaster preparedness.

AI is providing invaluable data and insights that help conservationists protect the environment. As AI advances, it will further enhance efforts to preserve natural resources and biodiversity.

Education

AI is transforming education by making learning more personalized and accessible. AI tailors' educational content to fit individual students' learning styles and paces, offering real-time feedback and support. This is especially helpful in addressing educational disparities:

- **Customizing learning materials**: AI analyzes student performance and preferences to adjust the lessons' complexity, pace, and content. For example, a student who excels in math but struggles with reading can receive more challenging math problems while getting support in reading.

- **Providing personalized feedback**: AI systems give immediate feedback to students, helping them understand their mistakes and improve faster. For example, AI can correct language students' pronunciation in real-time, allowing them to adjust and improve their skills more effectively.

- **Supporting diverse educational needs**: AI helps students with special needs by adapting learning environments to accommodate disabilities. Tools like voice-to-text and text-to-speech support students with difficulty reading or writing, making education more inclusive.

AI is making education more adaptive, inclusive, and effective. It helps bridge gaps in learning and ensures that all students, regardless of their background, receive quality education. As AI continues to develop, it promises to revolutionize the educational landscape further.

AI's integration into various sectors highlights its transformative power. AI is reshaping industries and opening up new possibilities from healthcare to agriculture, finance, environmental conservation, and education. As AI technology advances, its applications will continue to grow, introducing innovations that will further improve our world.

Evolving role of LangChain

LangChain is becoming an important tool as AI continues to transform different industries. This paper explores how LangChain is adapting and growing alongside the AI field, and it looks ahead to what new features and improvements could make it even more valuable in the future.

Originally, LangChain was created to facilitate developers' work with AI technologies. As AI continues to improve, LangChain has evolved to meet new challenges and help businesses use AI more effectively.

In the future, LangChain may offer better integration with emerging AI technologies. These updates could provide more user-friendly interfaces, allowing people with less technical knowledge to use AI. LangChain is also expected to add more customization options, making it a flexible solution for various industries. As AI becomes more widely used for real-time decision-making, predictive analytics, and automation, LangChain will likely incorporate features that support these areas, making it an even more essential tool for developers and businesses.

Overall, as LangChain continues to grow, its capabilities will strengthen, ensuring it plays a key role in bringing AI into various industries.

Anticipation of LangChain's adaptation in the AI ecosystem

As AI technology advances, LangChain is in a strong position to adapt and grow within this ever-changing landscape. Initially built to use language models for practical purposes, LangChain is ready to evolve by integrating the latest AI technologies and techniques. This adaptability is key to unlocking the full potential of language models and ensuring AI tools remain accessible and effective across a wide-range of industries.

One important area of development for LangChain is the integration of more specialized, domain-specific models. As ML models become more advanced and focused on specific industries, LangChain plans to incorporate these innovations to improve its applications. This will allow LangChain to offer more accurate, tailored solutions for the healthcare, finance, legal, and education industries.

LangChain aims to expand its usefulness by providing precise and effective solutions for diverse sectors. By continuously adapting to the latest advancements, LangChain will stay at the forefront of AI progress and become an even more valuable tool for real-world applications.

Predictions on potential features and enhancements

LangChain is expected to undergo several key improvements, making it even more versatile and user-friendly. Here are some of the anticipated enhancements:

- **Better integration with other AI tools**: In the future, LangChain will likely prioritize improving its compatibility with various AI systems. This will make it easier for users to connect LangChain with other AI platforms, allowing for smooth data exchange and better workflow efficiency. For example, users could link LangChain with market analysis or financial forecasting tools, streamlining operations and enhancing decision-making.

- **More customization and control**: As AI use grows, users will seek greater control over language models. LangChain may offer more customization features, allowing users to adjust settings to align with their needs and goals.

- **Commitment to ethical AI**: With rising concerns about AI's ethical implications, LangChain may incorporate features that promote responsible AI use. These could include tools to prevent bias, safeguard user data, and help users manage the risks and consequences of AI applications.

- **Support for collaborative AI projects**: LangChain may introduce new features that encourage collaboration, such as shared libraries, community-driven model creation, and collaborative platforms for working on complex AI projects. These additions could help users come together to build and improve AI solutions.

- **Improved language and cultural sensitivity**: To expand its reach globally, LangChain is expected to support more languages and dialects and become more attuned to cultural differences. This would make LangChain an even more valuable tool for businesses and users worldwide.

Ethical considerations and responsible AI

As AI advances quickly, it brings exciting opportunities and important ethical concerns. This section explores the moral issues related to AI's growth and suggests ways to ensure AI technologies are developed and used responsibly.

Analysis of the ethical implications of advancing AI

The ethical concerns surrounding AI are wide-ranging and complex, touching on privacy, security, fairness, and transparency. As AI becomes more integrated into our daily lives, questions arise about how these systems use personal data, make decisions, and sometimes reinforce biases. For example, AI algorithms may unintentionally reflect societal biases, leading to unfair outcomes in hiring, law enforcement, and loan approvals. Also, the lack of transparency in some AI systems makes it hard to understand how decisions are made, raising the need for accountability and trust.

Another big concern is AI's effect on jobs and the workforce. While AI can improve efficiency and create new job opportunities, it also risks displacing employment and increasing economic inequality. The ethical challenge is maximizing AI's benefits while minimizing its negative impact on workers and communities.

Strategies for promoting ethical and responsible AI development

To tackle the ethical concerns surrounding AI, a comprehensive approach is needed to ensure AI is developed and used responsibly. Here are some strategies that can help guide AI towards positive and fair outcomes:

- **Create and enforce ethical guidelines**: Ethical rules for AI development and use are essential. These rules should focus on fairness, transparency, accountability, and privacy. Governments and organizations can play a major role in setting and enforcing these standards.

- **Ensure transparency and explainability**: Building trust requires making AI systems more transparent and easier to understand. AI models should be able to explain their decisions in simple terms, and tools should be developed to help users inspect and question how these systems work.

- **Encourage diverse and inclusive AI teams**: Including people from different backgrounds, cultures, and areas of expertise in AI development can help identify and reduce biases. A more diverse team can ensure AI reflects various societal experiences and is inclusive of everyone.

- **Conduct impact assessments and audits**: Regular assessments and audits should be conducted to spot any potential ethical issues with AI systems before they are used. These checks should examine the social, economic, and environmental impacts of AI to ensure responsible decisions.

- **Promote public awareness and discussion**: Educating the public about AI and its potential effects is crucial for informed conversations and decision-making. Public discussions can also help understand society's values and expectations, guiding AI development in the right direction.

- **Work together globally on AI ethics**: AI affects people worldwide, so countries need to collaborate on setting ethical standards and regulations. This joint effort can help address challenges like data privacy and security and ensure the benefits of AI are shared fairly across borders.

By adopting these strategies, everyone involved in AI development—governments, businesses, developers, and the public—can help ensure that AI is used ethically, promoting fairness and positive societal outcomes.

Note: This use case illustrates how AI and LangChain can revolutionize agriculture by enabling real-time data analysis, predictive insights, and automated decision-making. Farmers and agronomists can easily access and apply complex insights without needing deep technical expertise by integrating AI models with NLP capabilities. This approach improves crop yield and resource efficiency and helps mitigate risks associated with climate change and market fluctuations. As AI and LangChain evolve, their role in smart farming will become even more impactful, making agriculture more data-driven, sustainable, and resilient.

How LangChain and AI work together in predictive crop management:

1. **Data collection and integration**:

    a. LangChain helps connect and process data from multiple sources, such as:

        i. Satellite imagery (weather patterns, soil conditions)

        ii. IoT sensors (moisture, temperature, nutrient levels)

        iii. Government and research databases (historical yield patterns, pest outbreaks)

    b. AI models analyze this vast dataset to identify patterns and correlations.

2. **NLP for querying data**:

   a. Farmers can interact with AI-driven assistants using natural language. For example:

      i. `What is the best time to plant wheat in my region?`

      ii. `Predict the risk of pest infestation for next month.`

   b. LangChain enables AI chatbots to understand these queries, fetch relevant data, and provide precise recommendations.

3. **ML for crop prediction**:

   a. AI models use historical and real-time data to predict:

      i. Optimal sowing and harvesting times

      ii. Expected crop yield based on weather and soil conditions

      iii. Potential risks such as drought, diseases, and pests

   b. LangChain integrates predictive models (e.g., regression models, deep learning) into AI pipelines, making the insights accessible via APIs and chat interfaces.

4. **Automated decision-making and recommendations**:

   a. LangChain helps orchestrate multiple AI tools to provide actionable recommendations.

   b. **Example**: If an AI model predicts drought risk, LangChain can:

      i. Suggest irrigation strategies

      ii. Generate a report with mitigation steps

      iii. Send alerts to farmers via SMS or chatbot

5. **AI-powered crop disease diagnosis**:

   a. Farmers can upload images of crops affected by disease.

   b. LangChain connects image recognition models (e.g., TensorFlow, OpenAI's CLIP) to detect diseases.

   c. The AI assistant suggests treatments based on research papers and expert recommendations.

6. **Integration with smart farming systems**:

   a. LangChain enables AI tools to work with automated farming systems:

      i. AI-powered drones for precision spraying.

ii. Smart irrigation systems that adjust water supply based on AI predictions.

iii. AI-driven marketplaces that suggest the best time to sell produce for maximum profit.

For the best understanding:

```
import os
import json
import numpy as np
import open
from langchain.chat_models import ChatOpenAI
from langchain.schema import HumanMessage
from sklearn.linear_model import LinearRegression
from PIL import Image
import torch
from torchvision import models, transforms

# Set OpenAI API Key (Replace with your key)
os.environ["OPENAI_API_KEY"] = "your_openai_api_key"

# Initialize LangChain AI Model
chat_model = ChatOpenAI()

def query_ai(question):
    """AI Chatbot for answering farming-related queries."""
    response = chat_model([HumanMessage(content=question)])
    return response.content

# Simulating IoT sensor & satellite data collection
def collect_data():
    """Simulating weather, soil, and sensor data."""
    data = {
        "temperature": np.random.uniform(15, 35),  # Degrees Celsius
        "humidity": np.random.uniform(20, 90),  # Percentage
        "soil_moisture": np.random.uniform(10, 60),  # Percentage
        "rainfall": np.random.uniform(0, 200),  # mm
        "historical_yield": np.random.uniform(1, 5),  # Tons per hectare
    }
    return data
```

```python
# Machine Learning for Crop Prediction
def predict_yield(data):
    """Predicts crop yield using a simple ML model."""
    model = LinearRegression()
    X_train = np.array([[15, 20, 10, 50], [30, 80, 50, 100], [25, 60, 40,
75]])  # Mock training data
    y_train = np.array([1.5, 4.0, 3.2])  # Mock yield data
    model.fit(X_train, y_train)
    X_test = np.array([[data['temperature'], data['humidity'], data['soil_
moisture'], data['rainfall']]])
    yield_prediction = model.predict(X_test)
    return yield_prediction[0]

# AI-Powered Crop Disease Diagnosis
def diagnose_disease(image_path):
    """Classifies crop disease using a pre-trained AI model."""
    model = models.resnet18(pretrained=True)
    model.eval()
    transform = transforms.Compose([
        transforms.Resize((224, 224)),
        transforms.ToTensor()
    ])
    image = Image.open(image_path)
    image = transform(image).unsqueeze(0)
    output = model(image)
    _, predicted_class = torch.max(output, 1)
    return f"Predicted Disease Class: {predicted_class.item()}"

# Automated Decision-Making
def generate_recommendations(data):
    """Provides AI-generated recommendations based on sensor data."""
    if data['soil_moisture'] < 20:
        return "Increase irrigation to prevent drought stress."
    elif data['temperature'] > 30:
        return "Consider heat-resistant crop varieties."
    else:
        return "Conditions are optimal for crop growth."

# Example Use Case Execution
sensor_data = collect_data()
```

```
yield_prediction = predict_yield(sensor_data)
decision_recommendation = generate_recommendations(sensor_data)
farm_query = "What is the best time to plant wheat in my region?"
chat_response = query_ai(farm_query)

# Print Results
print("Sensor Data:", json.dumps(sensor_data, indent=2))
print("Predicted Yield:", yield_prediction, "tons per hectare")
print("Farming Recommendation:", decision_recommendation)
print("AI Chatbot Response:", chat_response)

# Uncomment and add an image path to test crop disease detection
# print(diagnose_disease("path_to_crop_image.jpg"))
```

Output:

The output of the provided code depends on the randomness of the data collected and the AI responses. Below is an example output with mock values:

```
Sensor Data:
{
  "temperature": 22.78564821531997,
  "humidity": 57.73298279447029,
  "soil_moisture": 34.07257021525368,
  "rainfall": 94.85217029552093,
  "historical_yield": 3.40993589047745
}
Predicted Yield: 2.9871275959911463 tons per hectare
Farming Recommendation: Conditions are optimal for crop growth.
AI Chatbot Response: The best time to plant wheat depends on your region's climate. Generally, wheat is planted in early spring or fall. For optimal growth, make sure to plant it before the first frost.
```

Key notes:

1. **Sensor data**: The data (temperature, humidity, soil moisture, rainfall, historical yield) is generated randomly within specified ranges, so the values vary each time the code runs.

2. **Predicted yield**: Based on the mock training data in the linear regression model.

3. **Farming recommendation**: The recommendation is based on the current sensor data (in this case, optimal conditions).

4. **AI chatbot response**: A generic response to the farming-related query (**best time to plant wheat**).

5. **Crop disease detection**: The part where crop disease is diagnosed has been commented out. If uncommented and provided with a valid image path, it will return a prediction of the disease class based on a pre-trained ResNet-18 model.

To run the provided code efficiently in a cloud environment, you should consider the following key points about the cloud setup:

1. **Cloud provider selection**:

   a. Choose a cloud provider that offers the necessary infrastructure for ML, AI, and IoT applications. Examples:

      i. **AWS**: Use services like *AWS SageMaker* (for ML model training and deployment), *AWS Lambda* (for serverless functions), and *Amazon EC2* (for scalable compute resources).

      ii. **Azure**: Use *Azure ML* (for ML workflows), *Azure Functions* (for serverless computing), and *Azure Virtual Machines* (*VMs*) (for scalable compute).

      iii. **Google Cloud**: Leverage *Google AI Platform* for training and deploying ML models, and *Google Compute Engine* for VMs.

2. **Compute resources**:

   a. **VMs**: Use scalable VMs to run your Python code, especially for processing heavy tasks like AI model predictions (e.g., crop disease classification).

   b. **Serverless functions**: Use serverless architectures like AWS Lambda or Azure Functions for automating the data collection, AI query, and decision-making process without worrying about managing the underlying infrastructure.

   c. **GPU instances**: Since the code includes deep learning models (e.g., ResNet-18 for disease classification), you might need GPU-enabled instances (e.g., *AWS P3* instances or *Azure N-series* VMs) to handle image classification efficiently.

3. **Storage**:

   a. **Object storage**: For storing sensor data and images (e.g., crop images for disease detection), use cloud object storage like *AWS S3*, *Azure Blob Storage*, or *Google Cloud Storage*.

   b. **Database**: If you plan to store and manage historical data or sensor data, use cloud databases like *AWS RDS*, *Azure SQL Database*, or *Google Cloud Firestore*.

4. **Networking**:

   a. Ensure that your cloud resources are properly connected to enable seamless communication between different components (IoT sensors, AI models, and storage). You can use cloud networking services like *AWS VPC* or *Azure virtual network* for isolated and secure networks.

5. **ML services**:

   a. **AI model training and deployment**: Use managed services like AWS SageMaker or Azure ML for training and deploying ML models. These services provide an end-to-end workflow, from training to deployment. If you want to deploy the models manually, you can use Docker containers and deploy them using Kubernetes (e.g., *AWS EKS*, *Azure AKS*, or *Google GKE*) for container orchestration.

6. **AI/ML model support**:

   a. Ensure that the cloud provider supports deep learning libraries like PyTorch (for ResNet), TensorFlow, and scikit-learn. You can use cloud environments with pre-configured AI environments (e.g., *AWS Deep Learning AMIs* or *Azure ML environments*).

7. **Serverless and event-driven architecture**:

   a. You can setup an event-driven architecture where sensor data triggers certain actions automatically. For instance:

      i. **IoT sensors**: Use services like *AWS IoT Core* or *Azure IoT Hub* to connect and manage IoT devices for data collection.

      ii. Trigger events such as data collection, model prediction, and AI query generation when new data arrives or a certain threshold is met.

8. **Cost management**:

   a. Monitor the cloud costs associated with running the compute-intensive tasks. Leverage auto scaling to scale resources dynamically based on demand, and use services like *AWS Cost Explorer* or *Azure Cost Management* to track your usage.

9. **Deployment pipeline (Optional)**:

   a. If you plan on automating the workflow, use CI/CD pipelines such as *AWS CodePipeline* or *Azure DevOps* to continuously deploy and monitor the application.

10. **Security and access management**:

   a. Ensure proper security measures such as access control (via IAM roles), data encryption (in-transit and at-rest), and secure communication channels between services.

Sample architecture diagram:

    i.   IoT sensors | cloud storage (S3/Blob) | ML model (SageMaker/AML) | compute instance (EC2/VM) | prediction and recommendations | chatbot (OpenAI API) | farming advisory system.

11. **Cloud environment setup example (AWS)**:

    a.   AWS EC2 instance for running the Python script.

    b.   Install Python, necessary libraries (**torch**, **langchain**, **scikit-learn**, etc.), and setup the environment.

    c.   AWS Lambda can trigger model predictions when new data is received from IoT sensors.

    d.   AWS S3 to store crop images and sensor data.

    e.   AWS SageMaker for running pre-trained models or custom ML models like ResNet.

    f.   *Amazon API Gateway* to create REST APIs for serving the AI model for the chatbot queries.

By leveraging cloud infrastructure, you can scale the system based on demand, efficiently manage sensor data, and handle the computational load of ML models for crop prediction and disease diagnosis.

Conclusion

This chapter explores the growth and future of AI and LangChain, showing their broad impact across different industries and the ethical issues that come with their use. AI is advancing through new ML techniques, creating opportunities in healthcare and sustainability. The chapter highlights how AI is transforming industries like healthcare and agriculture and addressing global challenges. LangChain is also becoming more important in connecting AI's potential with practical uses.

Ethical concerns, such as the need for clear guidelines, transparency, and diverse development teams, are crucial as AI evolves. The future of AI looks promising, with continued innovation expected to benefit society. LangChain will play a key role in making AI more accessible and effective, helping responsibly integrate these technologies into our daily lives.

Points to remember

- **Innovation in ML**: The core of AI's future lies in the ongoing advancements in ML technologies. These innovations are technical achievements and pathways to solving complex problems and increasing various aspects of human life.

- **AI's expansion into new industries**: AI's influence expands beyond traditional tech spaces into healthcare, agriculture, and environmental conservation sectors. This diversification showcases AI's versatility and capacity to drive significant changes across the global economy.

- **LangChain's evolving role**: LangChain is not just adapting, but innovating in the dynamic AI ecosystem. Its future enhancements are poised to revolutionize the accessibility, efficiency, and industry-specific capabilities of AI tools. This progress in LangChain's development mirrors the broader trend of AI becoming more integrated and essential in various applications, including agriculture.

- **Ethical and responsible AI development**: As AI technologies advance, ethical considerations become increasingly critical. Addressing privacy, bias, and accountability issues is essential for fostering trust in AI systems and ensuring their benefits are distributed equitably.

- **The importance of collaboration**: The future of AI and LangChain will be shaped by collaborative efforts across disciplines, industries, and borders. Sharing knowledge, resources, and ethical guidelines will be key to harnessing AI's full potential while mitigating risks.

- **Educating and engaging the public**: Public understanding and engagement are crucial and integral for the responsible development and deployment of AI. Educating society about AI's benefits and challenges can empower individuals to shape a future where technology aligns with human values and needs.

- **International cooperation on AI standards**: Given AI's global impact, international cooperation is vital for establishing standards and regulations that ensure the safe, ethical, and effective use of AI technologies worldwide.

Multiple choice questions

1. **What is a key area of advancement in machine learning?**

    a. Decrease in data usage

    b. Simplified algorithms for easy understanding

    c. Improvements in image and speech recognition

    d. Reduction of computing power needed

2. **How is AI impacting the healthcare industry?**

    a. By reducing the number of healthcare workers

    b. By providing personalized treatment plans

    c. By eliminating the need for physical hospitals

    d. By decreasing the accuracy of diagnoses

3. **Which of the following is a focus for future LangChain enhancements?**

   a. Decreasing user customization options

   b. Limiting the number of languages supported

   c. Enhancing interoperability with other AI systems

   d. Reducing transparency in AI decision-making

4. **What is a significant ethical concern in the development of AI?**

   a. The overproduction of AI models

   b. The potential for AI to amplify existing biases

   c. The complete automation of all jobs

   d. The reduction of internet speeds

5. **AI's expansion into new industries showcases its:**

   a. Limited application to specific fields

   b. Dependence on traditional computing methods

   c. Versatility and transformative potential

   d. Inability to process large datasets

6. **Which strategy is important for promoting ethical AI development?**

   a. Ignoring public opinion on AI uses

   b. Developing and enforcing ethical guidelines

   c. Focusing solely on maximizing AI efficiency

   d. Limiting AI applications to entertainment

7. **The future of LangChain might include:**

   a. Reduced focus on ethical AI features

   b. Increased barriers to AI accessibility

   c. Collaborative AI development tools

   d. A shift away from language-based models

8. **One potential innovation in machine learning is:**

   a. Decreasing algorithm accuracy for faster outputs

   b. Personalized healthcare applications

   c. Phasing out reinforcement learning

   d. Eliminating the need for data in AI training

9. **A crucial aspect of responsible AI involves:**

    a. Keeping AI development within a single country

    b. Ensuring AI systems are transparent and accountable

    c. Avoiding the use of AI in public sectors

    d. Prioritizing AI applications in gaming

10. **LangChain's future role in AI: LangChain is anticipated to play a central role in bridging practical applications and AI capabilities in the future. Its unique framework and platform, leveraging language models and AI, are expected to facilitate the development and application of AI-driven solutions across various domains.**

    a. Diminishing in importance as other technologies take precedence

    b. Becoming obsolete due to advancements in other areas

    c. Central to bridging practical applications and AI capabilities

    d. Limited to theoretical research without practical applications

Answers

1	c
2	b
3	c
4	b
5	c
6	b
7	c
8	b
9	b
10	c

Key terms

*   **AI**: Is the reproduction of human intelligence processes by machines, notably computer systems. It encompasses learning, reasoning, and self-correction.

*   **ML**: A subset of AI that develops algorithms to learn and make predictions or decisions based on data.

- **LangChain**: a framework or platform that leverages language models and AI to facilitate the development and application of AI-driven solutions across various domains.

- **Deep learning**: Is a ML style that uses layered (deep) neural networks to analyze patterns in data. It is often used for image and speech recognition.

- **RL**: Is an area of ML where an algorithm learns to make decisions by performing certain actions and assessing the outcomes to maximize some notion of cumulative reward.

- **NLP**: Is an AI field that aims to improve the interface between computers and humans through natural language. It enables computers to understand, interpret, and generate human language.

- **The significance of ethical AI**: Ethical AI involves designing, developing, and deploying AI systems that are morally sound and respect human rights and values. This approach is crucial for ensuring the responsible and equitable use of AI.

- **The value of transparency in AI**: Transparency in AI is a fundamental principle that AI systems should be understandable and their operations should be easily explained. This promotes trust and accountability, key factors in the responsible use of AI.

- **AI bias**: Systematic and unfair discrimination embedded within AI algorithms often reflects existing societal prejudices or stems from biased datasets.

- **Interoperability**: Refers to the capability of various systems, devices, applications, or artifacts to connect and transmit seamlessly without requiring effort from the end user.

- **Predictive analytics**: Employs old data, statistical algorithms, and ML practices to assess the probability of future outcomes.

- **Responsible AI**: Is an approach to AI development that aims to ensure AI systems are dependable, safe, fair, and respectful of privacy and human rights.

- **Data privacy**: The right of individuals to control or influence what information related to them is collected and used.

- **Algorithmic transparency**: is the principle that algorithms' processes, decisions, and operations should be open and understandable to users and stakeholders.

- **Sustainable AI**: The pursuit of AI technologies and practices that are environmentally responsible and sustainable, aiming to minimize the ecological footprint of AI systems.

APPENDIX 1
Additional Resources and References

Introduction

Welcome to the appendix section of our journey through LangChain and the broader **artificial intelligence** (**AI**) world. As we have navigated through AI's concepts, applications, and potential with the aid of LangChain, the learning continues. AI is constantly evolving, and there is always more to discover. We have compiled a list of more resources and references to help you continue your exploration and deepen your understanding. These resources are designed to provide you with various perspectives, deepen your knowledge, and inspire your AI projects.

Structure

The chapter covers the following topics:

- Books and academic journals
- Online courses and tutorials
- Websites and blogs
- Conferences and workshops
- Community and forums

Objectives

This chapter aims to equip readers with a curated list of educational materials and platforms that foster further exploration and deepening knowledge in AI and LangChain. It provides diverse avenues for learning, from foundational texts and cutting-edge research to practical courses and vibrant communities, thereby supporting continuous growth and innovation in AI. This appendix serves as a bridge for readers eager to expand their AI journey beyond this book, offering resources catering to various expertise and interest levels.

Books and academic journals

Books and academic journals form the bedrock of any intellectual pursuit, offering foundational knowledge and cutting-edge insights. For AI enthusiasts, these resources provide a structured path to understanding complex topics, from introductory concepts to specialized domains like deep learning and ethical considerations. Below, we highlight seminal texts and journals pivotal to mastering AI and driving impactful research:

- **AI**: *Artificial Intelligence: A Modern Approach* by *Stuart Russell* and *Peter Norvig*

    o A detailed textbook that explores the basics of AI, covering its historical development, key concepts, and diverse methodologies.

- **Deep learning**: *Deep Learning* by *Ian Goodfellow, Yoshua Bengio*, and *Aaron Courville*

    o It focuses on deep learning, one of the key technologies behind recent advances in AI, including image and speech recognition applications.

- **Journal of Artificial Intelligence Research** (JAIR): Edited by *Craig Boutilier,* this journal explores foundational theories and applications in AI.

    o It is an open-access journal that publishes high-quality research articles in all areas of AI.

    o **Journal of Artificial Intelligence Research (JAIR)**: A leading academic journal focusing on theoretical and applied AI research. Edited *by Michael L. Littman* and others, it covers a wide array of topics, from foundational theories to real-world applications.

Online courses and tutorials

Online learning has revolutionized how individuals access knowledge and skills in various fields, including AI. Platforms like *Coursera, edX*, and *Fast.ai* offer comprehensive courses catering to beginners and advanced learners. These platforms provide an accessible gateway for anyone looking to understand and apply AI concepts in practical settings. Here is a detailed look at some of the top courses and tutorials available for AI education:

- **Coursera (AI For Everyone by Andrew Ng)**:

  o **Overview**: This course, designed by *Andrew Ng*, a prominent figure in the AI community, demystifies AI for non-technical audiences. It covers the basic concepts of AI, its applications, and its potential impact on society.

  o **Key features**:

    ▪ **Broad audience**: It is aimed at a wide range of learners, including those without a technical background, making AI concepts accessible to business leaders and everyday consumers.

    ▪ **Real-world applications**: The course illustrates how AI is integrated into industries like healthcare, transportation, and customer service, providing learners with a clear sense of how AI is transforming the world.

    ▪ **Ethical considerations**: This section discusses the moral implications of AI development and deployment, fostering a responsible approach to AI technologies.

- **edX (Introduction to Artificial Intelligence)**:

  o **Overview**: This introductory course provides a foundation in AI, covering key principles and techniques, including machine learning, reasoning, and robotics. It is suitable for learners who wish to understand the technical aspects of AI.

  o **Key features**:

    ▪ **Comprehensive curriculum**: This program offers a deep dive into the core topics of AI, ensuring that students gain a solid foundation in the field.

    ▪ **Interactive learning**: Includes interactive quizzes and hands-on projects that help solidify the concepts taught in lectures.

    ▪ **Expert instructors**: These courses are instructed by professors who possess profound knowledge of AI and deliver extensive insights into its theoretical foundations and practical applications.

- **Fast.ai**:

  o **Overview**: Fast.ai is a learning platform that makes deep learning accessible to coders who want to learn by doing. The courses are designed to be practical and based on implementing models from scratch.

  o **Key features**:

    ▪ **Hands-on approach**: Encourages learning by doing, with courses designed around coding exercises and real-world projects.

- **Community support**: It boasts a vibrant community of learners and experts who contribute to forums, share insights and help troubleshoot issues.

- **Free resources**: All courses are free, including additional resources like reading materials and lecture videos, making them highly accessible.

Additional learning resources

Let us look at some more sources that can help you polish your knowledge:

- **Google for Education**: *Google* offers a range of courses and resources for learning AI and machine learning, catering to various skill levels. These resources are particularly useful for learners who apply Google's AI tools in their projects.

- **Microsoft Learn for AI**: This platform offers learning paths and modules focused on AI engineering and data science, utilizing *Microsoft's Azure* platform. It is ideal for learners looking to integrate AI solutions in business environments.

- **IBM AI Learning**: *IBM's* cognitive class provides courses in AI and data science, emphasizing the application of AI in enterprise settings using IBM's technology stack.

- **Udacity's Artificial Intelligence Nanodegree**: Offers a more intensive, project-based learning environment. Students work on practical AI problems and projects that can be incorporated into their professional portfolios.

- **AI for Medicine by Coursera**: This specialized course, also by *Andrew Ng*, focuses on how AI can be leveraged to improve medicine and patient care. It covers medical imaging, diagnosis, and personalized medicine.

Websites and blogs

AI, keeping abreast of the latest trends in research and applications, is crucial. Websites and blogs are essential in disseminating knowledge and fostering community engagement among AI enthusiasts, researchers, and professionals. Here is a closer look at some leading platforms where cutting-edge AI discussions and insights are shared:

- **Towards Data Science on Medium**:
  - **Overview**: Medium platform is a hub for data scientists and AI enthusiasts to share insights and knowledge. It includes articles authored by various contributors, from seasoned experts to those new to the field.
  - **Key features**:
    - **Wide range of topics**: Covers everything from basic data science techniques to complex AI research, making it suitable for readers at all levels.

- **Community-driven content**: Articles are contributed by a community of writers, providing a variety of perspectives and voices.

- **Practical advice and tutorials**: Many posts include useful tips, code snippets, and tutorials, particularly valuable for those looking to apply AI in their projects.

- **Google Blog**:

  - **Overview**: This official Google blog offers a behind-the-scenes look at how one of the world's leading tech companies applies AI in various projects and research initiatives.

  - **Key features**:

    - **Cutting-edge research**: Featuring updates on the latest research and innovations in AI being developed by Google engineers and scientists.

    - **Real-world applications**: Showcases how Google integrates AI technologies into products and services that people use daily, such as *Google Assistant, Google Photos*, and more.

    - **Insights from experts**: Featuring posts written by Google's AI researchers and developers, who provide expert insights into the technology and its future.

- **OpenAI News**:

  - **Overview**: OpenAI maintains this blog to document its research and advancements in AI, particularly focusing on deep learning and **artificial general intelligence (AGI)**.

  - **Key features**:

    - **Research updates**: Provides detailed accounts of ongoing research projects, including machine learning models and algorithm developments.

    - **Commitment to safety and ethics**: OpenAI strongly emphasizes the ethical implications of AI, which is often a key theme in its blog content.

    - **Open-source contributions**: Regularly feature updates on new technologies and tools that have been open-sourced, encouraging community participation and collaboration.

Some additional resources are mentioned below:

- **AI Trendz**: This website offers up-to-date news, analysis, and insights into current AI technologies and industry trends. It is particularly useful for professionals who understand how AI can impact their businesses.

- **The AI Report by Synced**: It provides a global perspective on AI developments, highlighting significant research, policy, and market moves in the field.

- **MIT Technology Review (Artificial intelligence)**: This *MIT* resource covers the latest discoveries, trends, and controversies in AI, written and curated by some of the leading thinkers in the field.

- **DeepMind Blog**: As a leader in AI research, *DeepMind*'s blog shares insights into their latest research papers, breakthroughs in AI, and discussions on the broader implications of AI technology.

- **The Gradient**: This site aims to be a voice for discussion in AI, offering thoughtful commentary and deep dives into current AI technology and trends.

Conferences and workshop

Conferences and workshops are crucial in disseminating new knowledge and fostering collaborations in AI. They serve as platforms where academics, researchers, and industry professionals can share insights, discover new advancements, and discuss the future directions of AI technologies. Two of the most significant conferences in this field are the **Neural Information Processing Systems (NeurIPS)** and the **International Conference on Machine Learning (ICML)**, each of which caters to various facets of AI research and applications. Let us read about them in detail:

- **Conference on NeurIPS**:
  - **Overview**: NeurIPS is one of the most highly regarded AI conferences, especially focusing on neural networks and their practical applications. It brings together a diverse group of participants from academia and industry to explore various aspects of neural information processing systems.

  - **Key features**:
    - **Broad spectrum of topics**: Covers a wide range of topics from machine learning, computational neuroscience, statistics, and cognitive science, reflecting the interdisciplinary nature of AI.

    - **Innovative research presentations**: This section features presentations on the latest research advancements, often revealing breakthroughs in neural networks, deep learning techniques, and their applications.

    - **Workshops and tutorials**: Includes numerous workshops and tutorials, which provide more interactive and focused sessions on specific topics, facilitating deeper understanding and skills development.

- **ICML**:
  - **Overview**: ICML is a globally recognized conference highlighting machine learning innovations and developments. It is known for its rigorous

peer review process and high-quality research contributions, making it a must-attend event for those involved in machine learning research and development.

o **Key features**:

- **Premier research**: It showcases cutting-edge research in machine learning, encompassing supervised and unsupervised learning, reinforcement learning, and deep learning methods.

- **Industry and academic participation**: Attracts a balanced mix of academia and industry leaders, providing a rich environment for networking and collaboration.

- **Diverse formats**: The conference offers a variety of formats, including paper presentations, poster sessions, and invited talks, catering to different learning and communication styles.

Additional notable AI conferences and workshops are mentioned below:

- **Conference on Computer Vision and Pattern Recognition (CVPR)**: This leading annual conference focuses on advancements in computer vision and pattern recognition and showcases pioneering scientific research within these domains.

- **Association for the Advancement of Artificial Intelligence (AAAI)**: Held annually, this event covers a wide spectrum of AI topics and applications, making significant contributions to both the theoretical and applied dimensions of AI.

- **Conference on Knowledge Discovery and Data Mining (SIGKDD)**: This conference is centered on data science and covers data mining, knowledge discovery, large-scale data analytics, and big data, presenting the newest algorithms and their applications.

- **Annual Meeting of the Association for Computational Linguistics (ACL)**: This conference is dedicated to natural language processing and computational linguistics, providing a platform for researchers from around the globe to discuss computational techniques for linguistic analysis.

- **Robotics: Science and Systems (RSS)**: This annual academic conference covers many robotics-related topics, providing a platform for discussing recent innovations and progress in robotic systems and science.

Community and forums

AI, communities, and forums are essential for creating a collaborative environment where individuals can collectively exchange knowledge, address challenges, and innovate. Platforms, like *Stack Overflow* and *GitHub* are at the forefront of this collaborative environment, offering spaces where newcomers and experienced professionals can learn, contribute, and grow. Here is an expanded look at how these platforms support the AI community:

- **Stack Overflow**:
  - **Overview**: Stack Overflow is one of the most reputable online communities for developers. It offers a platform where users can pose questions, exchange knowledge, and benefit from each other's experiences across various programming-related topics, such as AI and machine learning.
  - **Key features**:
    - **Q&A model**: Stack Overflow's **questioning and answering (Q&A)** format allows users to post specific programming issues they are facing and receive answers from the community. This model helps keep the information organized and searchable.
    - **Tagging system**: Users can tag their questions with specific topics such as Python, machine learning, deep learning, or TensorFlow, making it easier to find and solve AI-related issues.
    - **Reputation and badges**: The platform encourages quality contributions through a reputation system. Users earn points and badges for helpful answers, which helps establish credibility within the community.
- **GitHub**:
  - **Overview**: GitHub is a leading software development platform, millions of developers use it to share code and build projects. It is particularly significant in the AI field for hosting open-source projects related to machine learning, deep learning, and data science.
  - **Key features**:
    - **Repository hosting**: GitHub provides a platform for developers to host and review code, oversee projects, and collaborate on software development alongside millions of other users.
    - **Collaboration features**: Tools like pull requests, branches, and commits facilitate collaboration among developers working on the same projects.
    - **Open-source community**: Many AI projects are open-sourced on GitHub, allowing anyone to contribute to their development, fork the project, or use the code in their projects.
- **Impact on AI community**:
  - **Resource for learning and collaboration**: This provides access to cutting-edge AI projects and the opportunity to collaborate with other developers worldwide.

- o   **Innovation and development**: It facilitates the rapid development and dissemination of AI technologies, lowering barriers to entry for developers who want to experiment with new ideas.

Additional AI communities and forums are mentioned below:

- **Kaggle**: Known for its machine learning competitions, Kaggle also provides a forum where data scientists and AI researchers can connect, discuss, and collaborate on data science projects and competitions.

- **Machine learning**: A subreddit dedicated to machine learning where enthusiasts and experts discuss trends, research, and various AI-related topics.

- **AI forums by major AI research institutes**: Many institutions, such as DeepMind, OpenAI, and MIT, have forums or community pages to share updates and engage with the community on various AI research topics.

- **LinkedIn Groups and Special Interest Groups (SIGs)**: Professional networking sites like *LinkedIn* host numerous groups and forums dedicated to AI topics, providing networking opportunities and professional discussions.

Conclusion

The resources and references listed here serve as an invaluable foundation for anyone venturing into the expansive realm of AI. However, it is important to remember that the journey into AI is continuous learning and adaptation. The field is dynamic and rapidly evolving, with new methodologies, frameworks, and areas of application being developed at an unprecedented pace.

To truly excel in AI, it is crucial to maintain a curious mindset and a proactive approach to learning. Regular interaction with various resources, including academic journals, interactive online platforms, and community involvement, can help you connect with others who share a passion for AI. These interactions foster collaborations, ignite innovation, and result in groundbreaking projects or startups.

Join our book's Discord space

Join the book's Discord Workspace for Latest updates, Offers, Tech happenings around the world, New Release and Sessions with the Authors:

https://discord.bpbonline.com

APPENDIX 2

Glossary of Terms

- **Abstraction layers**: Computational layers that separate functionalities in software or algorithms to simplify architecture, making systems easier to manage.

- **Activation methods**: Functions in neural networks determining whether a neuron should activate to influence the model's output.

- **Adaptive learning systems**: They are models that adjust to changes in incoming data dynamically without needing to be retrained from scratch.

- **Adversarial neural frameworks**: Architectures where neural networks are trained in opposition to enhance their accuracy and robustness.

- **AI implementations**: Applications or systems utilizing **artificial intelligence** (AI) for specific problem-solving or task execution.

- **Algorithmic efficiency metrics**: Measures evaluating an algorithm's use of computational resources like time and memory.

- **Analytical modeling**: Creating models to test hypotheses or predict new phenomena based on statistical analysis and data analytics.

- **Artificial cognition**: The simulation of human thought processes and problem-solving capabilities in a computational model.

- **Attribute identification**: Identifying specific characteristics from data that aid in analytical tasks.

- **Batch learning techniques**: They involve training a neural network on data groups simultaneously to enhance performance and stability.

- **Behavioral cloning**: A technique where a **machine learning** (**ML**) model mimics human actions to perform tasks similarly.

- **Biometric authentication**: The use of unique physiological features to identify individuals.

- **Blockchain technology**: It is a distributed digital record system that records transactions across multiple computers. This architecture ensures that each entry is secure and tamper-resistant, enhancing data integrity and reliability.

- **Categorization models**: ML strategies that assign inputs into predetermined categories or labels.

- **Cluster coefficient analysis**: It is a measure in network theory that assesses how closely nodes in a graph tend to group.

- **Cluster computing**: A system of connected computers that work together as a single system to perform complex computations.

- **Cloud-based services**: Systems that use internet-hosted servers to manage, process, and store data.

- **Cognitive analytics**: Using advanced analytics techniques and cognitive computing to interpret data and generate insights.

- **Collaborative learning models**: Scenarios in ML are where different tasks are learned simultaneously, and insights are shared across models.

- **Data enhancement methods**: Strategies to artificially increase data volume through modifications or synthetic generation.

- **Data entity frameworks**: Systems designed to define and categorize the basic entities within a specific domain.

- **Data federation**: Integrating data from disparate sources creates a more cohesive and manageable analysis environment.

- **Data integrity processes**: Techniques for identifying and correcting errors or inconsistencies within a dataset.

- **Data transformation techniques**: Methods for converting raw data into a more suitable format for analysis.

- **Data visualization techniques**: Techniques for creating visual descriptions of data to facilitate understanding and communication of information.

- **Decision support systems**: Tools that aid in making informed decisions by simulating the decision-making process.

- **Deepfakes**: Synthetic media where one person's likeness is replaced with another using neural networks.

- **Distributed model training**: Training models across multiple devices without centralizing data to improve learning efficacy.

- **Dynamic programming algorithms**: They solve problems by breaking them into simpler subproblems and storing the results to avoid redundant calculations.

- **Elastic computing**: The capability of systems to adapt to workload changes by automatically adjusting resource allocation.

- **Embedding strategies**: Techniques that represent categorical variables as continuous vectors within neural networks.

- **Ensemble methods**: Techniques combining multiple learning algorithms to realize better predictive performance than any single model could be obtained.

- **Entity recognition**: It is a task of **natural language processing (NLP)** that identifies and classifies key information (entities) within text.

- **Explainable AI (XAI) strategies**: It enhances AI system's transparency, making their decisions understandable to humans.

- **Feature construction**: It is the process of creating new variables from raw data to boost the performance of ML models.

- **Feature significance analysis**: Determining the impact of different variables on a model's predictions.

- **Feature space compression**: Techniques that reduce data complexity by distilling it to its most significant features.

- **Forecast error analysis**: Methods for measuring the differences between forecasted and observed values to refine forecasting models.

- **Functional programming**: In AI, it is a paradigm where computation is treated as evaluating mathematical functions, avoiding state changes and mutable data.

- **Generalization capacity**: The ability of a model to perform accurately on new, unseen data, demonstrating its applicability beyond the training set.

- **Genetic algorithms**: Search heuristics that mimic natural selection to solve optimization and search problems efficiently.

- **Geospatial analysis**: It analyzes spatial and geographic data using satellite imagery, GPS, and historical data to identify and map spatial patterns and relationships.

- **Gradient-boosting machines**: They are a technique for regression and classification that builds an ensemble of predictive models, like decision trees, to improve predictions.

- **Gradient optimization**: An algorithmic approach applied in ML to reduce the loss function by iteratively moving towards the steepest descent.

- **Hash functions in data science**: Functions that map data of arbitrary size to fixed-size values are commonly used to speed up table lookup or data comparison tasks.

- **Heuristic evaluation**: A usability inspection method where user interfaces are evaluated by experts using recognized usability principles.

- **High-dimensional data handling**: Techniques and strategies for managing and analyzing data with many variables, focusing on dimensionality reduction to simplify models without losing essential information.

- **Hyperbolic tangent function**: An activation function used in neural networks that scales input values to a range between -1 and 1, facilitating effective training by normalizing the input.

- **Hyperparameter optimization**: It is the procedure of tuning the parameters of a model that monitors the learning process to achieve optimal performance.

- **Incremental learning**: It is a learning process in which the model updates continually as new data arrives, adapting to new trends without forgetting previous knowledge.

- **Information retrieval systems**: They are systems designed to collect, organize, index, and retrieve information from large datasets, facilitating quick and efficient data access.

- **Interactive data applications**: They allow users to interact dynamically with and manipulate data, often providing deep analysis and visualization tools.

- **Interactive learning environments**: They facilitate dynamic interaction between the algorithm and the user, enhancing the learning experience through real-time adaptations.

- **Interoperability**: It describes the capability of diverse information technology systems and software applications to effectively communicate, exchange data, and utilize shared information for operations and decision-making.

- **Jacobian matrix**: A matrix representing all first-order partial derivatives of a vector-valued function, essential in studying dynamical systems and control theory.

- **Joint learning**: It is a ML scenario in which multiple tasks are learned simultaneously, leveraging commonalities across functions to improve learning efficiency.

- **Just-in-time compilation**: It is an optimization technique that compiles certain program parts at runtime to enhance performance by taking advantage of the system's current state.

- **Kernel methods**: They are a cluster of algorithms for array analysis. The best-known technique is the **support vector machine (SVM)** for classification and regression tasks.

- **Knowledge-based systems**: AI systems that apply specialized information and reasoning procedures to solve complex problems with high expertise.

- **Knowledge Discovery in Databases (KDDs)**: It identifies valid, novel, potentially useful, and finally understandable patterns in data, which is integral to data mining processes.

- **Knowledge engineering**: AI involves integrating knowledge into computer systems to solve complex problems requiring high human expertise.

- **Knowledge extraction**: It is the process of deriving high-quality information from text by identifying patterns, relationships, and computational facts in textual sources.

- **Knowledge transfer techniques**: They are methods used in ML to apply knowledge gained from solving one problem to different but related issues.

- **Lagrange multipliers**: It is a method used in optimization to find the local maxima and minima of functions subject to equality constraints. They help manage and solve constrained optimization problems.

- **Latent semantic analysis (LSA)**: It is a technique in NLP that extracts and represents the contextual usage meaning of words by applying numerical calculations to a large corpus of text.

- **Latent variable models**: They are statistical models that assume an underlying, unobservable variable structure influences the observed variables. They are commonly used in psychology and the social sciences.

- **Localization in robotics**: Techniques used in robotics to determine a robot's position in its environment using various sensors and algorithms.

- **Logical deduction systems**: They are systems used in AI that apply logic to derive conclusions from a set of premises. They are fundamental to developing expert systems and automated reasoning.

- **Loss metrics**: They are functions that measure the discrepancy between the actual outcomes and the predictions made by a model. They guide the optimization of ML algorithms.

- **Machine perception**: It is the capability of a system to interpret data in a manner that mimics human sensory perception. It is essential in fields like computer vision and speech recognition.

- **Model compression**: It refers to strategies for reducing the computational resources required by a ML model without significantly compromising its performance.

- **Model fitting**: It is the process of adjusting a ML model's parameters during training so that it can accurately predict outcomes.

- **Multilayer Perceptron (MLP)**: They are a brand of neural network composed of multiple layers of neurons that learn to map input datasets onto appropriate outputs.

- **Multitask learning**: It is a ML approach in which numerous learning tasks are solved simultaneously, sharing representations to improve generalization.

- **Neural network pruning**: It reduces network complexity by removing weights or neurons that have little impact on the output, thereby improving efficiency.

- **Neuromorphic computing**: Designing computer architectures inspired by the human brain's structure and function, aiming to improve efficiency and processing power dramatically.

- **Non-linear optimization**: It solves optimization problems where the objective or some constraints are non-linear functions, which is common in many scientific and engineering applications.

- **Normalized data**: It is the data that has been adjusted to ensure consistency in scale and distribution and is often a prerequisite for many statistical analyses and ML algorithms.

- **Object detection algorithms**: They are computer vision techniques that identify and locate objects within images or videos. They are used extensively in applications like video surveillance and autonomous driving.

- **Operational intelligence**: It is real-time analytics that provides visibility and insight into business operations, enabling better decision-making and performance monitoring.

- **Optimization algorithms**: In AI, these are algorithms designed to find the optimal solution from a set of possible solutions. They are used in scheduling, resource allocation, and route planning tasks.

- **Out-of-sample testing**: It evaluates a model's performance on a data set not used during the training phase to gauge its ability to generalize to new data.

- **Outlier detection**: It involves identifying data points that deviate significantly from the average data distribution. It is crucial in fraud detection, network security, and fault detection.

- **Parallel processing**: The technique of dividing a problem into subproblems that can be processed simultaneously, typically on multiple processors, to speed up computing tasks.

- **Predictive maintenance**: Utilizing data analysis tools and techniques to identify anomalies and forecast equipment failures in advance, thus preventing downtime and prolonging the life of the equipment.

- **Predictive modeling (ConPredictive maintenance)**: Using data analysis tools and techniques to detect anomalies and predict equipment failures before they happen, thereby preventing downtime and extending equipment life.

- **Predictive modeling**: Constructing models to predict the likelihood of future outcomes based on historical data, commonly employed across industries like finance, marketing, and healthcare.

- **Precision-recall metrics**: Evaluation metrics measure the accuracy of prediction models, specifically in classification problems where the balance between precision and recall is critical.

- **Principal component analysis**: It is a statistical technique for simplifying the complexity of high-dimensional data while retaining trends and patterns.

- **Probabilistic language prediction**: Using statistical methods to predict the likelihood of word sequences is fundamental in tasks such as speech recognition and text auto-completion.

- **Quantile regression**: It is a regression method that estimates the response variable's conditional median or other quantiles, providing a more comprehensive view than average modeling.

- **Quantitative modeling**: The application of mathematical and statistical techniques to model real-world scenarios, allowing for the prediction and interpretation of complex phenomena.

- **Query optimization**: It is the process of enhancing the performance of a database querying system to improve response time and resource usage.

- **Recursive algorithms**: They are procedures or formulas that solve problems by repeatedly breaking them down into smaller, more manageable subproblems.

- **Reinforcement feedback**: Utilizing rewards or penalties as signals for positive or negative behavior in decision-making is crucial for learning in AI.

- **Robotic process automation (RPA)**: Technologies that allow businesses to automate routine tasks across applications and systems by mimicking human interactions.

- **Semantic data structures**: They are structures that organize data meaningfully, considering the semantics of the data.

- **Sensory data interpretation**: Analyzing data gathered from sensors to help systems understand their environment or context.

- **Sequence modeling networks**: They are neural networks that predict future states in sequence data, such as language sentences, stock prices, and genetic sequences.

- **Solution heuristics**: Techniques that provide a practical method for solving problems that are more about finding an acceptable solution rather than an optimal one. These techniques are often used when an exact solution is difficult or impossible to determine within a reasonable timeframe.

- **Spatial data analysis**: It is used in mapping, **geographic information systems (GIS)**, and satellite imagery interpretation.

- **Stochastic modeling**: This technique utilizes probability and random variables to model and analyze uncertain systems. It is common in fields like finance, physics, and biology.

- **Structuring models**: They are used to predict the likelihood of future outcomes based on historical data, widely used in fields such as finance, marketing, and healthcare.

- **Structured neural networks**: These are advanced types of neural networks designed for specific tasks, where the network architecture is deliberately organized to perform optimally, such as convolutional neural networks for image processing.

- **Supervised learning algorithms**: ML algorithms that learn a function from labeled training data, including input data and the correct outputs.

- **TensorFlow**: It is an open-source software library created by *Google* for research and development in ML and deep neural networks. It provides a comprehensive, flexible ecosystem of tools, libraries, and community resources, allowing researchers to advance ML/DNN technology and developers to build and deploy ML-powered applications.

- **Time series forecasting**: It is a method that analyzes a series of data points ordered in time to predict future estimates based on historical trends.

- **Unbiased estimation**: Statistical methods that ensure parameter estimates are correct on average are critical for maintaining the integrity of inferential statistics.

- **Unstructured information handling**: Techniques for managing data that only fits into traditional row and column databases, such as texts, videos, and images.

- **User experience design in AI**: Crafting AI applications with a focus on the user's interaction experience, ensuring that the AI components are intuitive and enhance the overall usability of the application.

- **Variable selection**: It is selecting which variables to include in a model, which is crucial for improving the model's efficiency and accuracy.

- **Variational techniques**: Statistical methods used in Bayesian inference to approximate complex probability distributions.

- **Version control systems**: They are package tools designed to track and manage modifications to documents, computer programs, and various other forms of data. These systems enable effective collaboration by allowing multiple individuals to work on shared files, recording changes, and managing conflicts efficiently.

- **Visualization tools**: Software applications that allow users to create, manipulate, and view graphical representations of data, helping to uncover patterns, trends, and correlations.

- **Web scraping tools**: They are designed to extract data from websites automatically. They are widely used in data gathering and analysis.

- **Weight initialization methods**: Techniques used to set the initial values of weights in neural networks at the start of training, influencing how effectively a network will learn.

- **Weight regularization**: It is a ML technique that adds penalties to the weight sizes in a neural network to reduce the model's complexity and prevent overfitting.

- **Workload automation**: It uses software to automatically manage, schedule, and operate business processes and transactions.

- **Extreme Gradient Boosting (XGBoost)**: It is a sophisticated gradient boosting library that optimizes processes across distributed systems. It efficiently implements gradient boosting techniques to enhance speed and performance in model training and prediction tasks.

- **You Only Look Once (YOLO) integration**: Methods for using XML to structure, store, and transport data, facilitating complex data exchanges and storage solutions.

- **Yarn cluster management**: It is a technology within the Hadoop ecosystem that manages resources in cluster environments and optimizes resource utilization and schedules.

- **Yield management systems**: They are techniques used to adjust prices based on expected consumer behavior to maximize revenue or profitability, particularly in the hospitality and transportation industries.

- **Yield optimization approaches**: They involve strategies designed to enhance the productivity and efficiency of production processes. Commonly applied in manufacturing and supply chain management, these methods focus on maximizing output while reducing waste to achieve optimal operational performance.

- **YOLO algorithms:** They are real-time object detection systems that process images in one evaluation, quickly and accurately identifying and classifying objects.

- **Zero-inflated models**: These statistical models account for excess zeros in count data. They are useful in fields where the absence of an event can dominate observational data.

- **Zero-shot learning methods**: They are ML techniques that allow models to recognize objects or concepts they have not been explicitly trained to identify, extending the model's ability to generalize from known to unknown categories.

- **Zero-trust architecture**: It operates on the security principle that no individual or device, whether inside or outside an organization's network boundaries, is granted trust by default. Instead, every attempt to access the system must be rigorously authenticated and authorized before permission is granted.

- **Zigbee technology**: It is a high-level communication protocol for creating personal area networks with small, low-power digital radios commonly used in home automation.

- **Normalize the data**: By subtracting the mean and scaling it to the standard deviation, data can be normalized. This method is commonly used to prepare data for ML algorithms, where data needs to be in a standard format.

Join our book's Discord space

Join the book's Discord Workspace for Latest updates, Offers, Tech happenings around the world, New Release and Sessions with the Authors:

https://discord.bpbonline.com

Index